Integration, Diversity and the Making of a European Public Sphere

NEW HORIZONS IN EUROPEAN POLITICS

Series Editor: Julie Smith, *Robinson College, Cambridge, UK*

The New Horizons in European Politics series is an invaluable forum for original research across the spectrum of European politics, promoting innovative cross-disciplinary analysis of contemporary issues and debates. Covering a diverse range of topics, the series examines issues such as: the impacts of the severe challenges brought about by the financial crisis; economic issues, including integration and monetary union; the politics of the EU and other governmental and nongovernmental institutions; environmental politics and the ongoing struggle to mitigate climate change; and the politics of trade, energy and security in Europe. Both international and comparative in its approach, this exciting series encompasses theoretical and empirical work from both well-established researchers and the next generation of scholars.

Titles in the series include:

Building the Knowledge Economy in Europe
New Constellations in European Research and Higher Education Governance
Edited by Meng-Hsuan Chou and Åse Gornitzka

The EU and the Global Financial Crisis
New Varieties of Capitalism
Christian Schweiger

Shaping EU Policy from Below
EU Democracy and the Committee of the Regions
Simona Piattoni and Justus Schönlau

Integration, Diversity and the Making of a European Public Sphere
Edited by Hakan G. Sicakkan

Integration, Diversity and the Making of a European Public Sphere

Edited by

Hakan G. Sicakkan

Department of Comparative Politics, University of Bergen, Norway

NEW HORIZONS IN EUROPEAN POLITICS

EE Edward Elgar PUBLISHING

Cheltenham, UK • Northampton, MA, USA

Published by
Edward Elgar Publishing Limited
The Lypiatts
15 Lansdown Road
Cheltenham
Glos GL50 2JA
UK

Edward Elgar Publishing, Inc.
William Pratt House
9 Dewey Court
Northampton
Massachusetts 01060
USA

A catalogue record for this book
is available from the British Library

Library of Congress Control Number: 2016944281

This book is available electronically in the **Elgar**online
Social and Political Science subject collection
DOI 10.4337/9781785360916

Printed on elemental chlorine free (ECF)
recycled paper containing 30% Post-Consumer Waste

ISBN 978 1 78536 090 9 (cased)
ISBN 978 1 78536 091 6 (eBook)

Typeset by Columns Design XML Ltd, Reading
Printed and bound in the USA

Contents

Figures

Tables

Contributors

Jan H. van de Beek
Researcher at the Institute for Migration and Ethnic Studies (IMES), University of Amsterdam, the Netherlands.

Wanda Dressler
Associated researcher at LADYSS, CNRS, Paris West University Nanterre La Défense, France.

Deniz Neriman Duru
Postdoctoral research fellow at the Media, Cognition and Communication Department, University of Copenhagen, Denmark.

Martina Klicperová-Baker
Research fellow at the Institute of Psychology, Czech Academy of Sciences, the Czech Republic.

Jaroslav Košťál
Research fellow at the Institute of Psychology, Czech Academy of Sciences, the Czech Republic.

Monika Mokre
Senior research associate and lecturer at the Institute for Culture Studies and History of Theatre, Austrian Academy of Sciences, Austria.

Marybel Perez
Senior researcher, Center for Philanthropy Studies (CEPS), University of Basel, Switzerland.

Robert Sata
Research fellow and lecturer at the Department of Political Science, Central European University, Hungary.

Hakan G. Sicakkan
Associate professor at the Department of Comparative Politics, University of Bergen, Norway.

Hans-Jörg Trenz
Professor, Department of Media, Cognition and Communication, University of Copenhagen, Denmark, and adjunct professor at ARENA, Centre for European Studies of University of Oslo, Norway.

Floris Vermeulen
Associate professor at the Department of Political Science, University of Amsterdam, the Netherlands.

Preface

> Directeur général honoraire à la Commission européenne et créateur, en 1973, de l'*Eurobaromètre*, je souhaiterais recevoir une documentation aussi complète que possible sur les recherches réalisées dans le cadre du Programme 'Eurosphère'. Je me permets de rappeler que le concept d''Eurosphère' semble avoir été introduit dans la recherche socio-politique dès le début des années 60; cf. *Science politique et intégration européenne*, par Jean Meynaud et Dusan Sidjanski, Institut d'études européennes, Genève, 1965. J.-R. Rabier.[1]

I received this message on 23 August 2012. The sender of the e-mail was Jacques-René Rabier, the founder of two central European institutions – Eurobarometer and the Press and Information Service of High Authority of the European Coal and Steel Community. At the time, I was writing the final scientific reports of Eurosphere, an international research project that I was leading in the period between February 2007 and July 2012 with funding from the European Union's Sixth Framework Programme.[2] Not only because high-standing politicians' attention to the project results was desirable in order to increase its impact, but also out of personal curiosity, my correspondence with Mr Rabier continued for a few rounds more. I had certainly hoped current leaders of the European Union would come across at least an executive summary of the results of my project along with other projects. What I did not expect was to be micromanaged by a prominent member of the founder generation who still retained an enthusiastic and impatient curiosity about the current state of their artwork.

Writing to me that the term 'Eurosphere' was introduced into the academic literature in a book by Jean Meynaud and Dusan Sidjanski in 1965, Mr Rabier was being too modest by omitting to mention that the authors had actually written that the term 'Eurosphere' had been invented by Jacques-René Rabier and Jean Meynaud (Meynaud and Sidjanski 1965: 25). They defined the concept as the sphere of those who participate in the European integration processes actively, those who are directly affected by its consequences, and those who affect the integration process by expressing solidarity with the European. With the Eurosphere they aimed to spread and catalyse European integration. Later, although the name was forgotten, the European Community and the European Union continued to build on the founding generation's work and use the Eurosphere as a core element of European integration policies.

This book is about the outcome of the efforts of a handful of visionary and engaged Europeanists who strove, and are still doing so, to institute a transnational European public sphere in order to connect Europe's supranational institutions with individual citizens. Its ten chapters assess the outcomes of the Eurosphere's introduction into the European Union system, looking at its impacts in different dimensions of the European public sphere. With a view to discovering the preconditions for linking European citizens with the EU political institutions through the emerging European public sphere, the roles of various public sphere participants in the formation of a European public sphere are studied. This is done by mapping and explaining the extent to which participants of public debates in Europe (including citizens, public interest organizations, political parties, think tanks, media and the EU institutions) are interconnected through political cleavages, transnational networks, collaboration, discourses, mass media, and policymaking structures and processes.

The ten chapters in this book, taken together, have discovered a central feature of European integration, namely a particular system of Europe-wide political cleavages with integrative effects, which is manifest in the networking webs and discursive patterns of the collective actors participating in public debates in Europe. These political cleavages have been brought about by the very existence of the Eurosphere. To say the last thing first, the conclusion of this book is as follows.

A European public sphere can be said to exist when the already existing public spaces (at transnational, national and sub-national levels) come into resilient patterns of relationships of collaboration, conflict and contestation with the EU-initiated, pro-European, elite-dominated supranational public and its vertically organized, top-down trans-European public space, that is, the Eurosphere. In other words, the European public sphere is a constellation of historically existing and new ethnic, religious, minority-related, national and transnational public spaces and publics which constitute (and which are welded to each other by) a system of contesting discourses, alliances and polarizations. This conceptualization is entrenched in an agonistic pluralism perspective of a public sphere.

The chapters in this volume systematically compare the ways in which the European Union, national public sphere participants (media, civil society organizations, political parties and policy research institutes) and transnational networks of these are trying to create links (or break them) between citizens and the political institutions of the European Union across many boundaries. The main focus is on the European Union policies aiming to create a common European public sphere, and how the EU policies on this matter are (mis)aligned with the priorities of other participants (including individual citizens) in public debates. Although the chapters address a variety of political cleavages, the common cleavage dimension that all chapters address is the centre–periphery cleavage, that is, collaboration, conflict and contestation between elites at European and national levels.

The volume is organized along particular dimensions of politics identified through a synthesis of the theory of agonistic pluralism on democracy, the theory of the deliberative public sphere and the theory of political cleavages on party systems. Thus, Chantal Mouffe, Jürgen Habermas and Stein Rokkan are the theoreticians and analysts who have partly inspired the overall analytical approach of this book. Additional inspiration comes from our own findings and the researchers who contributed to this project. Rokkan successfully incorporated the aggregative, deliberative and agonistic dimensions of politics in his conceptual maps. The analytical distinctions he made in his typology of citizen intervention in politics were used as one criterion when selecting the contributions to be included and structuring the chapters in this book. Rokkan identifies two channels of citizen intervention in democratic politics. The first is the numerical channel, as he calls it, which is about elections, political parties and voters. The second is the corporate-plural channel, which concerns the direct interventions by civil society, including both corporate and public interest groups, into government's decision-making processes. This channel is about negotiation, deliberation and policymaking. The media channel, on the other hand, concerns citizens' and civil society's uninterrupted critical voice. Today, empirical studies of the public sphere mainly revolve around the media channel, and the concepts and method tools deployed are devised to map and understand the media channel. This book diverges from this current trend by studying the three channels under a common conceptual frame, which is presented in Chapter 1.

These three channels are competitive. In the numerical channel parties try to gain government power through elections. In the corporate-plural channel, public and corporate interest groups strive to get the attention and recognition of governments and citizens for their causes. In the media channel, different media organizations try to win readers and audience by creating widely appealing news framings, whereas political and social actors strive to get the media's attention. Social and political actors that are competing in one of these channels have to be active speakers in public debates if they want to survive and win, because they can only achieve their goals by making themselves and their causes visible to the general public through participation, persuasion and legitimation in mediated public debates. Therefore, they are the most obvious speakers and listeners in the European public sphere. The actors that are studied here are political parties, non-state organizations (public interest groups: non-governmental organizations and social movement organizations), think tanks (policy research institutes including advocacy think tanks), and newspapers and TV channels. The channels that they use to intervene in public debates are, as noted, the numerical channel, corporate-plural channel and media channel. Chapters 3 to 5 focus on the media channel (the European Union's media policies, traditional mass media and social media). Chapters 6 and 7 assess the corporate-plural dimension (think tanks and minority organizations); it should be noted that, in addition to assessing the traditional media dimension, Chapter 4 addresses issues of political cleavages in the corporate-plural dimension when comparing national and European elites' discourses with media framings. Chapters 8 and 9 contribute to understanding the numeric channels of the European public sphere (political parties and formation of an agonistic European demos).

The volume opens with theoretical and conceptual reflections in Chapter 1, authored by Hakan G. Sicakkan, inquiring into the relationship between the Eurosphere, a pro-EU public space constructed by the supranational institutions, and the formation of the European public sphere. He posits the constitutive role of the Eurosphere in the ongoing formation of a European public sphere. The chapter presents a brief history of the making of the Eurosphere by the founding fathers of the European Union. Linking the Eurosphere and the European public sphere to each other causally in the conceptual framework of a pluralist-agonistic perspective, the author argues that the Eurosphere has a constitutive role in the formation of the European public sphere. Finally, he identifies the public spaces, publics, social and political actors (adversaries) and political cleavages (agons) that constitute the agonistic European public sphere.

In Chapter 2 Wanda Dressler maps the territorial spread and diversity of the European publics that the European Union is currently aiming to link with its political structures. This chapter should be regarded as an exploration into the highly complex territorial basis of the publics and public spaces of Europe, and the policies that the European Union deploys both to respect and to transcend the internal boundaries that territorial diversity maintains. The chapter shows how the regionalization process brought about a new diversity structure within a transformed, integral European territorial space. Because the current multi-level and cross-border territorial organization and increased poly-ethnic features within it are far too complex and considerably more conflict-laden than aggregative and deliberative public sphere theories assume, Dressler concludes by pointing to the newly emerging agonistic features of the transformed European territorial space as an important feature of the European public sphere.

After these two chapters focusing on the theoretical and historical background of the European Union's public sphere and territorial transformation policies, the book starts its empirical contributions with three chapters devoted to analysis of the mediated public sphere (Chapters 3, 4 and 5).

Chapter 3 by Monika Mokre analyses EC/EU policies from a European public sphere perspective, asking how media structures and their framing conditions affect the political function of media for the European public sphere and, especially, the emergence of an agonistic European public sphere not exclusively structured by national cleavages. In her historical overview of the European Union's media policies and an evaluation of their impact on the European public sphere, Mokre finds that media policies have proven successful in reducing national barriers for broadcasting and establishing a single European media market but that they did not succeed in providing centralized forms of information distribution and exchange. Following this, the chapter presents empirical results of the Eurosphere project on the preferences of European actors with regard to the European public sphere. These preferences are compared with the actual activities of the European Commission. Mokre argues that the results of the Eurosphere project have shown a possible alternative to the European Union's centralized approach to transnational exchange of news and the attempts of journalists to include a European dimension in media coverage. In the long run, this could lead to an agonistic European public sphere not exclusively structured by national cleavages. Concluding, the chapter discusses possible future developments of media policies furthering inclusive European public spheres.

In Chapter 4 Hakan G. Sicakkan asks to what extent the Eurosphere has succeeded in constituting a European public sphere. The author develops an analysis frame deriving from the neo-functionalist assumption that ongoing European integration is similar to historical state and nation building processes. He posits that, for this to be true, we must observe that the European Union's perspectives on significant issues are at least partly embraced by trans-European and national elites and national mass media. He compares the citizenship and diversity discourses of national and trans-European elites with media framings and EU policies. National media seem to reflect the preferences of national elites and the premises behind the European Union policies better than they do the preferences of trans-European elites. This is because trans-European elites are exposed more to the European Commission, which is the most transnationalized political institution in the European Union's political system, whereas European Union laws and policies are directly affected by national elites through the Council of Ministers, an institution with more intergovernmental features. If we recognize that the European Commission and the Eurosphere represent the spirit of European integration to a greater extent than the latter, European elites' integration ambition is partly reflected in national public spheres.

Chapter 5 by Deniz Neriman Duru and Hans-Jörg Trenz turns to new media and another type of elite group that contributes to the formation of the European public sphere. They discuss the role of social media and 'expats', mobile foreign citizens (both EU and non-EU), in the formation of a European public sphere. The authors explore the ways in which social networking media provide platforms for transnational encounters between expats and other groups in a local public space, Copenhagen in Denmark. By analysing the socialization and cultural self-representation of expats, they argue that social networking media shift the frontiers of identities between expats and locals, and catalyse a new spirit of hybridity and creative 'playing with diversity' that become characteristic for the local public sphere. Mobility and citizenship rights as facilitated by the Europe of free movement contribute in this sense to the consolidation of a European public sphere, which is not based on sharp distinctions but where transnational encounters are rather kept in flow with an elite group of EU mobiles and other less privileged people (EU and non-EU migrants) in constant exchange with each other.

The next three chapters concern the corporate-plural channel of non-state organizations that are active in the national and European public spheres. These are organizations that are engaged in influencing government policies directly through conducting and disseminating policy analyses, lobbying, participating in consultations and policy proposals, mobilizing citizens and organizing grassroots events. Here, we concentrate particularly on the EU think tanks (Chapter 6) and minority organizations (Chapter 7).

Chapter 6, authored by Marybel Perez, assesses the extent to which national think tanks and their trans-European networks contribute to the articulation of a European public sphere. Drawing on think tank scholarship and research conducted in the Eurosphere project, the author discusses how think tanks contribute to the moulding of the public sphere at the transnational and global levels where structures of communication are complex and fragmented. To this end, the analysis focuses on EU think tanks' participation in EU policymaking. Perez seeks answers to a range of questions about the ways in which policy research institutes and think tanks create public spaces of communication between the EU and other stakeholders, and how they in turn are constrained by the specific features of the EU policymaking mechanisms. She also considers the conditions under which trans-European think tank networks and the EU have a socializing effect on national think tanks. Think tanks contribute to the definition and reproduction of ideas through the dissemination of books and reports, appearing in interviews, lecturing at educational institutions, and so on. Through these activities, think tanks create links between different kinds of actors, and through their policy analysis they contribute to the definition and reproduction of discourses that shape the public sphere. The chapter poses that EU think tanks' most significant contribution to the trans-European public sphere is creating platforms for interaction and socializing ideas.

In Chapter 7 Jan H. van de Beek and Floris Vermeulen assess the European Union's public consultation mechanisms from the perspective of the representation needs of minority organizations. After mapping the EU's objectives concerning its consultation system, the discrepancy between these objectives and what minority organizations want is assessed. The minority groups that are considered are regional national minorities, Roma, Jews, Muslim immigrants and non-religious immigrants. Mainstream political parties in each country are used as a control group. Large differences between groups are found in the degree of institutionalization of the EU consultation system, which is most developed for national regional minorities and Roma, and least for non-religious immigrants, where Jews have a proactive attitude and consultation of Muslim immigrants is increasing. Seen from the perspective of the ethnic groups, consultation is driven by the wish to participate (regional national minorities), protect religious rights (Jews, Muslim immigrants), influence EU foreign policy (Jews) and seek protection against discrimination (Roma). Seen from the perspective of EU institutions, gaining legitimacy (through being more representative, and protecting minority rights) is the driving force, though the EU is not very successful in this respect.

Chapters 6 and 7 should be read in parallel with the comparative analysis of non-state organizations and media actors in Chapter 4. The first part of Chapter 4 assesses the differences in discourses of national and trans-European elites. These three chapters show the main political cleavages and the patterns of collaboration and polarization between the trans-European and national elites working in different kinds of non-state organizations.

Next come two chapters about the social and political actors that are operating in the numeric channel, that is, political parties (Chapter 8) and citizens (Chapter 9). Chapter 8 looks at the ways in which the preferences of national elites are aligned or de-aligned with European party groups in the European Parliament, whereas Chapter 9 maps the discrepancy between the preferences of national elites and individual citizens. In this sense, these two chapters are complementary in showing the links from citizens to the European Union institutions in the numeric channel. Chapter 9 can also be read synchronously with Chapter 4 in order to track the links between citizens and the European Union institutions through the corporate-plural channel.

Robert Sata focuses in Chapter 8 on the question of whether parties contribute to or hinder the democratic performance of the European Union and what roles national parties and European party groups play in aggregating political preferences in the European Parliament. Literature on European integration frequently states an elite–citizens gap in European politics partly due to the fact that European political parties do not compete on European but domestic issues. At the same time, national parties successfully formed European party groups to compete in the European arena, and access to European Parliament, Council or other institutions of the EU is mainly through the channels of party politics. Yet it is unclear whether parties manage to link national constituencies with the EU or national loyalties impact negatively on the possibilities of a European public sphere. The chapter analyses these issues by examining alignments and misalignments between stances and objectives of national political elites and European party groups. Enlisting the stances and objectives of the national and European party elites enables us to analyse how the European public sphere is articulated and, even more importantly, to identify possible areas of contestation among the different arenas. An examination of differences between positions of the national political elite and the European party groups provides a deeper insight into the actual importance of European parties, and the feasibility and acceptability of a common European public sphere of political elites.

In Chapter 9, Martina Klicperová-Baker and Jaroslav Košťál estimate the preconditions of European integration, the European demos and the European public sphere. Democracies are conflict resolution systems; they are defined by the constructive solution of multiple political cleavages. The attitudes and values of their citizens should not be in a destructive antagonistic clash but, instead, in an agonistic, benign competition. The European demos was operationalized in terms of democratic spirit, tolerance and civility; the public sphere was assessed by analysis of ideologies. The European Values Study (EVS) served as the data source. The results suggest that each of the countries under study differs by its preconditions for the democratic demos. At the same time, there is a significant level of commonality. The existence of a European public was assessed by an analysis of ideologies representing various political orientations of European citizens. The ideologies appear to be fragmented by countries and by geopolitical regions. Thus, as expected, rather than the existence of a general European public we observed the partitioned ideology of individual countries or regions. Yet, at the same time, we identified significant clusters of democrats, which were particularly numerous among the elites. The democratic elites appear as most instrumental in the formation of a benign, agonistic system at the European level. It is concluded that the European demos has the necessary preconditions in the tolerant democratic mentality which is abundant in Northern and Western Europe while also to some degree represented in all other nations. In contrast, the preconditions for a unified public were not confirmed, as ideologies appeared to be geopolitically partitioned.

Taken together, these two chapters uncover the issues of conflict and contestation in the numeric channel between different segments of society and different levels of the EU political system, from individual citizens and national parties to the European Parliament party groups, giving a rather detailed picture of the extent to which the European numeric channel actually gives voice to the citizens and transmits their concerns to the European level, that is, to the European Parliament and EU policymaking.

The final chapter draws general conclusions beyond what each chapter provides. It depicts the outcomes of the European Union's policies aiming to form a European public sphere and puts these empirical findings in the theoretical context developed in Chapter 1. It draws the general lines between the new links and political cleavages generated by the European Union policies. Based on these, the chapter briefly reflects on the current state of the art pertaining to the theorization of the transnational public sphere, with a focus on its conceptualization and explanation of its emergence. Focusing on the outcomes of the relationships of collaboration, conflict and contestation between national collective actors and pan-European networks, the main contribution of this volume is, thus, to introduce and evaluate the Eurosphere's constitutive role in the formation of the European public sphere. We show how the intended and unintended outcomes of the European founding fathers' Eurosphere initiative sparked the formation of an agonistic European public sphere.

I would like to express my gratitude to those who contributed to the making of this book. Thanks to the European Commission for a research grant that covered our Eurosphere project activities in 16 countries for five and a half years in the Sixth Framework Programme. Thanks also to the Norwegian Research Council and the University of Bergen, my home university, which contributed with additional resources for funding Ph.D. scholarships and for the management and coordination of the overall project. The Meltzer Research Fund provided generous resources for my sabbatical leave to be spent at the European University Institute, Sciences Po and the Humboldt University, which made it possible for me to write Chapters 1, 4 and 10 of this book. I would also like to thank Rainer Bauböck (European University Institute), Riva Kastoryano (Sciences Po) and Gökçe Yurdakul (Humboldt University), who made the Meltzer Research Fund grant possible by kindly inviting me to hold visiting fellowships at their universities.

Finally, this book would not be possible without the contribution of the 138 senior and junior researchers who worked in the Eurosphere project. Only a couple of them have authored the chapters of this volume, but there is a huge amount of work done by the other researchers who do not appear in this book, including research design, data collection and registration, data analysis and report writing. Unfortunately, I do not have enough space to list their names here. However, a list of their names can be found on the Eurosphere project's website.[3]

Hakan G. Sicakkan
26 March 2016
Badia-Fiesolana, Florence

NOTES

1. 'As Honorary Director General at the European Commission and the creator in 1973 of the *Eurobarometer*, I would like to receive as much documentation as possible on the research conducted under the program "Eurosphere". Allow me to recall that the concept of "Eurosphere" seems to have been introduced into the socio-political research in the early 60s; cf. *Political Science and European Integration*, by Jean Meynaud and Dusan Sidjanski, Institute of European Studies, Geneva, 1965. J.-R. Rabier'.
2. The project's full title was Diversity and the European Public Sphere: Towards a Citizens' Europe. With the Eurosphere project, we sought answers to the question of 'Under what conditions and to what extent is a transnational public sphere possible in Europe?' The project was funded by the European Union's Sixth Framework Programme. A total of 138 researchers working at 17 research and higher education institutions in 16 European countries contributed to its different components. Comprehensive information about the project and the final reports presenting its results can be accessed at https://eurosphere.b.uib.no/.
3. See https://eurosphere.b.uib.no/ or http://eurospheres.org.

REFERENCE

Meynaud, J. and D. Sidjanski (1965) *Science politique et intégration européenne*, Genève: Institut d'études européennes.

1. An agonistic pluralism approach to the European public sphere

Hakan G. Sicakkan

The 'Eurosphere' is of crucial importance if we want to properly understand what the European public sphere is. For without the Eurosphere, a European public sphere might not emerge. The term 'Eurosphere' was invented by Jacques-René Rabier and Jean Meynaud (Meynaud and Sidjanski 1965: 25). They defined it as the sphere of those who contribute to the European integration processes, those who are directly subjected to its consequences, and those who further the integration process by expressing solidarity with the idea of a united Europe. In other words, the Eurosphere was the vertical, top-down, trans-European communicative space of European-minded, pro-EU and pro-diversity elites and citizens.

In this chapter, I posit the constitutive role of the Eurosphere in the ongoing formation of a European public sphere. In the first section, I extend Rabier and Meynaud's definition of the Eurosphere in terms of its relationship to the European public sphere. I proceed in the same section by presenting a brief history of the making of the Eurosphere by the founding fathers of the European Union. In the second section, by linking the two terms causally in an agonistic pluralist perspective I argue that the Eurosphere has a constitutive role in the formation of the European public sphere. An agonistic pluralist approach to the public sphere requires due attention to, and recognition of, both the adversarial and the harmonious features of politics and society and strives to abandon imperfect assumptions that entail only consensus or dissension. In section three I identify the social spaces, institutions, structures and political actors (adversaries) that constitute the agonistic European public sphere. I conclude by suggesting an analytical framework which is based on an extended agonistic pluralist notion of a European public sphere.

1 WHAT IS THE EUROSPHERE?

The term 'Eurosphere' is often used by Mark Leonard and others to connote the EU's zone of influence in the international political arena:

> [T]he next wave of European transformation is only just beginning. The European Union is starting to develop an enormous sphere of influence, extending way beyond its borders that could be called the 'Eurosphere'. This belt of eighty countries covering the former Soviet Union, the Western Balkans, the Middle East, North Africa, and Sub-Saharan Africa accounts for 20 per cent of the world's population. (Leonard 2005: 4)

Indeed, as I underlined, the term 'Eurosphere' was introduced by Jacques-René Rabier and Jean Meynaud in 1965, and their usage of the term refers to quite another thing:

> Selon une expression suggérée par J.-R. Rabier et J. Meynaud et qui maintenant est devenue courante, l'eurosphère désigne les diverses sphères de personnes ou de groupes qui participent activement à l'intégration ou qui étant directement touchés par ses effets réagissent d'une manière significative. Ces individus ou groupes manifestent donc des solidarités européennes en influant sur le movement d'intégration ou en s'en défendant. (Meynaud and Sidjanski 1965: 25)

In Rabier and Meynaud's approach, the Eurosphere is defined as the communicative public space of those individuals and groups who participate in European integration processes actively, who are directly affected by the consequences of European integration, and who affect the European integration processes by expressing solidarity with 'the European'. To be more precise, in addition to affected elites and citizens these categories include the European Union's political, bureaucratic and technocratic elites. In this form, Rabier and Meynaud's definition of the Eurosphere primarily corresponds to the features of one of the public spaces that we study in this book, that is, the vertical, top-down, trans-European communicative space of pro-EU elites and citizens. Thus, throughout this chapter the Eurosphere does not relate to the European Union's zone of influence, but to the European public sphere. It was invented and initiated by the European Union's founder generation in order to be used as a launch pad in the construction of a comprehensive European public sphere.

At this juncture, it is in order to preliminarily delineate what a European public sphere is and its relationship to the Eurosphere. The European public sphere is more encompassing than the Eurosphere. The Eurosphere is one of the multiple types of public spaces within the

European public sphere. It entails simply one public: the transnational public of pro-EU elites and citizens. The European public sphere, on the other hand, contains multiple subnational, national and transnational public spaces and multiple publics that are in alliance, contestation and conflict with each other. Among these the Eurosphere is special because it constitutes the European public sphere by connecting the multiple public spaces and publics of Europe to each other through extension of collaboration, contestation and conflict to the European scale. As this volume empirically shows, the Eurosphere (and the European elites who are operating within it) generates positive and negative reactions to itself at all levels of European society, which brings about common political cleavages at the European scale with respect to which individual citizens, social groups and collective political actors take stances and engage in Europe-wide public debates. In this sense the Eurosphere has a causal status in the processes leading to the formation of a European public sphere.

1.1 A Brief History of the Making of the Eurosphere

Although the term 'Eurosphere' was not introduced into the literature before 1965, the history of the European public sphere is at least as old as the European Union itself. To some, it is even older than the European Union's history (Kaelble 2002). The idea of a transnational public sphere transcending the boundaries of the EU member states is, on the one hand, one of the main building blocks of the European integration project. On the other hand, it is an umbrella concept that links different EU integration objectives and policies under a common conceptual frame. Important examples of such objectives and policies that form a coherent, integral whole under the concept of the European public sphere are European citizenship, European identity, European demos, European solidarity, European territory, European networks, European communication strategy, European civil society, the four freedoms and European institutions.

If we accept that the main ingredients of a political public sphere are the state (including all its political institutions), civil society, individual citizens, the means and channels of political communication between them and the content of public communication, it would not be incorrect to assert that the formation of the Eurosphere started in the early 1950s with the arrival on to the scene of European history of the Europeanist political elites who were involved in the establishment and running of the European Coal and Steel Community (ECSC). More concretely, through the ECSC they initiated a supranationalization process, that is, the creation and strengthening of transnational decision-making bodies that are relatively independent of national states, by instituting a High Authority (today's European Commission), a Common Assembly of national parliamentarians (today's European Parliament), a Special Council of national government ministers (today's Council of the European Union) and a Court of Justice (today's European Court of Justice).

In spite of the fact that the ECSC introduced the world's very first international institutions which were based on the principle of supranationalism, the surrounding international environment was still a world of sovereign nation states weary of war. Mainstream international relations paradigms at that time regarded national governments as the sole legitimate representatives of citizens. Still under the influence of the legacy of strong charismatic political leaderships that were necessitated by the conditions of the last two world wars, international politics was seen as an exclusive task for the elite layer of governments. At such a time, when citizens' and civil society's involvement even in their own countries' international politics and international relations was quite a remote idea, the ECSC introduced indirect citizen involvement, or representation, in supranational decision-making through the Common Assembly. The Common Assembly was composed of nationally elected parliamentarians who were appointed to represent their voters in the Common Assembly in dual mandate. Despite operating basically in consultative capacity until 1979, the Common Assembly was the beginning of a radical break with the government elites' monopoly on transnational decision-making by including nationally elected parliamentarians, from parties in government and opposition alike, in a transnational assembly.

Also, with the establishment of the High Authority and the Court of Justice in addition to the Common Assembly, the ECSC planted the first seeds of a transnational political system and its checks-and-balances scheme. Under the subsequent arrangements of the European Community and the European Union, the European Commission and the European Court of Justice retained and further strengthened their supranational features. Since the 1990s, the Council of Ministers has been gradually transforming from an intergovernmental to a supranational institution with a steady increase in the number of policy areas being decided through qualified majority voting. As research on voting behaviour in the European Parliament shows, European parliamentarians are acting with an increasingly transnational mindset, voting in line with the ideology and preferences of their European party groups rather than on the basis of national interests (cf. Sata, this volume, Chapter 8). While key political institutions of the European Union are becoming gradually more supranational, citizens' influence on transnational policymaking has been progressively, yet far from sufficiently, increasing as the European Parliament is empowered vis-à-vis the Council and the Commission in the decision-making procedures.

Within the conceptual frame of the notion of the public sphere, two important advances in the formation of the Eurosphere were the direct links established between individual citizens and the legislature and the judiciary of the European Union. The former link happened through the introduction of direct elections to the European Parliament in 1979. The latter was realized with the Lisbon Treaty, which came into force at the end of 2009, making it easier for individual citizens to bring an action before the General Court of the Court of Justice of the European Union (CJEU) against EU decisions which affect them directly.

However, the linking of the European Commission, the executive organ of the European Union, with individual citizens followed a less direct path. Harrison and Pukallus (2015) claim historians of European integration writing about the European Community (EC)'s communication with citizens are operating with mistaken frames of understanding when stating that the early leaders of the ECSC and EC were not interested in communicating with citizens. It is believed that they wanted less citizen involvement for the sake of efficiency in European integration work. Based on original archive data, Harrison and Pukallus (2015) convincingly document the opposite was the case in a thorough historical study of EU leaders' ways of communicating with citizens and the EU's public communication policies and strategies between 1951 and 1967.

That is, the ECSC (1951–1957), EEC (1957–1992), EC (1993–2009) and EU (1993 onwards) have been conscious of the necessity of introducing measures to communicate with the citizens. Communication measures that started in the 1950s were a one-way conduit from the Information Service of the High Authority (which was named the Press and Information Service in 1955) in order to inform the citizens directly about the ECSC and its decisions, policies and activities through all available means, including mass media. Jacques-René Rabier was the person who founded this institution (Baisnee 2007). Whereas one of the two divisions of this institution gave information services to the trade unions sector, the other division aimed to 'inform the European public "in its widest extension"' (Harrison and Pukallus 2015: 242).

However, a 1962 Gallup poll showed that, despite the ECSC's efforts, citizens' knowledge of European affairs was extremely low. Recognizing the difficulty of reaching the public directly with limited resources, the ECSC decided to transmit their messages to citizens through influential public figures. This was a critical juncture, leading the European leaders from a 'popularist approach' (1951–1962) to an 'elitist opinion leader approach' (1963–1967) in their efforts to construct a European public sphere (Harrison and Pukallus 2015). This was also the beginning of the formation of the Eurosphere, the communicative space of European elites and citizens, which became the driver of the formation of the larger European public sphere. An 'opinion leader approach' meant reaching the public through public figures who were influential in different sectors. The Commission gathered leaders from a wide range of sectors, including civil society, research and education, media, politics, businesses and trade unions. The selected leaders were invited to different activities in order to be socialized as intermediaries between the EEC and the public. These public figures were supposed to constitute the backbone of what Rabier and Meynaud called the 'Eurosphere'.

In contrast to what most research on European integration claims, there was a strong and sincere 'civil aim' in the European leaders' communication efforts (Harrison and Pukallus 2015). The concern was certainly to increase the legitimacy of European political institutions by gaining public recognition for their political performance. However, although top-down communication from supranational institutions to citizens through opinion leaders was thought to improve the supranational institutions' visibility and transparency, this was hardly enough to allow us to call what was being instituted a public sphere, for the High Authority's public communication was mainly a one-way conduit, and citizens' voice and influence were missing in the ongoing elite deliberation and communication. It was once again Jacques-René Rabier who set out to institute Eurobarometer in 1973 in order not only to incorporate citizen input, that is, public opinion, as a source of supranational decision-making, but also to spark the construction of a European public by exposing the different nations' features, opinions and attitudes to each other (Baisnee 2007).

This approach, which incorporates public opinion measurements with top-down message transmission through intermediary transnational elites, forms the basis of today's more advanced European Union strategies to connect with citizens. Both components became more advanced over the years, turning into more comprehensive policies seeking legitimacy for the European Union as a political system. By initiating and sponsoring pan-European networks of civil society organizations, including European federations of political parties and European networks of NGOs, the transnational elite layer in the Eurosphere was widened even more and specialized in different sectors. These attempts were based on the stipulations of the European Union's policy initiatives on communication strategy, governance and democracy and dialogue.[1] The pan-European civil society component comprised both public interest groups and corporate interest groups. This process extended also to efforts to build trans-European networks of higher education and research institutions and think tanks. Some pan-European networks became the European Union's regular dialogue and consultation partners in policymaking processes in their expertise areas, for example, among others, the European Women's Lobby (EWL), the Social Platform of European NGOs (SocialPlatform), the European Network against Racism (ENAR) and the European NGO Confederation for Relief and Development (CONCORD).

The pan-European non-state networks are European-level counterparts of national organizations. A majority of them have headquarters in Brussels. National non-state organizations are members of the pan-European networks that entrench their legitimacy in both their roots at the national level and the normative power and moral legitimacy of their causes. They claim to perform three functions – voicing a specific public interest toward the European Union, influencing EU policymaking in a special policy area, and increasing their member organizations' awareness about the supranational policies that affect them – though they do not claim to represent the national civil societies (Sicakkan 2012b). In conformity with the notion of the Eurosphere, pan-European networks are supposed to function as intermediaries between national civil societies and the European Union. While they perform these roles, they constitute themselves as the transnational civil society of Europe on a European scale.

To summarize, with the founding of the European Union's political institutions (the European Council, the European Parliament, the European Commission and the European Court of Justice), the first component of the Eurosphere, and of the European public sphere, was established. The Eurosphere, the vertical communicative public space of European and national elites and citizens, can be regarded as established when the European Union's institutions and national civil societies interact with each other regularly and over a long period of time through the pan-European civil society networks. As empirically shown in the chapters of this volume, one observes such regular Europe-wide interactions across national and European levels of civil society.

1.2 What Was the Purpose of the Architects of the Eurosphere?

There is no doubt that the Eurosphere was an initiative led by the European Union's founding fathers, who aimed to catalyse the European integration processes. Their initial design constituted a one-way, top-down communication style, simply aiming to inform the European public about the European Union. After 1974, Eurobarometer targeted generating mutual knowledge about national public opinions. Although we know that the founding fathers thought the Eurosphere would advance European integration, the depiction given by historians is inconclusive as regards whether they foresaw a causal link between the Eurosphere and the European public sphere. Baisnee (2007) seems, on the other hand, to have captured this in an interview given by Rabier:

> The goal was, first, to better know [public] opinion in order to orientate information policy and, secondly, to contribute to revealing European citizens to one another. It was a matter not only of knowing public opinion but also of informing that public opinion about what citizens from other countries thought about common topics. (J.R. Rabier, quoted in Baisnee 2007: 499)

Thus, 'the goal was to create a European public opinion by measuring it and publicizing it ... [T]he Eurobarometer created European public opinion' (Baisnee 2007: 499). What does this actually involve? We need to get help from Habermas to answer this question. Habermas asserts an almost deterministic relationship between the concepts of 'public sphere', 'public opinion' and 'public' when he defines a public sphere as 'a realm of our social life in which something approaching public opinion can be formed' and a public as a 'bearer of public opinion' (Habermas et al. 1974: 49–50). The statements by an architect of the Eurosphere partly indicate that he might be aware of this presumed relationship. In the ideal case of theory corresponding perfectly to facts, this implies that the outcome of creating a European public opinion by measuring and publicizing it was expected to be the making of a European public and a European public sphere in the longer term.

Keeping in mind that Habermas was talking about national public spheres, and not a transnational public sphere of deep, complex diversity, I want to draw attention to the last point made by Rabier about 'common topics'. It is quite frequently argued by scholars and policymakers that a European public sphere does not exist because there are no common European topics in which citizens are interested. Thus, Baisnee (2007) might be right when he argues that research on the European public sphere has been built on the concepts generated by the European Union itself. On the other hand, it might be the case that Rabier imported the idea of 'common topics' from the first generation of public sphere researchers like Habermas. No matter where it originates from, common topics as an indicator of the existence of a public sphere fits better with the reality of non-heterogeneous nation states than diverse societies and transnational entities.

2 CONCEPTUALIZING THE EUROPEAN PUBLIC SPHERE

Indeed, the elements of the public sphere listed in mainstream theories, that is, a (pan-European) civil society, a (European) citizenry that acts as a public capable of generating a public opinion, a (European) public opinion and a (pan-European) mass media, have been empirically sought by researchers without much success. The conclusion arrived at through such approaches was that a European public sphere does not (and cannot) exist. But is it so that a European public sphere really does not exist? Or is it that our nation-state-oriented concepts were not capable of detecting a transnational public sphere of diversity? As Habermas has repeatedly stated, his conceptual tools on the public sphere were not developed to study postnational entities like the European Union.

In order to understand a transnational public sphere, for example the European public sphere, one needs to take into account its ‘composite’ (non-homogeneous), ‘multi-lingual’, ‘less institutionalized’, ‘political centreless’ (polycentric) and ‘elitist’ (multi-level) traits (Kaelble 2002). An adequate indicator of the existence of a transnational public sphere entailing multiple publics and public spaces is rather the existence of European-scale political cleavages. I will turn back to the interview with Rabier in order to make this point more clear. When asked whether a European public opinion existed, Rabier answered:

> This is built. European public opinion is the extent to which Europeans think the same way on a number of issues: on democracy, on human rights, on the status of women. This is a general support, tacit, with this distinction, however, that young people and highly educated people are closer to each other in different countries than are other categories of population. This is partly because they are more politicized and read newspapers, etc. The divide is there, in terms of information and training, hence the need for European education.[2]

The above quotation reveals a perception of European public opinion as a singular, aggregative phenomenon. This approach to European public opinion, hence to the European public sphere, was adopted rather uncritically by some politicians and researchers. Consequently, not only in public opinion surveys led by the European Union’s political institutions, but also in academic research on the European public sphere, similarities rather than European-scale political cleavages were sought across European societies and nations. This concerned similarity in opinions, attitudes, values, discourses and reactions regarding different issues. The search for similarity was doomed to fail even at the point of departure.

Thus, until structuralist media research came on to the scene, the European public sphere was gauged on partly inadequate premises. Media research that offers structural approaches conceptualized the European public sphere in terms of one or more of the following indicators: (1) national media's attention to 'European themes' (e.g. Gerhards 2000; Trenz 2003); (2) the degree of reporting the same events at the same time (e.g. Eder and Kantner 2000); (3) whether news is reported with a 'European framing' or 'similar framing' (Peters et al. 2005); (4) the visibility and resonance of news beyond national borders (Eder and Kantner 2000; Eder and Trenz 2003; Koopmans 2004; Olesen 2005); and (5) the legitimacy of foreign speakers in national public spheres (Risse and Van de Steeg 2003). This line of research has documented that media's attention to Europe-related themes has gradually increased. Media research that deploys 'common/similar discourses' or 'common/similar meaning frames' as an indicator of the European public sphere either reports contradictory findings because the degree of transnational similarity in discourses and meaning frames varies with respect to the 'policy fields one studies' (Koopmans and Erbe 2004, 114) or reports a 'halting' process of Europeanization (Peters et al. 2005).

In addition to deploying national mass media as the empirical equivalent of the concept of the European public sphere while overlooking other options (cf. Baisnee 2007), another, and more serious, predicament of media-focused approaches is their conception of the European public sphere as Europeanization of national public spheres (Eriksen 2005; Koopmans 2007), or as expanding overlaps between national public spheres (Schlesinger 1999), or as a mechanism whose different parts are interconnected in such a way that they respond in a timely way to stimuli received or produced by one part (Eder and Kantner 2000). They presume that national and subnational public spheres will gradually fade away and be replaced by a Europe-wide public sphere through overlaps and/or Europeanization. On the contrary, the political crisis of extremism and populism that the recent financial crisis triggered revealed the strong presence of the national public spheres and national publics after the Eurosphere elites' 60 years of efforts at building a European public sphere. Further, the political crisis of Europe also revealed the interdependent, agonistic coexistence of various public spaces in Europe, for example the public spaces of nativists, nation-statists, Europeanists and minorities (cf. Sicakkan forthcoming). Then, what is an agonistic public sphere?

2.1 The Agonistic Public Sphere

The agonistic relations between the vertical trans-European public (the Eurosphere) and the other publics of Europe (transnational, national and subnational) are constitutive. On the one hand, they constitute the European public sphere by introducing common, integrative 'political cleavages' (Rokkan 1975) on a European scale. On the other hand, they constitute the sub-European public spaces by transforming the publics of Europe in particular directions. On the individual level, multiple and multi-dimensional belongings including the European identity are increasingly spreading. As these three features have increased the complexity of the conflictual relations and become its core characteristics, the European public sphere cannot be properly understood through lenses provided by harmony-seeking consensual, deliberative or aggregative approaches that tend to overlook conflicts and suppress adversarial behaviour and that imply a democratic public sphere cannot develop in conflict-laden diverse societies (cf. Mouffe 1999, 2002, 2007). Therefore, an important task when conceptualizing the European public sphere in agonistic terms is incorporation of the conflict dimension into the concept.

> I propose to distinguish between 'the political' and 'politics'. By 'political' I refer to the dimension of antagonism that is inherent in all human society, antagonism that can take many different forms and can emerge in diverse social relations. Politics, on the other hand, refers to the ensemble of practices, discourses and institutions which seek to establish a certain order and to organize human coexistence in conditions which are always potentially conflictual because they are affected by the dimension of 'the political'. (Mouffe 2007: 42)

This distinction does not only explicitly reveal and embrace the conflict dimension in our understanding of politics, democracy and the public sphere; it also points at where to observe agons, that is, adversary contestations, and agonistic relations when doing empirical research: practices, discourses and institutions. Further, in an attempt to domesticate antagonism in public affairs, Mouffe distinguishes between 'enemies' and 'adversaries', and conceptualizes 'them' and 'us' as adversaries, and the relationship between them as agonistic rather than antagonistic: 'the aim of democratic politics is to construct the "them" in such a way that it is no longer perceived as an enemy to be destroyed, but an "adversary", i.e. somebody whose ideas we combat but whose right to defend those ideas we do not put into question' (Mouffe 2002a: 126). Thus, in an imperfectly truncated form, what constitutes the public sphere is the agons, agonistic relations, conflict structures, adversaries (actors), discourses, and the politics they do. This is the tangible material that the public sphere is made of. In this framework Mouffe does not specify how the constitutive elements of the agonistic plural public sphere are to be assured coexistence against interest-based aggregative or morality-infused deliberative democracy attempts to eradicate or suppress them. Nor do the two other important varieties of the agonistic theory that are developed by James Tully (cf. 2002, 2007, 2008, 2014) and William Connolly (cf. 2002, 2004, 2005, 2010) explicitly and systematically develop this topic beyond the critique that democratic theory has to take account of conflictual relations and accept their eternal existence in politics and society (Mannon 2014). For the purposes of this book, I identify the constitutive elements of the European public sphere in section 3 below. It is important to note that this is an agonistic conceptualization exercise that targets the European public sphere rather than a theory development attempt. However, as the Eurosphere research adopted a grounded theory approach, some of our empirical findings can also be regarded as having some degree of generality beyond the European Union case.

2.2 Extending the Agonistic Pluralist Notion of the Public Sphere

In an agonistic pluralist approach the focus is not only on similarity and conformity but also on difference and conflict. In addition, as mentioned, Mouffe points to practices, discourses and institutions as the core elements of an agonistic public sphere. This specification of empirical themes entails two predicaments. First, it derives from an understanding of the public sphere as a single, unified space. Agons and adversary relations can be integrative or divisive. Regardless of this, they are among the constitutive elements of a public sphere. Incommensurabilities may, on the other hand, lead to severe segmentation and fragmentation. If we accept the whole spectrum of conflict as an inevitable part of social relations as agonist theories do, it is reasonable to acknowledge that the public sphere will be at least partly fragmented and segmented. The public sphere does not cease to exist because of fragmentation and segmentation. Second, Mouffe's analytical specification derives from a structuralist approach that places actors, if not agency, in the background. This renders the actors participating in the public sphere anonymous, concealing the wide spectrum of different collective actors in the public sphere behind the notion of agency.

Thus, a constitutive agonistic dimension, that is, political cleavages generated by the coexistence of multiple public spaces within one public sphere, cannot be adequately included in the conceptual framework without extending Mouffe's agonistic pluralist approach. Such an extension would be to recognize not only the plurality of individuals, groups and conflicts but also the plurality of public spaces in the public sphere. An agonistic pluralist approach has to search the agons in discourses, institutions, public spaces, collective actors, structures and political cleavages that entail both adversarial and harmonious states of affairs, relationships and interactions.

The extension concerns the multiplicity of publics and public spaces that coexist in a public sphere, which is not necessarily unified in the same way as the public sphere of a relatively homogeneous citizenry. This is about recognizing and accepting the very possibility of a public sphere divided or segmented along various incommensurabilities, but still strongly integrated through a 'modus vivendi' (Gray 2000). In order to incorporate this, my agonistic pluralist approach to the public sphere distinguishes between the notions of 'public space' and 'public sphere', where public space is a constituent element of a public sphere. Observing the historical patterns of new public sphere formations and in contrast to what interest-based aggregative and morality-based rational deliberative approaches imply, I assert that existing public spaces need not fade away or overlap with each other for new ones to emerge, and that a public sphere is constituted by publics and individuals trespassing over the boundaries between multiple historical and new public spaces that coexist.

Such an agonistic public sphere is distinguished from other public spheres by its incorporation of a co-constitutive transcendent public space which is all-inclusive, and a boundary-transgressing public that is in collaboration, conflict and contestation with other co-constitutive publics (e.g. transnational, national, subnational). This includes society-initiated and state-initiated publics and the new spaces of communication, interaction and collective action that they create. The special set of agonistic relations between multiple publics that inhabit the co-constitutive public spaces sharply distinguishes an agonistic public sphere from a notion of the public sphere as a unified and open space of communication. This distinction also incorporates the 'subaltern public spaces' and the element of 'emancipation' into the conceptual frame (cf. Fraser 2007).

The co-constitutive public spaces are distinguished from each other on the basis not primarily of their publics' collective identities but of the dominant ideologies and discourses of political order within them (e.g. nationalizing, transnationalizing, globalizing, essentializing, individualizing, genderizing discourses). Agons, that is, contestations, between the publics on determining the common principles on which the political order is to be entrenched are the core theme of the politics between the publics. Discourses of political order are formed and reconstructed by publics within their respective public spaces. They are communicated and negotiated outwards between the public spaces and publics by the boundary-trespassing elites and citizens.

Thus, what constitutes an agonistic public sphere is multiple public spaces, multiple publics, at least one transcendent public space, at least one boundary-trespassing public, boundary-transgressing groups and individuals in all types of public spaces, discourses of political order and political cleavages. It is the agons, platforms, institutions and boundary-trespassing actors that are the integrative forces in an agonistic public sphere. The integrative role of the transcendent public space materializes through different publics' positions and stances, as well as the actions they take for or against the trespassing public and transgressing groups and individuals. That is, it is the politics occurring across and between the public spaces that makes them parts of a public sphere, politics that is made possible by transgression and the trespassing of boundaries. In the context of the agonistic European public sphere, the transcendent public space is the Eurosphere, and the trespassing public is the trans-European public of pro-EU and pro-diversity elites and citizens. It is the agonistic coexistence of the Eurosphere with the historically existing other public spaces that makes a European public sphere possible.

2.3 The Eurosphere as the Defining Component of the European Public Sphere

Following the depiction of the extended notion of an agonistic public sphere, the European public sphere should be conceptualized as a sphere that consists of several different types of public spaces that coexist at different levels, where the top-down trans-European public sphere, that is, the Eurosphere, is the defining constituent public space. The same holds true for the conceptualization of a European public: a trans-European public is the defining public among the multiple types of public that constitute the European public. Note that I am not deploying 'European', 'transnational' and 'trans-European' interchangeably. The condition for imagining this complex set of public spaces and publics as components of the European public sphere is that they constitute a unique cleavage system comprising discourses, alliances and polarizations that contest each other.

Thus, from an extended agonistic pluralist perspective, the European public sphere has come into being with the emergence of a trans-Europeanizing public space (the Eurosphere) and a trans-European public (Eurosphere elites and citizens and their networks and non-state organizations) that stretch over different levels of the EU political and social systems and that coexist, interact and contest with the other current public space types. The European public sphere is radically different from national public spheres. In contrast to national public spheres, it is level-wise and territorially more polycentric; it is not as intrusive and permeating as the national public sphere is; it does not aim to dominate all publics of Europe; its driving force, that is, the trans-European public in the Eurosphere, largely appears as of equal worth in relation to other publics through a geographical understanding of Europeanness, though in contrast to its own egalitarian discourse it displays elitist exclusiveness and a depoliticizing moral superiority in its practices, networks and institutions.

Exploring the role of the European Union's policies in the puzzle that the Eurosphere has brought about, I have already shown in the beginning that the Eurosphere was intentionally built by the European elites to facilitate the formation of a unified European public sphere. A quick glance at the European Union's and the trans-European networks' webpages will show that the European Union's institutions interact intensively with the pan-European networks and trans-European elites. In this sense, part of the Eurosphere's objective has been achieved.

However, although their connections with the European Union's political institutions are fairly good and in some areas also structured and formalized, the scope of their links with national and local civil societies do not seem to match this (Sicakkan 2012b). The pan-European networks and the elites leading them are trying to justify their role with respect to the moral power of the normative ideals that they are advocating – for example human rights, minority rights, citizen rights, individual rights, gender rights, environmental values, the rule of law, democracy, and so on – rather than as representatives of national civil societies. They do not justify their existence based exclusively on the participation of national civil society organizations in the networks and the support that they get from national civil societies. Despite this, the pan-European civil society networks are working to ensure the participation of national civil society organizations in their networks.

On the other hand, civil society organizations operating at the member state level foresee the danger of pan-European networks of civil society becoming merely the messengers of the European Union, conveying values and discourses only downwards and not upwards in the multi-level civil society system that has been created (Sicakkan 2012b). This is a structural conflict between the pan-European networks' headquarters and the non-state organizations that are their members.

Another structural conflict concerns transnationalist, Europeanist non-state organizations operating at the national level that are categorically against collaboration with pan-European networks. They resist joining or collaborating with the pan-European networks, and some even work against them because they regard these networks and the European Union as undemocratic and not capable of protecting the citizen and human rights earned within the nation state, since they exist as top-down initiatives by the European Union. They are suspicious of the pan-European networks also because these networks use a technocratic terminology, which affects ways of thinking, and that they transmit messages one way, from the European Union to national civil societies. In addition to these liberal-democratic and left-leaning objections to the trans-European networks that are partly sponsored by the European Union, we find also nationalist, populist and right-wing extremist groups that are organized transnationally against the postnational, permissive and all-inclusive inclinations in the Eurosphere (Sicakkan 2012b).

In other words, the formation of the European public sphere continues and is still advancing. This is so not only because the trans-European elite layer was partly a successful intermediary carrying messages from the supranational institutions to national civil societies, but also because of the widening and transnational networking of grassroots and other types of political actors that are for and against the normative ideals of the European Union. In particular, certain national-level non-state organizations that are critical about the elitism, permissiveness and top-down communication through the Eurosphere formed their own trans-European networks within the European public sphere (Sicakkan 2012b).

3 THE COMPONENTS OF THE AGONISTIC EUROPEAN PUBLIC SPHERE

The above examples of structural conflict and contestation were an introductory foretaste exemplifying the agons in the European public sphere. In this section, I identify the publics, public spaces and actors of the European public sphere. What is meant by public spaces? What are their features? Which discourses of political order do they entail? Which publics do they accommodate? Which networks link them outwards?

Which actors transgress their boundaries? How does the Eurosphere render them constituents of a European public sphere? In the following, I will briefly answer these questions.[3]

3.1 Publics, Public Spaces and Discourses of Political Order in Europe

Historically, different types of public spaces have emerged in Europe. In order of their appearance in European history, the major types of public spaces that currently coexist are (1) essentializing ethnic, religious or national spaces, (2) nationalizing public spaces of the modern nation states, (3) trans-Europeanizing public spaces, and (4) globalizing or transnationalizing public spaces, which correspond respectively to ethnic and religious publics, national publics, trans-European publics, and transnational or global publics (cf. Sicakkan 2006). Through European integration, each of these public space types has found its expression and representation at different levels.

Before proceeding, the fluctuations in terminology below such as 'national' and 'nationalizing' or 'trans-European' and 'trans-Europeanizing' need some explanation. This concerns the distinction between being, becoming and making. Whereas 'trans-European space' means what a social space is, 'trans-Europeanizing' may connote either what it is making the European public sphere into or what it is becoming itself. Here, I only deploy the distinction between being and making. Thus, a nationalizing public space means a public space whose coexistence in the European public sphere contributes to making the European public sphere a sphere of national public spaces. This distinction applies to the other public space categories in a similar way.

Throughout processes of state formation and nation building, the notion of the public sphere evolved from being the legitimizing aspect of states' sovereignty and political organization to serving as a tool of collective identity promotion and citizen intervention, which led to a conception of the public sphere as a reference and a space of belonging and citizen politics. To the already existing ethnic and religious essentializing spaces, these processes added the national spaces of interaction. National spaces comprise mass political parties, political and economic interest organizations, nationwide media, and elites. However, the national spaces have not necessarily expressed the existing diversities within societies, something which resulted in the survival of the essentializing spaces as well as provoking the emergence of new subnational public spaces. These essentializing public spaces created their own modes of meaning, interaction and participation both within and beyond the frames of the nation states. Essentializing spaces are those spaces that accommodate singular forms of ethnic, religious or diasporic belongings; they are organized in ethnic and religious political parties, organizations, and ethnically and religiously oriented media as well as elite and expert forums.

The forms of belonging reaching beyond the boundaries of nation states and beyond essentializing spaces led to the emergence of new public spaces – transnationalizing spaces. Transnational spaces accommodate cross-border political belongings based on common values that challenge the boundaries of national and essentializing spaces. They represent cross-border social political organizations that exclude singular ethnic, religious, national and diasporic modes of belonging. The transnational space is, thus, different from various versions of 'transnational politics' where national references of meaning persist and constitute the basis for political action. Transnational spaces are also different from diasporic spaces that relate to physically de-territorialized singular belongings. They are about people, and their actions and interactions, which are also psychically de-territorialized. The transnational space comprises transnational organizations and associations with non-spatial expressions and de-essentializing symbolisms. This symbolism relates to misalignments between transnational spaces and other types of spaces, including also national and European public spheres. Transnational spaces accommodate people with multiple references of identification. They find their concrete expressions in trans-border organizations and networks as well as corporative organizations that function as channels of communication with national elites and governments and with the EU institutions.

Conceptualized as a gradually growing process of merging of markets and politics within and beyond the boundaries of nation states, globalization has further affected national states' normative, instrumental and symbolic influences on public sphere formation. The concept of glocalization has in our terminology come to mean the processes of mirroring, protrusion, and appearance of the new ethics, symbols, loyalties, and references of meaning created in globalization, beyond the nation state's frames, and in concrete 'places' located within nation state territories. The glocal space is thus the facade of globalization in our concrete localities. The proliferation of alternative references of identification through globalization has added new, alternative belonging modes and citizenship practices to people's lives. These stretch beyond nationality, ethnicity, religion, nation, minorities, majorities, and territorial belongings. The distinguishing characteristic of the new forms of belonging and new practices of citizenship is the mobility of subjects' minds and bodies between different references of identification (Sicakkan 2006). Coupled with conventional politics' insufficient capacity to respond to citizens' interests emanating from these new modes of belonging, the consequence of this proliferation to politics is the emergence of glocal spaces. Glocal spaces accommodate essentializing belongings, national modes of belonging, transnational modes of belonging, and belongings inspired and informed by the idea of a diverse society. Glocal spaces entail a variety of local incipient forms of all-inclusive organizations.

To these, we can add the trans-European spaces which are in formation as a consequence of the processes of European integration. Trans-European spaces are quite similar to glocal spaces in terms of facilitating the diversity and equality of belongings. People with glocal and European belongings see the European Union as a better political entity than the nation state because they believe it gradually eradicates the existing national boundaries in Europe (Sicakkan 2006: 111–114). However, whereas people with European belongings stop reasoning at this point, persons with glocal belongings continue: They perceive the European Union as another political entity that divides humanity with new boundaries, like nation states did. Yet the European Union, for them, is better than nation states because its borders are broader (Sicakkan 2006: 111–114). This adds a new distinction to our analytical categories, namely the distinction between 'the global subject' and 'the euro-subject' accommodated in, respectively, 'glocal spaces' and 'trans-European spaces'.

To summarize, in order of chronological appearance in political history, the first type of public space is that of essentializing spaces. Essentializing spaces are observed in some of the European states' religious and ethnic minorities which view their own and other identities as unalterable and fixed for all time. In Europe, they have formed their own spaces of interaction, meaning, and channels of participation in politics and in the society at large. The dominant discourse of political order in essentializing spaces is entrenched in primordialist assumptions of identity and ethnicity. The second type comprises the nationalizing spaces, which were created by the nation states. The national space entails state-building peoples and minorities that have been assimilated into the national mode of belonging. The discourse of political order derives from a naturalistic idea of the nation state which takes the international system of nation states as granted. Also national public spaces may appear with an essentializing belonging-content, and historically this has happened in states with a high degree of ethnic homogeneity. The third type is the transnationalizing spaces, which exclude essentializing and territorialized forms of belonging. The discourse of political order that upholds transnationalizing spaces is entrenched in an assumption of identity, belonging and state that is detached from territory and state. The interactions in transnational spaces are cross-border, organized in transnational organizations, and aimed at bypassing the existing political and territorial boundaries between humans. The fourth type of public space is glocal spaces, where all the above-mentioned modes of belonging and participation forms coexist. The fifth type is the emerging trans-European spaces, which comprise belongings situated in local contexts that are characterized by a high degree of identification with Europe either instead of or in addition to the aforementioned references of identification. Glocal spaces and trans-European spaces constitute an alternative to the traditional notions of public space, and they may be seen as prototypes of the diverse societies of the future. They both are inclusive of essentialized, national, transnational, glocal and European modes of belonging. Glocal spaces are localized in local incipient organizations throughout Europe (Sicakkan 2006), whereas trans-European spaces are manifested in Europe-oriented political parties, organizations, social movements and incipient organizations.

The reality is that these public spaces coexist, and emerging public spaces do not necessarily replace the currently existing ones. When operationalized in terms of their political order discourses, actors and their networks, the publics and public spaces reach beyond their own boundaries to constitute a cleavage system of discourses and alliances, in competition with each other to dominate the public sphere. It is the identification of such a cleavage system of contesting discourses and alliances at the European level that allows us to assert that, with the emergence of a trans-European public sphere of elites and citizens (the Eurosphere), and its encounters of conflict and contestation with other public spaces and publics, a European public sphere has emerged.

3.2 Actors and Networks in the Agonistic European Public Sphere

Pan-European networks – both those that are initiated by the European Union and those that have emerged either independently from the European Union or as a reaction to its attempts to form a political elite-led civil society – are the backbone of the European public sphere keeping the already existing collective actors and their public spaces linked. As mentioned, this is due to the existence of the Eurosphere.

Analytically, the network dimension of the European public sphere can be approached in two ways. The first approach focuses on 'horizontal' (Koopmans and Erbe 2004) networks where social and political actors seek and get involved in transnational collaboration and communication without attempting to build a higher hierarchical level that structures their interactions. The second approach emphasizes 'vertical' (Koopmans and Erbe 2004) networks that seek to articulate more structured, and often institutionalized, channels of collaboration and communication, at the European level. The second approach can be further elaborated in terms of bottom-up and top-down networks. Bottom-up networks emerge through social and political actors' own initiatives to build trans-European networks seeking to structure and/or institutionalize their collaboration at the European level. Top-down networks emerge through elite-led European-level initiatives that attempt to bring different social and political actors together under their umbrella (Sicakkan 2012b).

Each process and mechanism for forming a trans-European network implies a specific preference for a particular model of a European public sphere. Different preferences concerning involvement in horizontal and vertical trans-European structures, on the one hand, and in bottom-up and top-down structures, on the other hand, imply different approaches to diversity, as well as different attributions of ontological priority to the individual, the collectivity (of different types), the subnational, the national and the European. For instance, some actors deliberately rule out participating in vertical structures because they do not want to contribute to a hierarchical European public sphere structure. Therefore, in trans-European constellations of national-level organizations, we find not only pro-European orientations but also diverging ideas and strategies concerning how the European public sphere should be structured (or not be structured at all), for example a strictly segmented European public sphere along the lines of a Europe of nations, or a European public sphere as an arena that facilitates only limited transnational collaboration on certain issues that cannot be dealt with only at the national level, or a European public sphere of overlapping publics that follows the multi-level governance structure of the EU, or an ideally integrated single European public sphere, and so on.

The network dimension of trans-European political spaces can be measured by deploying rather simple indicators: (1) the operative level of the networks (regional, national, trans-European interactions); (2) the scope of collaborative interaction (collaborative projects or actions, joint projects or actions, attempts to formulate common objectives, efforts to formulate common actions to address common concerns, synchronizing existing project or action plans, mutual information sharing); and (3) membership status in networks (active membership, passive membership, observer status).

The actors interacting with these networks cover the whole spectrum of social and political actors, including individual citizens, political parties, non-state organizations such as social movement organizations, corporate and public interest organizations, NGOs, think tanks, print and broadcast media actors and state institutions. They operate within one of the public space types mentioned in the previous section. Some of them operate, in addition, across different public spaces. They may be open to or sceptical of the existence of one or more of the public space types. They may be for or against the European Union, the European public sphere, the nation state, an ideology or any social group. They may be involved more or less in trans-European collaboration and communication and in European-level public debates. By studying these factors, one may elucidate to what extent actors contribute to the formation of a European public sphere. Further, some features of these collective actors may affect citizen involvement in the European public sphere. It is in order to mention some important public sphere players at this point.

Think tanks and their trans-European networks are important players in the European public sphere because they are involved in work with policy analysis and opinion formation and consultation to decision-makers at different levels. Another important type of public sphere actor is political parties. Political parties include all sorts of political organizations and political alliances that contest for government power in democratic elections. Social movements and non-governmental organizations are also among the central collective actors participating in public debates. They are political organizations with defined political objectives around clear issue orientations which do not run for government power, but attempt to influence the political decision-making processes and their outcomes in other ways. Media organizations are central entities, both as actors participating in the public sphere and as a channel of communication in the public sphere.

Different features of these collective actors are expected to have different impacts on citizens' involvement in political processes. In this respect we can define two types of collective actors: social and political actors that operate within, from, on behalf of and across communicative public spaces. They constitute and are accommodated by the aforementioned types of communicative public spaces; and they are amongst the key determinants of the structuring quality of such public spaces, which in turn impact upon citizens' involvement and participation at different levels. In this respect these collective entities should be treated both as (1) political and social actors that shape the communicative public spaces and (2) components of communicative public spaces that are shaped by these spaces.

Regarding the former, the relevant feature is collective social and political actors' orientations to different communicative public spaces.

With their positive, negative or neutral orientations towards singular and multiple types of communicative public spaces (essentializing, nationalizing, transnationalizing, trans-Europeanizing) – combined with their potential structuring, guiding and mobilizing capacity – collective social or political actors influence citizens' ability to think and act as 'co-others', that is, the ability to treat oneself as just another other (Sicakkan 2006), and thus citizens' ways and substance of involvement. The structuring and guiding relationships between communicative public spaces and the mentioned types of social and political actors thus gain relevance, though as an indirect (spurious) explanatory factor. Another relevant feature of social and political actors participating in the public sphere is the type of their collective vision of political society and the public sphere. This is operationalized with the following models: a single protected sphere, multiple segmented spheres, a single shared sphere, multi-level overlapping spheres, multi-level differential spheres, and composite civic spheres (cf. Sicakkan 2012a).

Regarding the latter, physical presence of collective actors as organizations or as incipient organizations in these communicative public spaces constitutes the concrete manifestation of these spaces. In other words, with their presence, they make the communicative public spaces real, tangible and physically and locally available to citizens. In this sense, their locales and organized activities become arenas, channels and ways of citizens' participation and involvement. Thus, channels, forms, issues, events and discourses of involvement that these collective actors make available for citizens are imperative in an analysis of the European public sphere and the public spaces that form it.

Social and political actors subsisting and operating within and across different public spaces and their networks create the publics and public spaces of Europe as well as the European public sphere through the political cleavages they generate on different scales, local, national, European and global. The agonistic pluralist perspective of the public sphere requires identification of the actors that create the constitutive political cleavages and agons by transgressing and trespassing over public space boundaries. An agonistic pluralist approach to transnational and global public spheres requires identification of the networks of actors that emerge as a consequence of their transgression and trespassing.

4 CONCLUSION

There are few widely recognized facts to help explain the processes of change in today's Europe, but those facts that are established depict a remarkable picture. The European territory is owned and politically structured by nations and nation states. The relations between the European states are to a significant extent characterized by an unprecedented degree of supranational and intergovernmental institutionalization through the European Union and other European organizations and treaties. Although these international institutions increasingly shape their lives, citizens continue to play a minuscule role in European-level decision-making. Next, Europe is inhabited by a complex diversity of historical and new publics. These publics, for example minority publics, national publics, transnational publics, European publics, and new publics that are more challenging to categorize, create their distinct, internal discursive and interactive spaces. The institutional and other collective actors emerging from and operating in these spaces, and giving voice for the publics inhabiting these spaces, interact increasingly beyond their own and other boundaries.

Some of these trans-boundary communications and interactions – be they collaborations, conflicts, exchanges or contestations – can be explained by common past, shared cultural heritage, collective identities, geographical proximity, practical suitability, exit and voice possibilities, political opportunity structures, and elite initiatives. This chapter addressed the ingredients of this reality that cannot be explained exclusively by such factors, but also, with the increasing transgression and trespassing of the boundaries of their immediate surroundings, something which allows them to identify with more distant political entities, hard-to-imagine collectivities, and less tangible ideas about their own belongings.

In order to incorporate these insights, this chapter proposed a conceptual and analytical framework for studying the ongoing formation and structuring of the European public sphere. From an extended agonistic pluralism perspective of the public sphere, which pronouncedly recognizes the plurality of publics and public spaces within a public sphere as well as specifying the institutions and different types of actors participating in it, it conceptualized the European public sphere as a web of (1) existing historical and new publics, public spaces and discourses of political order, (2) networks and social and political actors and, most importantly, (3) a transcendent public space (the Eurosphere) of a transgressing public and the new European-scale political cleavages and agons that they generate in interaction with the other publics and public spaces of Europe.

This approach gives a fresh understanding of postnational public spheres in general and the transnational European public sphere in particular. In the current chaotic picture of citizens, organizations, communicative public spaces and political institutions that interact, interconnect and interlink with each other, social and political actors are facilitating or inhibiting the emergence of an inclusive European public sphere in different ways. In this chapter, actors' roles in and contributions to the formation of a European public sphere are understood in terms of the interconnectedness of existing public spaces and interlinkages between organizations (collective actors) beyond a variety of borders and boundaries. It is agons generated by actors' transcendence and transgressing of boundaries that create interconnectedness between Europe's communicative public spaces. On the other hand, it is the different degrees of openness or closure of the existing communicative public spaces that facilitate or obstruct such transcendence and transgression.

Thus, the social and political dynamics of the emergence of a European public sphere must be sought in the tension between the architects, gatekeepers, transgressors and transcenders of borders and boundaries within the existing and newly emerging European publics. Through compliance, endorsement, resistance and opposition, and through boundary-making, gatekeeping, transgression and transcendence, they create multiple poles and polarizations in the very same European political space. This makes them all architects of the European public sphere.

NOTES

1. White Paper on a European Communication Policy (COM(2006) 35 Final), European Governance: A White Paper (COM(2001) 428 Final) and Plan D for Democracy, Dialogue and Debate (COM (2005) 494 Final).
2. See ec.europa.eu/public_opinion/docs/entretien_rabier.pdf.
3. For a more elaborate discussion of these questions see Sicakkan (2006).

REFERENCES

Baisnee, O. (2007) The European Public Sphere Does Not Exist (At Least It's Worth Wondering …), *European Journal of Communication* 22(4): 493–503.

Connolly, W.E. (2002 [1991]) *Identity/Difference: Democratic Negotiations of Political Paradox*, expanded edn, Minneapolis: University of Minnesota Press.

Connolly, W.E. (2004 [1995]) *The Ethos of Pluralization*, Minneapolis: University of Minnesota Press.

Connolly, W.E. (2005) *Pluralism*, Durham, NC: Duke University Press.

Connolly, W.E. (2010) A World of Becoming, in Alan Finlayson (ed.), *Democracy and Pluralism: The Political Thought of William E. Connolly*, pp. 222–235, London: Routledge.

Eder, K. and C. Kantner (2000) Transnationale Resonanzstrukturen in Europa: Eine Kritik der Rede vom Öffentlichkeitsdefizit, in M. Bach (ed.), *Die Europäisierung nationaler Gesellschaften*, Sonderheft 40 der *Kölner Zeitschrift für Soziologie und Sozialpsychologie*, pp. 306–331, Wiesbaden: Westdeutscher Verlag.

Eder, K. and H.-J. Trenz (2003) The Making of a European Public Space: An Inquiry into Relating Supranational Politics and Transnational Spaces of Communication: The Case of Justice and Home Affairs, in B. Kohler-Koch (ed.), *Linking EU and National Governance*, pp. 111–134, Oxford: Oxford University Press.

Eriksen, E.O. (2005) An Emerging European Public Sphere, *European Journal of Social Theory* 8(3): 341–363.

Fraser, N. (2007) Transnationalizing the Public Sphere: On the Legitimacy and Efficacy of Public Opinion in a Post-Westphalian World, *Theory, Culture and Society* 24(4): 7–30.

Gerhards, J. (2000) Europäisierung von Ökonomie und Politik und die Trägheit der Entstehung einer europäischen Öffentlichkeit, in M. Bach (ed.), *Die Europäisierung nationaler Gesellschaften*, Sonderheft 40 der *Kölner Zeitschrift für Soziologie und Sozialpsychologie*, pp. 277–305, Wiesbaden: Westdeutscher Verlag.

Gray, J. (2000) *Two Faces of Liberalism*, Cambridge: Polity Press.

Habermas, J., S. Lennox and F. Lennox (1974) The Public Sphere: An Encyclopedia Article (1964), *New German Critique* 3: 49–55.

Harrison, J. and S. Pukallus (2015) The European Community's Public Communication Policy 1951–1967, *Contemporary European History* 24(2): 233–251.

Kaelble, H. (2002) The Historical Rise of a European Public Sphere? *Journal of European Integration History* 8(2): 9–22.

Koopmans, R. (2004) Movements and Media: Selection Processes and Evolutionary Dynamics in the Public Sphere, *Theory and Society* 33(3–4): 367–391.

Koopmans, R. (2007) Who Inhabits the European Public Sphere? Winners and Losers, Supporters and Opponents in Europeanised Political Debate, *European Journal of Political Research* 46(2): 183–210.

Koopmans, R. and J. Erbe (2004) Towards a European Public Sphere? *Innovation: The European Journal of Social Science Research* 17(2): 97–118.

Leonard, M. (2005) *Why Europe Will Run the 21st Century*, London: Fourth Estate.

Mannon, W. (2014) Applying Principles of Agonistic Politics to Institutional Design, Paper proposed to ECPR Conference, http://ecpr.eu/Filestore/PaperProposal/6a607c02-3a40-493d-abbc-a0c0bd587551.pdf (accessed 16 March 2016).

Meynaud, J. and D. Sidjanski (1965) *Science politique et intégration européenne*, Genève: Institut d'études européennes.

Mouffe, C. (1999) Deliberative Democracy or Agonistic Pluralism, *Social Research* 66(3): 745–758.

Mouffe, C. (2002) Which Public Sphere for a Democratic Society? Intellectuals, Justice and Democracy, *Theoria: A Journal of Social and Political Theory* 99: 55–65.

Mouffe, C. (2002a) For an Agonistic Public Sphere, in O. Enwezor (ed.), *Democracy Unrealized: Documenta 11, Platform 1*, pp. 87–97, Berlin: Hatje Cantz.

Mouffe, C. (2007) Democracy as Agonistic Pluralism, in Elizabeth Deeds Ermarth (ed.), *Rewriting Democracy: Cultural Politics in Postmodernity*, pp. 36–45, Aldershot: Ashgate.

Olesen, T. (2005) Transnational Publics: New Spaces of Social Movement Activism and the Problem of Global Long-sightedness, *Current Sociology* 53(3): 419–440.

Peters, B., S. Sifft, A. Wimmel, M. Brüggemann and K. Kleinen-von Königslöw (2005) National and Transnational Public Spheres: The Case of the EU, *European Review* 3(1): 139–160.

Risse, T. and M. Van de Steeg (2003) An Emerging European Public Sphere? Empirical Evidence and Theoretical Clarifications, Paper presented to the conference Europeanization of Public Spheres, Political Mobilization, Public Communication and the European Union, Science Center Berlin, 20–22 June.

Rokkan, S. (1975) Dimensions of State Formation and Nation-building: A Possible Paradigm for Research on Variations within Europe, in C. Tilly (ed.), *The Formation of National States in Western Europe*, pp. 562–600, Princeton, NJ: Princeton University Press.

Schlesinger, P. (1999) Changing Spaces of Political Communication: The Case of the European Union, *Political Communication* 16(3): 263–279.

Sicakkan, H.G. (2006) Glocal Spaces as Prototypes of a Future Diverse Society: An Exploratory Study in Six European Countries, in H.G. Sicakkan and Y. Lithman (eds), *What Happens When a Society Is Diverse?* pp. 105–148, New York: Edwin Mellen Press.

Sicakkan, H.G. (2012a) Diversity, Polity and the European Public Sphere, *Javnost – The Public* 19(1): 5–18.

Sicakkan, H.G. (2012b) Trans-Europeanizing Public Spaces in Europe, *Javnost – The Public* 19(1): 103–124.

Sicakkan, H.G. (forthcoming) Is the European Public Sphere Good for Democracy? in Y. Peters and M. Tatham (eds), *Democratic Transformations in Europe 31: Challenges and Opportunities*, Abingdon: Routledge.

Trenz, H.-J. (2003) Media Coverage on European Governance: Testing the Performance of National Newspapers, EUSA Biennial International Conference, Nashville, TN, 27–29 March.

Tully, J. (2002) The Unfreedom of the Moderns in Comparison to Their Ideals of Constitutional Democracy, *Modern Law Review*, 65(2): 204–228.

Tully, J. (2007 [1995]) *Strange Multiplicity: Constitutionalism in an Age of Diversity*, Cambridge: Cambridge University Press.

Tully, J. (2008) *Public Philosophy in a New Key*, Vol. I: *Democracy and Civic Freedom*, Cambridge: Cambridge University Press.

Tully, J. (2014) On Global Citizenship, in J. Tully, *On Global Citizenship: James Tully in Dialogue*, pp. 1–100, London: Bloomsbury.

2. Europe's territorial transformation, regions and diversity: towards a common European public sphere?

Wanda Dressler

This chapter analyses two dimensions of the EU's approach to territorial diversity with an impact on the formation of a European public sphere. The first dimension relates to the variety of the novel institutional ways in which territories of the member states are transformed into an open common space, while crafting at the same time a European unity within the diversity of territorial cultural traditions, groups, institutions and political systems and integrating the migrant groups coming from European and non-European countries. The second dimension concerns the various ways in which the EU seeks to accommodate diversity, understood as respect for and recognition of differences related to gender, sexuality, ethnicity, religion, race, nationality and handicap, from the European to the national and local scales, through diverse European instruments. These two dimensions may potentially seem to serve contradictory ends, but combined they contribute to the emergence of a new set of political interactions across national borders, administrative levels and territorial scales. This happens by making a variety of European, national and sub-national territories interact in a subsidiary way. Thus, this chapter discusses whether the new plural set of political relations arising from the EU's territorial transformation and diversity accommodation policies may facilitate the creation of an agonistic European public sphere (see Sicakkan, this volume, Chapter 1).

In an effort to answer this question, I focus on the EU's regional and diversity policies and the normative and legislative processes and instruments that are devised to contribute to the still ongoing vast territorial transformation. I put special emphasis on the norms in use and the capacity of the EU's instruments to energize a dual political logic in the member states which combines the processes of regionalization and diversity accommodation with the amalgamation of the national spaces.

The EU's main legal and institutional instruments that have focused on territory include, among others, euro-regions, regionalism, the European Committee of the Regions, Council of Europe policy, Helsinki agreements, CSCE (today the Organization for Security and Cooperation in Europe, OSCE), laws on minority protection at the international level, and widespread laws on national decentralization. These were set up in parallel with linguistic and cultural instruments such as the Charter on Minority Languages, the Convention on Cultural Diversity and the Directive against Racism and Anti-semitism[1] (2004–2005), the Charter and the last Law of European Fundamental Rights in 2009 included in the Lisbon Treaty.

Approached from a multidisciplinary perspective, my evaluations of the impacts of the EU's territorial diversity policies are based on an important body of fieldwork on national and cross-border regions, micro- and macro-regional levels, and numerous texts from the EU (see Dressler 1999, 2005, 2007, 2009). I start with a brief history of the reform process of regionalization that put the member states into a process of change from national states to postnational states. I continue with an assessment of the international and European instruments adopted and the necessary theoretical and geopolitical reflection which led to their implementation. I deploy examples of different types of territories to evaluate the efficiency of EU multilevel governance in dealing with diversity. Next, I show how the regionalization process brought about a new diversity structure within the transformed European territorial space. Finally, I conclude that, because the current multilevel and cross-border territorial organization and the increased poly-ethnic features within it are far too complex and considerably more conflict-laden than mainstream public sphere theories assume, an agonistic perspective is a more realistic approach to the European public sphere (cf. Sicakkan, this volume, Chapter 1).

1 EUROPE'S TERRITORIAL TRANSFORMATION INTO A COMMON SPACE

Since the post-war era, we have seen various policy initiatives for the deconstructing and rebuilding of European territories on different scales in order to create a Europe without borders and facilitate the flux of goods, services and persons. These initiatives emerged through different institutions producing new norms (national, European and supranational entities, most of the time concurrently) and imposing a new key role on the member states in facilitating exchanges, which in turn contributed to the weakening of their own sovereignty. The region, conceived initially as the new category of practice and analysis in the rebuilding of Europe, has since the 1950s been expected to reproduce European integration, accommodation of native minorities and integration of new migrant minorities in compliance with a new, transformed national logic that was entrenched in both European laws and the member states' own dynamism and political will.

During the period 1970–1990, the regional policies that deployed regions as a new management level (among other things, by enabling the member states to obtain EU funding based on regional needs) have generally been quite successful in the old member states, under the top-down pressure of European institutions and the bottom-up demands coming from various social movement organizations. The latter took a new political turn in the 1970s and forced the new and old elites, both from countries and from regions, to renew the regionalist discourse inherited from the interwar period.[2] Except in some cases such as the Basque Country and Corsica, where violence continued for decades in search of independence, the formal frames were not put in question at the institutional level, each country shaping the regionalization process the way it wanted, according to social demand.

The member states' own regional policies and European regional policies (regionalism, partnership, subsidiarity in the Maastricht Treaty) were further transformed through the reforms of Structural Funds which started in 1988, giving the regions an opportunity to exist at different levels and to benefit politically, financially and economically from this opportunity to deepen European integration.

The EU also reached a consensus for the 2004 enlargement process among the new members, decentralization and regionalization being elements of conditionality for entering the EU as well as the problem of integration of different migrant minorities which arose with greater intensity during the period 1990–2010.

Since 2008, the quasi-zero growth rate that characterized the years after the onset of the crisis has had consequences for the goals of minority protection and equality of rights and social status in relatively more vulnerable regional contexts, increasingly centred around regional or global metropoles. Macro-regions also became an efficient policy implementation context where regions facing similar economic challenges could be addressed cross-nationally in common policy frames. Indeed, the EU regional policy that was based on the member states' own territorial-administrative divisions enabled the regions to interact with the European Union directly.

Along with the different sorts of territorial rescaling and regional interconnectedness across national borders, the current demographic decline in the EU and the relative intensity of migratory flux adds complexity and challenges to the old and recurrent issue of regional, territorial and linguistic diversity within all the European member states. The challenge is how to evolve smoothly from the context of national states, still so vivid and closed in on themselves, to a competitive multilevel, postnational society in a shared European political space, peaceful and open to the diversity of European and non–European cultures.

1.1 Regions as the Basic Instrument of Europe's Territorial Transformation

The regionalization of national spaces started through the regional reform in Western Europe in the 1960s and in Eastern Europe in the 1990s, during the different phases of the European Union enlargement. Further, the setting up of larger regional scales, for example the macro-regions, aimed to facilitate the implementation of Euro-regulation and to consolidate cohesion. The general process which explains the significant rise of the region as a means of territorial transformation across Western Europe lies first in the uneven economic development in the post-war era. Well established in the interwar period, the phenomenon of the 'depressed region', increased by declining industry or uncompetitive agriculture, stood out in greater contrast. It caused a deeper distortion between the rich and poor or underdeveloped territories, contrary to what the numerous liberal adepts of market self-regulation predicted. Pressure built up for measures to address the handicaps of relative disadvantages, giving a new meaning to regions: economic interest supplying collective bonds. Uneven economic development not only promoted regional identification, but also gave rise to regionalist claims. The emergence of supranational administration, more distant from immediate experience than any previous authority, put an understandable premium on sub-national administration as a compensating mechanism.

After the end of the war, which led to the Treaty of Rome (1951) and to a common market that ended unconditional sovereignty, the new European institutions – the Commission and the Parliament – tried to bypass the national authorities in pursuit of a closer union and had an interest in promoting regional institutions as power-level partners. The values of nationality receded to a secondary plane compared to the claims of liberty. The European Charter of Regionalization in 1988, foreseeing that regions would be actors in member-state policymaking within the EU, aimed to formally enjoin member states to institutionalize regional identities. Proposed mainly by Germany to ensure the *Länder*'s role in the future of European construction, however, this initiative was rejected (Marcou 1999). The regionalization process was not mature and consistent enough throughout the Western European territories to institutionalize the role of the region. Nevertheless, the further rise of democracy offered a positive opening to the recognition of regions and regional administrations as legitimate policy actors. Parliamentary systems based on universal suffrage and civil rights, boosted by political movements in favour of difference in 1968–1970, provided a compelling model of self-government.

The pattern of regionalization applied to the different institutional and political structures of the member states yielded variable results. On reflection, it showed that the number of areas with a powerful sense of their own separate character was far smaller than that of the regions into which most of the EU is divided today. For every 'large' entity like Bavaria, Brittany or Catalonia, there are many more 'small' units such as the administrative region of Rhones-Alpes, Lower Saxony, or Murcia in Spain. The process whereby such distinct kinds of zoning have acquired a common political reality is to be found in the political history of these territories.

The social turbulence of the late 1960s and early 1970s increased the pressure for liberties beyond the agenda of parliaments and shook the established order. The new pattern of democratic pressure, connecting territorial and industrial democracy, explains the way that regions came on to the political agenda in these countries. The range of state traditions among them was critical in determining the outcome. The hierarchy of effective regionalization corresponds closely to the institutional and ideological bequests of an earlier age. That is why it seems preferable not to speak of regions but rather of a process of regionalization which took different forms according to state traditions and the choice made by the states of the institutional form to mobilize as partners to the EU: it could be territorial communities other than non-existing regions, endowed with specific traditional powers (more or less financial and institutional autonomy) or granted more competencies to fulfil the EU funding criteria.

The European Structural and Investment Funds, especially the European Regional Development Fund and the European Cohesion Fund, were the mechanisms adopted in 1975 by the supporters of social regulation of liberal economic trends in order to stimulate regional policy (NUTS 2) and reduce the disparities linked to uneven development and the economic trends of spatial concentration of more advanced technology and infrastructures of industries and services. The regional policy, representing 7.8 per cent of the EU budget in 1980, was in rapid progression after the various enlargements of Greece, Spain, Portugal and the cohesion policy (Agenda 2000: 213 billion euros for 1999–2006; Marcou 1999: 7). It can be considered as the most notable innovation in the territorial administrative system. However, it must be said that spatial concentration mechanisms did challenge regulatory attempts during the first decades of the construction of Europe.

After centuries of centralization and authoritarianism, in the 1990s the regionalization and democratization processes went on in parallel to the implementation of affirmative action, following the debates on multiculturalism, in order to eliminate the regional disparities. This thinking on regions was supported by the Council of the European Union and pursued through the Committee of the Regions created in 1993–1994. Its aims were efficient transmission, increasing the understanding of European policy norms, and distribution of financial aid at all levels in order to implement the subsidiarity principle and the cohesion demands.

Faced with the impossible task of promoting one institutional model of region or defining it, the EU institutions have given a normative definition of regional entities as 'entities situated immediately below the state level, with a political representation carried out through an elected council, an association or an organ created at region level by an entity at a lesser level' (Article 3 in the Assembly of European Regions statutes). The result was that the Committee of the Regions membership comprised 95 representatives of communes or municipalities, 41 representatives of provinces and departments or similar units, and 86 representatives of regions. These are in charge of defining the eligibility of regions and zones according to a common nomenclature of statistical territorial units (NUTS) which do not coincide with the states' political and administrative divisions. It was the only way to allow different kinds of actors to collaborate on the construction of a European common public sphere with shared norms, respectful of the respective administrative territorial ruling traditions.

On the other hand, the European Union could not operate alone in this process of reframing territorial dynamics. It was necessary to associate neighbouring countries such as the USSR during the Cold War, as it was interested in macro-regional cooperation and learning from the European model. The Helsinki agreements and the agenda of the OSCE supported the idea of setting up international standards on minority rights and implementation of cross-border cooperation. For a European continent split after the building of the Berlin Wall, it was necessary to build a common vision of territorial dynamics. The Helsinki agreements and the OSCE agenda supported the idea of setting up international standards on minority rights and implementation of cross-border cooperation. So, at different levels, the 'territory' connotes the many meanings generally defined by theoreticians of geographical and territorial management interested in spatial factors of endogenous development and the territories' potential (including networks, action capacity, identity mobilization, etc.). Sociologists, economists and geographers such as Henri Lefevre, Joël Bonnemaison, Michel Foucher (e.g. Foucher and Gonon 1993) and Paul Krugman (e.g. Krugman 2000, 2011) in particular all contributed to this effort. The territory is now considered as a social construction, invented or reinvented. Territoriality is a cultural relationship free from the links which constitute it.

1.2 Interconnecting the Regions: Cross-border Regions and Macro-regions

Countries do their territorial structuring by dividing their territorial spaces horizontally and vertically in different ways, and the NUTS system of the European Union is primarily based on the territorial administrative units of member states. Despite significant differences between the European countries in this respect, the regional administrative level has now become one of the key factors leading to the deeper anchoring and amalgamation of the sub-national, national and European spaces. The member states were expected to follow the subsidiarity principle. The building of new identities was expected to bring up to date the relationship of the groups to their territories and make it easier for them to readapt in a dynamic way.

Building on this complex system of regions, the bottom-up attempts to interlink these regions started at the beginning of the post-war period. Created in Western Europe in the 1950s, euro-regions are cross-border associations of municipalities with their own budget to develop permanent cooperation in a variety of domains. Started through a common agreement with European actors and implemented by national, departmental and/or regional bodies, the euro-regions have a consultative status. In the 1990s, cross-border cooperation also started to function in countries scheduled for membership accession to the EU. The Association for European Border Regions (ARFE) financed by the EU plays an active role through its pilot project Linkage Assistance and Cooperation for the European Border Regions (LACE), which aims to overcome historical difficulties. Since 1991, the EU has helped in the making of transborder networks on its territory and 'Median Europe' (Maurel 1997) through the Interreg II Programmes

(1995–1998).[3] They are starting to carry out an inter-community dialogue which had been interrupted for decades or even centuries.

After the region, which is considered as the vector of European linguistic, cultural and historical diversity (cf. Anderson 1994), the macro-region or interregional level came on to Europe's political scene, transcending national borders to create new economic-territorial units. The Committee of the Regions renewed, under the 2010 Spanish presidency, the Conference of European Regions with Legislative Power created in 2001 (REGLEG) as a powerful network (43 per cent of the EU population live in these regions). REGLEG participated in the implementation of the White Paper on Multilevel Governance written in 1999 as well as in the cohesion policy to ensure the future of the Lisbon strategy. The process began in 2007 with the publication of the Territorial Agenda and the Green Paper on Territorial Cohesion written for the European Commission in 2008. With the White Paper on Multilevel Governance, a new era of cooperation started across national, regional and local borders, between policy areas and different levels of governance. Concrete cooperation has happened through the strategy of macro-regions. Examples, including both existing and suggested macro-regions, are the Baltic Sea Region, the Danube Region, the Adriatic and Ionian Region, the Alpine Region, the North Sea Region, the Atlantic Arc Region and the Black Sea Region.

The macro-regions strategy experiments with a new way of thinking about multilevel governance and subsidiarity, the two key concepts at the heart of the Committee of the Regions' work. It corresponds to the triple objective of economic, social and territorial cohesion written into the Lisbon Treaty. Cross-border cooperation within macro-regions is considered to have 'an enormous potential', implying better coordination, shared solutions and so on. No longer identified as political or administrative entities, these levels rather aim to strengthen regional development policy and European integration. They are spaces, intellectually (and administratively) built to be actors of integration in the European economic and socio-political process, around a natural (geographical) or economic space or a historical past, and with the aim of reframing a pragmatic and operational identity.

Currently, Europe houses many types of regions that are interconnected through a wide range of collaboration arrangements and common action schemes. For example, out of 20 regions, five have a special status in Italy; there are 17 autonomous communities with 26 cantons in Switzerland, 16 *Länder* in Germany and nine in Austria. Now these are further connected to each other through the euro-regions, other cross-border regions and macro-regions, each of which accommodates different types and configurations of diversity.

The Council of European Municipalities and Regions (CEMR), founded in 1951 in Geneva, as well as many associations from these territories, have fought to anchor in the Lisbon Treaty the subsidiarity principle with instruments to implement it concretely (and financially) at the national legislative level to maintain or promote territorial cohesion. The territorial dimension added to the cohesion policy objectives in the Lisbon Treaty 'epitomises the full diversity of Europe', said the new European Commissioner for regional policy. The economic crisis, with its uneven territorial consequences, has shown that cohesion policy continues to play a central role in the balanced integration of Europe's regions, by enabling structural adjustments. Implementation of the cohesion policy also implies a strengthening of communication and cohesion between each level.

In December 2010, the President of the Commission said in a plenary session of the Committee of the Regions: 'I need you to convince the member states to sign territorial pacts with big towns and regions.' The regional and local elites are more and more considered as 'the indispensable links of the EU whose role must be extended as equal partners and not only executives with a revised budget to succeed to realize the objectives of 2020 strategy'. The bottom-up role of sub-national elites should be well considered in the future, through the homogenizing role of big metropoles which draw powerful forces of innovation and contestation around their surroundings. Europe's transnational public sphere is being constituted through these new urban actors in Western Europe mainly (e.g. Podemos in Spain, the forces around Tsipras in Greece).

These processes required a symbolic interconnection between the regions to strengthen their functional cohesion. The logic sustaining the production of these new territories is increasingly combined with the logic of networking, speeded up with new technology revolution to ensure cohesion through accommodation of diversity. The combination of these different logics appears necessary to satisfy the needs of economic and social integration.

2 EUROPE'S TERRITORIAL TRANSFORMATION, NEW COLLECTIVITIES AND ACCOMMODATION OF DIVERSITY

The two aforementioned logics were fused through parallel, synchronous implementation of various regional and diversity policies. Whereas regions were made the setting in which diversity accommodation would take place, regions themselves became a diversity element to be accommodated along with the other diversities in Europe. For example, the EU created new general instruments such as the European Charter of Regional and Minority Languages (1992) and the Committee of the Regions, established in 1994 with a consultative role. The European treaties bound the Commission and the European Council to consult the Committee of the Regions on all proposals having any implications at local and regional level on all domains, when deemed necessary by the European Parliament, the Commission and the Council. However, the EU position to respond to the social demands of regions and nations has led to a very great diversity of management modes, with more or less accepted constraints of the legislative and territorial frame: so many dissatisfactions and political activism are still on the agenda.

2.1 Territorial Rescaling, Old and New Identity References and Diversity Policies

With France and Germany as the historical prototypes, the civic and ethnic notions, respectively, of the nation have co-existed rather harmoniously in the European Union. Each country has been operating within its own collective identity and citizenship tradition, dissolving the potentiality for conflict in this matter. However, with the enlargement in 2004 and owing to the EU's regionalization policies, ethnicity was strengthened as a link or demarcation, redrawing the European spaces of collective identity, not only in the new member states but also in the old member states, for example the cases of Catalonia in Spain and Scotland in the United Kingdom. Even France, a country known for its notion of civic citizen identity based on the citizenship of France, is now increasingly referring to regional languages and cultures, whereas the concept of ethnicity is used rather to describe symbolic bonds and identity dynamics.

While the appeal of 'ethnicity' as a frame of reference has been growing and spreading, with the introduction of border regions, cross-border regions, euro-regions, macro-regions and territorial cohesion policies, which bring together a variety of languages, religions and countries in addressing common policy challenges across local, regional and national borders, 'territoriality' has indeed been a leaning wall for the European integration project. In some cases, the regionalization processes have also brought closer some linguistic minorities living in border regions divided by national borders, for example the border regions of Finland, Norway (although not a member state) and Sweden that are inhabited by the Sami people. On the other hand, the European Union's two important integration policy tools, internal mobility and open borders, which might at first sight be conceived as contradicting the territoriality principle, proved rather to be a link than a break-off point, with networks linking identities to their places of origin and to the places of presence simultaneously. Regionalism and transnationalization have created new links and new types of relationships and exchange, which are in the process of becoming an alternative and supplement to ethnic and civic affiliations of the member states. Some brief case summaries are in order to make these points clearer:

In Spain, the decentralization of power since the ratification of the new Constitution in 1978 was one of the more important factors of success. European Structural and Cohesion Funds have been the most significant instruments in the economic development of Spain and of its 17 regions in particular. The economic and employment improvements of some regions have, however, deepened the gap with the other regions. The integration of Eastern Europe has reduced in an important way the financial resources allocated to Spanish regions, worsening the social polarity since the financial crisis, which has revealed many inadequate investments conceived for a continuous growth which is no longer occurring.

The management of diversity at the micro-regional level has increased spatial fragmentation and inefficiency. Also, strong movements demanding secession of large-scale regions with ethnic identities, such as Catalonia and Scotland, might contribute in the future to further fragmentation. The new attempt at territorial reform in France seems valuable for those territories with a large metropolis (Bordeaux, Toulouse, Marseilles) which could develop new technologies and interregional dynamics, but is still very controversial in other parts of France which have fewer opportunities to develop the current dynamics and still rely on old ones such as public sector employment. National solidarity depends more than ever on European Action Funds that try to structure the European economy for the next ten years (300 billion euros from private and public sources required by the Juncker plan, targeting certain regions: NUTS 2). In most of the Western European countries, the growth has been very low and has forced a change in the growth model and the mechanism of the economy as well as the economic model itself (European Pact of Stability) with the help of the European Central Bank to reduce increasing inequalities. In Eastern European countries, on the other hand, this regionalization process had to be done rapidly and with difficulties, given the authoritarian tendencies inherited from communist times, and the conflict-heavy situations after the Second World War. Ireland and Spain were considered good models of democratic transition and an inspiration for them.

It has not been easy to implement an adequate degree of coordination between national, regional, linguistic and religious minorities and territorial units like regions, municipalities, euro-regions and border regions. Europe has known so many border changes, political units and movements of people that the mosaic of minorities it presents is very diverse (Yacoub 1998). It makes it challenging to carry out a synthesis. Most often, border regions are the location of the various minorities which have split from one nation. In Germany, for example, the Danish minority from Schleswig-Holstein provided a model which was strengthened by the 1955 federal law. Apart from its Magyar minority, Austria has two border minorities, who obtained their rights in 1955 and 1988. In Lithuania, a law dating back to 1991 treats Poles as foreigners, like the Russians from Estonia who came after 1945, and the country has rejected the Polish demand for an autonomous region, whereas in Poland the 1997 Constitution recognized the status of the Lithuanian, Belarusian and Ukrainian minorities.

The euro-regions, which were created in Western Europe in the 1950s, were later set up in Eastern Europe in the 1990s as the international border of Europe, first between Germany and Poland, and later on with the former USSR satellites. The previously mentioned cross-border networks created by the EU on its territory and Median Europe in the Interreg II Programmes are starting to carry out an inter-community dialogue which had been interrupted for decades or even centuries. However, most states found it difficult to allow some autonomy in this form of cooperation, mainly in fiscal matters. Differences in administrative traditions could also provide a pretext not to develop this cooperation. Dysfunction, distrust, old conflicts difficult to overcome, stereotypes, and fear of territorial re-colonization have been a handicap in border relationships between Poland and Germany, Poland and Ukraine or Lithuania, and Germany and Czechoslovakia (Sudeten conflict and the Beneš abrogation decree). Fear of economic pauperization linked to cross-border work is another deterrent to active cooperation (Lorraine/Luxembourg). German minorities even expected to recover the confiscated lands of the Second World War from such cross-border cooperation.

However, border minorities are not always the main actors in border cooperation. Elites at other levels have come forward with another logic, one which is sometimes more peaceful and more future-oriented than turned towards the past. For example, it was mainly young elites trained at foreign universities who promoted cooperation through NGOs with great dynamism at the Polish/Belarusian or Ukrainian borders. Church elites helped as well in the case of Ukraine and Poland. Border populations do need time to consider economic and other human benefits and break old stereotypes. In most cases, cooperation starts in a simple way with a common sport or cultural festival, a common radio or newspaper dealing with minority issues or more complex economic cooperation. The Interreg Programmes allow regular exchanges between actors of good will to promote new open relations. But, as older people do not forgive easily displacements or collective killings, there are still many dark memories to overcome.

An important tool furthering Europe's territorial transformation and at the same time increasing its diversity, the Good Neighbourhood and Friendship Treaty was proposed and signed between Germany, Hungary, Poland, Romania and so on after 1990 as a condition of entering the EU and NATO. In June 1991, the German–Polish Good Neighbourhood Treaty gave Polish citizens of German origin the right to express freely their identity. Media, school networks, and bilingualism with the financial help of Germany allowed a pacification of relationships between minority and majority (see also Lepesant 1997). The Hungarian minority question remained difficult, however, in the seven states where they are scattered (Austria, Ukraine, Serbia, Romania, Croatia, Slovenia, Slovakia). In Romania, it was only after 1990 that E.A. Iliescu (1989–1996) improved the democratic situation by creating the country's fourth democratic party, the Democratic Union of Romanian Magyars. This historic reconciliation was celebrated on 16 September 1996 with the signature of a Good Neighbourhood and Friendship Treaty between the two states, prior to their entry into NATO (Hungary in 1999, Romania in 2004) and the EU (Hungary in 2004, Romania in 2007). Since the partitioning of the Czech Republic in December 1992, the Hungarian minority in Slovakia has presented a difficult issue for the new state: the language law of 1995 is considered to be discriminatory, hiding the forced assimilation intent in the 1992 Constitution, which only reaffirms the rights of the Slovak people. In March 1995, a Good Neighbourhood Treaty like the one in Romania was signed between the two states in Paris, even if the idea of an autonomous region is still rejected, as it is in Lithuania. With the 1992 German–Czech Treaty, 53 418 German citizens now find themselves protected. In December 1996, the German–Czech declaration ended the question of the Sudeten expulsion from Nazi Germany in 1945 with the creation of an investment fund for common interest projects (cf. Lepesant 1997). In 1980, Hungary liberalized the protection of German minorities (220 000 in 1997) who benefited from the German–Hungarian treaty of June 1992, and in 1993 Hungarian law acknowledged and strengthened minority rights.

The restoration of independence for the three Baltic states posed again the question of Russian minorities present in these countries with a high rate of population (from 9.4 per cent in Lithuania to 34 per cent in Latvia). These states have chosen to adopt the status of citizenship acquired before the Russian occupation, so that those Russian citizens who came later have had no choice but to ask for naturalization and accept the linguistic constraints imposed by the Baltic States after independence. Today, peaceful co-existence does not mean that all problems are solved, as the two populations ignore each other and sometimes re-open conflicts, such as in 2008 with the episode of the Russian soldier's statue in Tallinn. Treaties were not signed with neighbourhood countries, but the neighbourhood policy initiated in 2003 used the same instruments as those deployed internally in the European Union (e.g. Interreg Programmes such as PHARE[4] and TACIS[5]). From then on, these instruments took on the same pattern for all neighbouring countries, being adapted through case-by-case negotiations such as with Moldova and Ukraine, in order to tighten links between them, if not for accession to EU membership. The respect for diversity through the Eurasian space was the basic issue here.

The EU tried in 2011 to impose a vote on respecting gender diversity in Moldova but faced the refusal of the orthodox clergy and of the population itself. Kazakhstan, through its 'new way for Europe', has built a model of interethnic and interreligious harmony well disseminated through the country's different regions, with assistance from EU advisers. A few years ago, Russia itself was adopting the model of interethnic concord pushed forward by the most democratic forces in order to cooperate with the EU on a variety of matters. Russia was mobilized before all other countries since the Helsinki agreement to protect its minorities in the new EU members, such as the Baltic states. But this strategy only worked in one sense, for the Russians: it protected them in the 'near abroad' (Rosenfeld 2009), as we can see in Ukraine. Minority groups are used as a springboard to regain control in the post-Soviet republics, such as Ukraine and Georgia, which are reluctant to re-integrate into the post-Soviet space. While the inner situation in Russia worsened with the financial crisis of 2008, Russian foreign policy in Europe in general has been to invest massively and even to build tight relations with some previous satellites such as Hungary, threatening in some cases the fabric of democracy and diversity.

The countries directly at the European border such as Belarus, Ukraine, Moldova and Georgia are all subject to increasing Russian pressure. Their ethnic heterogeneity is a factor of added fragmentation easy to manipulate from Russia. They have difficulties in formulating a common identity which will help to build a common project for the future. Moldova suffers partition from Transnistria, under Russian pressure, and now Ukraine has to face a separatist offensive, diminishing its will to move closer to the association project offered to it by Europe and which was the cause of the dismissal of the former president. Certainly, this does not necessarily mean that the peaceful cohabitation of religions and linguistic differences is threatened: the exacerbation of the identities divided between Russians and Ukrainians on Ukraine's territory comes mainly from the escalation of the war. Those who have Soviet Union nostalgia today are largely state-controlled and offer an account of events markedly different from that carried by the Western press. Russians seeing their own country's motivations are largely defensive about Georgian or Ukrainian aggression, finding it normal that order should be maintained throughout the former Soviet Union, or to protect and have other countries or privileged interests in the near abroad. We can now speak in terms of political and economic conflict rather than cooperation. These new developments in Russo-Ukrainian relations have destroyed years of patient efforts to build the new neighbourhood policy.

The energy dependency of Europe on Russia and all the complex issues around energy transit roads are making the matter of EU support quite difficult to foresee in the state of diplomatic negotiations which give the advantage to Russia and reduce to nothing the efforts of the new neighbourhood policy towards Ukraine. The energy issue remains central to equilibrate the relations of these regions with the EU.

The two logics of territorial transformation and diversity accommodation have thus not only introduced the various regional territories, their administrations, the national and cross-border local entities, and the shared niches around them as new identity references, but also reinvigorated the existing but formerly dysfunctional ethnic and imperial allegiances as parts of people's collective identities. In this context of simultaneous ethnicization, regionalization and territorial expansion of collective identities beyond the collective identity categories generated by the nation states, the new territoriality is made with nodes, roots, networks and a co-existence of identities. The nation states are now perceived through their diversity of forms, to which is attached a discourse directed at their diverse social strata. Consequently, they rebuild themselves through the relationship between culture and politics to maintain their feeling of belonging. This rebuilding is not done without conflict, something which can be seen as an integrative part of social dynamics at the European level from an agonistic perspective. Cultural and geographic identities are melted down within the same administrative space, that is, the region.

2.2 Diversity Accommodation between Solidarity and Competitiveness

Following its founding fathers, the EU has been built on the ideal of solidarity between the peoples of Europe, through slow maturation and specific historical conjectures, and the strong will of people sharing a common vision founded on consensus. The progressive implementation of regional policy expresses this will to oppose a counterweight to the very liberal vision, fight against the internal disparities of the European territory and build a European territory where the spatial organization inherited from the national territorial management logic should be reorganized. Meanwhile, the economic globalization context imposes a real adaptation of the entrepreneurs' territorial strategy as a response to global competition. Some regions benefit from the process; others do not and see their situation worsening with the border opening.

The Convention on the Promotion of Cultural Diversity was, for example, signed in 2005 by UNESCO to guarantee the survival of minority cultures as well as of majority cultures. This recognition of the specific nature of cultural groups' activities, goods and cultural services was considered a political act by the international community, demonstrating a new will to oppose an ever growing globalization. This Convention was a French and Canadian initiative, carried out under the Chirac presidency. It has the same power as other international instruments such as the WTO or bilateral treaties. A country could, for example, refuse to open its audio-visual and cinematographic market during international commercial negotiations. With this Convention, the smaller countries would get a tool which would enable them to resist outside pressure. However, the text does not put constraints in terms of means. The Cooperation Fund set up for underdeveloped countries relies on voluntary contributions by each country, but these are already making a lot of financial contributions. However, to be implemented, it must be ratified by at least 30 countries. The US was opposed to this process and tried to block it through bilateral treaties imposed on the most fragile countries.

Another important text on this issue is the Charter of the Fundamental Rights of the European Union, which includes social and environmental rights; the minority issue is quoted in three articles under the young, senior, sexual, ethnic, religious and philosophical categories. This text sets up a list of diversity criteria which are taken into account according to needs in each country and shows the emergence of a new consciousness about sexual diversity.

However, European people seem to be more reluctant towards cultural diversity concerning extra-Europeans or post-imperial countries. The recent wave of populism, nativism, xenophobia and racism, reappearing even in wealthier Northern Europe, shows that perceived economic deprivation and the rise of primordial collective identity references feed these trends more than ever, whatever the general level of prosperity. The Muslim communities, in particular, polarize the attention at the national as well as the regional level in terms of implementing diversity directives on these levels. In French regions, for instance, although many efforts are undertaken to integrate minority cultures, the social problems are so numerous that the state level is more and more required to apply coherently all national measures and European directives. This is mainly true for the second and third generations of Muslim immigrant groups since September 2001. Regarding migration and integration policies, the regions in the majority of the member states come into the picture at the stage of implementation, and there are important dissimilarities in their interpretation of migration and integration policies as well as in their approaches and attitudes towards the question of migrant minority integration. Most European countries share the same difficulties of integrating these minorities, even if they are open to asylum as in Sweden. The party systems mirror the centre–periphery conflicts and economic cleavages more than cultural cleavages. More open discourse on migration in political parties and the media is needed to face the new realities of competitiveness and democratic aspirations as well as the different waves of migrants who need cultural recognition at all levels of territory. Incentives like the Year of Intercultural Dialogue (2008) seem to be good instruments for this purpose, as they are also well supported by civil societies. They boost the creation of associations in this domain but need to be reproduced to have a deeper impact in the long run.

Trans-European networks help the migrant population to survive at different levels of society. The case of the Roma population is exemplary in this respect. The existence of elites able to defend their rights provides a new stratification which is emerging in the global exchanges and required recognition of their cultural specificity and of their professional skills. The Charter of Fundamental Rights is a positive step forward in this direction. The states are linked in a tight web of constraints that will improve its effectiveness and make it appear as an experimental model of future democratic, multicultural societies. The legislative corpus and bureaucratic structures are the big pillars of this building. They can allow pursuit of respect for diversity in territorial construction and cultural redefinition with the common legal tools proposed by the Council of Europe.

In addition to the abovementioned international pressure to 'globalize' and challenges posed by migration, European enlargement has also affected the EU's approach to diversity accommodation in the sense that it made the need for cross-national solidarity more visible. In this respect, the EU pedagogical method was exported to the East (e.g. Programmes for Peace and Reconciliation). By virtue of their membership of the EU, governments are under an obligation to implement EU policies in border areas, and this has been more binding under the Lisbon Agenda, pointing to a new and inclusive style of governance and interaction with citizens. The Lisbon strategy informs and engages citizens in the process through communication and coordination efforts at national to local levels and from national parliaments to local civil society to provide democratic legitimacy. To strengthen global competitiveness for all the regions of Europe, there is also a necessity to identify the various territorial potentials for sustainable economic growth and job creation in the EU: this means removing or mitigating constraints, mainly on lagging peripheral areas of the EU and on borders through intensification of cross-border and trans-national cooperation. The issue of good practice in partnership (such as symbolic structures and working processes) and collaborative working (intra-sectoral and cross-sectoral as well as organizational capacity) in cross-border regions to complement inter-governmental cooperation is highly topical for key strategic issues. Transferable models or good practices were proposed for the purpose of providing guidance to communities, group organizations and neighbours to achieve tangible results and develop the capacity to achieve goals.

The persistent weight of the nation states and their competitive behaviour within EU internal affairs appear as an obstacle to the progress of solidarity-based European integration. The citizens identify themselves primarily with this level. The persistence of nations in a European market at a time of globalization is a major fact: the 2008 crisis has enhanced the decisive role of the states, which retain the main instruments of economic regulation in Europe's labour market and financial and social redistribution, through their own regulation of sovereign debt. Their reluctance to function according to the subsidiarity principle and multilevel governance reduces the effectiveness of cohesion policy based on these principles. The proposal to create an inter-parliamentary commission for consulting national parliaments before passing new laws in order to produce a better understanding of the logic of European legislation to the national parliaments has been proposed but not discussed. Proposals to connect the regions more strongly, and the European Parliament as partner, have also been spoken about, but no concrete decisions have followed as yet.

The idea of devoting a year to a theme to focus on a problem of particular importance among these priorities in the EU, such as the Year of Intercultural Dialogue in 2008, has proved to be quite popular among European citizens. However, the concern is that the awareness-raising efforts devoted to a particular theme are given up the following year when another theme is chosen. This lack of continuity prevents the financing of any initiative needing to be followed up. We can focus on two examples, one about cultural diversity, the other the fight against poverty and social exclusion in the regional context. They usually concern the same target people. Migrants and minorities are usually more concerned by poverty and social exclusion and cultural ghettoization. More than 80 millions people live under the poverty threshold in the EU. It is a big issue for European towns and regions, because it is the local and regional powers which are responsible for devising, financing and implementing the integration policy of the socially, economically and culturally excluded (ethnic minorities, seniors, the unemployed, the handicapped, etc.).

On the other hand, outside the EU, while the law is placed at the heart of the process of European integration, solidarity implies that neighbours adopt some common rules and harmonize policies towards each other. In exporting its rules, the EU builds a new type of border, but the intensity of requirements and political conditionality and the level of transfer of the politico-legal European model are greatly put in question by the new evolutions. The reforms which the EU hoped would stabilize its neighbourhood are no longer fulfilled: the war between Ukraine and Russia and the situation in the Middle East show the failure of the continuous efforts in the past decades. The changing geo-strategic situations of all the neighbourhood countries and the current difficulties of members within the EU in finding a common solidarity strategy do not encourage much optimism in the building of a harmonious European public sphere.

The information revolution has contributed significantly to the growth of global metropoles that states are attempting to promote together as an alternative or supplement to regional territories, trying to evaluate what is the appropriate financially significant format to reduce growing inequalities. On the one hand, those are causing conflicts and disillusionment about the EU (the existence of ethnic networks, clusters, transnational networks) and, on the other, they create polarization, attraction and creativity in the new cosmopolitan entities. Whilst to a great extent the young, the poor and the rural people go to the metropoles in quest of jobs and welfare, adopting global values and lifestyles, many are left behind in the more rural territories in the North or the East, losing their collective references and developing anti-multicultural and anti-European populist trends threatening European democratic values. This process can be seen through the rise of the far-right parties even in rich countries such as Norway. This evolution represents a great challenge for European institutions, and these will need to evolve with the change of cultural and social frames of reference.

The territorial organization which ensured the conditions of economic growth and diversity accommodation simultaneously in the more dynamic territories through development of less productive economies seems to have worked well with respect to the objective of social cohesion from 1980 till recently. Laurent Davezies and Thierry Pech (2014) show, however, that this cycle has come to an end, owing to increasing metropole concentration and the strengthening of the knowledge and information-based society (see also Davezies 2014). The reduction of revenue disparity between territories, increasing the tension between solidarity and competitiveness, is rapidly changing through mutation of production models, turning more towards the immaterial economy, which brings with it the challenge of choosing between equality without growth and growth without equality. Less and less do the states deploy redistribution policies to decrease inequality.

Territorial cohesion policy is linked to the idea of 'social and societal cohesion', which has not been debated yet inside the EU. It is a concept which should be put alongside the implementation of the principle of competition. Combining tools for durable growth and resources for territorial cohesion and diversity accommodation seems essential to achieve a stable Europe. Consulting the territories as real decision-making partners is also needed as a preliminary to the legislative process to study the territorial impact of all legislative decisions. It implies a better coordination of economic policies at the EU level. Currently, it is the Committee of the Regions which stresses the strengthening of the cohesion policy in the wake of an increasing regional disparity in economic terms. It is looked upon as a development policy in itself, not as a simple financial tool.

The current evolution of the cohesion policy between solidarity and competitiveness and the capacity of the EU to propose new principles and norms, supported by a deeper reflection on the future of economic activities on its territory, seems crucial for the future of Europe in a period when all the states weakened by the financial crisis have strategic choices to make to reduce disparities and inequality. However, contrary to this fact, the use of the globalization theme in the regional policy frame hides more than ever today the ideological positions, which are fighting around two main concepts: that of territorial cohesion with its territorial redistributive policy and that of competition with its territorial cumulative policy (Didelon et al. 2011).

3 EUROPE'S TERRITORIAL INTEGRATION AS A STEP TOWARDS A COMMON EUROPEAN PUBLIC SPHERE?

The ongoing territorial transformation of Europe into one common transnational space, which actually derives from the European Union's concern for developing a common market and its effective governance, has already at this stage important consequences.

Firstly, in addition to national administrations, the regional level has entered into the multilevel governance equation as a determining factor more strongly than before. That is, regions and regional administrations became (1) a new addressee of EU policies, (2) a new level of authority to which citizens can direct their contention and grievances and which they can hold accountable on relevant policy issues, and (3) a new channel through which citizens can make themselves heard by the EU central authorities, bypassing the nation state.

Secondly, the multilevel structure of authority, with occasionally overlapping competences between the regional, national and European levels, increases the complexity of political communication and relations of accountability between citizens and the authorities at different levels. That is, the citizens have to relate to different levels of authority on different issues, which may sometimes mean mobilization against different addressees at different territorial scales on different issues, and sometimes even dealing with multiple authorities as the addressee of a single political claim. More importantly, sometimes citizens and civil society groups claim they do not find clear nodes of responsibility or accountability on policy issues that are dealt with by diffuse institutional alliances or policy partnerships within the complex EU governance system.

Thirdly, in addition to what is already achieved through eradication of national borders, introduction of free mobility and the common market, the regions of Europe have also contributed to transforming Europe into an aggregate of multilevel, postnational, multicultural and national societies. This reconstruction of the EU territory as an open common economic and socio-political space, organized in different types of regions that are linked through cross-border regions, macro-regions, open borders and free mobility of persons, goods and services, has also increased the multiplicity of poly-ethnic features and institutional polymorphism.

Fourthly, in contrast to the social and political organization of national states which is based on ethno-national or ethno-religious collective identities or state loyalty, shared natural resources and other common economic niches seem to be the basis of new regions and regional identity formations, at least in the EU's economy and common market-based terminology. Social organization around exploiting common economic niches might be conflict-minimizing between identity groups, but such organization also strengthens territorial identity and will potentially lead to either conflict-laden presence or exclusion of second- and third-country nationals who do not originate from the respective region's territory.

These features of the new European territorial space are quite far from and considerably more complex than what conventional theories of the public sphere presuppose about the citizenry and political system where political communication will occur. The mainstream public sphere theories, especially those that follow the Habermasian tradition, require a higher level of convergence between citizens' languages, religions, cultures and approaches to politics, and a smaller possibility of inter-group conflict, than what is currently the case in the European Union. If we need to speak about a transnational public sphere in the European Union, the more proper alternative is an agonistic understanding of the public sphere, recognizing the complex and conflictual character of the political affairs between citizens, diversity groups, boundaries and authorities (cf. Sicakkan, this volume, Chapter 1). Through conflict and compromise, the agonistic perspective will also advance new ways of sharing resources or niches and the formation of alliances around common objectives beyond the regional and national levels.

NOTES

1. The Convention method facilitates collaboration between national politicians and members of the European Parliament to take decisions through consensus building with an opening to civil society, contributing to the creation of a European public space.
2. Resolution on EU Policy and the Role of the Regions, 18 November 1988 (OJ No. C326, p. 289).
3. In addition to 150 million ECUs that was allocated to Median Europe countries for transborder cooperation internally within the EU, an additional 150 million ECUs was granted to the programme PHARE CBC for cross-border cooperation with non-EU countries in the region. The latter included 25 million ECUs per year for the Czech–German border, 6 million ECUs per year for the Austro-Czech border and 78 million ECUs per year for the Austro-Hungarian border between 1996 and 1999 in order to increase and improve the checkpoints. There are eight euro-regions only on the Germano-Polish and Germano-Czech borders.

4. PHARE has since 1994 been the main financial instrument of the pre-accession strategy for the Central and Eastern European countries which have applied for European Union membership.
5. The TACIS programme (since 1999) promotes, in Eastern Europe and Central Asia, the transition to a market economy and the reinforcing of democracy and the rule of law.

REFERENCES

Anderson, P. (1994) *The Invention of the Region, 1945–1990*, EUI Working Paper EUF 94/2, Firenze: European University Institute.

Commission of the European Communities (2006) *Territorial Agenda of the European Union: Towards a More Competitive Europe of Diverse Regions*, October, Brussels: Commission of the European Communities.

Committee of the Regions (2000) *The White Paper on Multilevel Governance*, 9, Brussels: Committee of the Regions.

Committee of the Regions (2001) *Regional and Local Government in the European Union: Responsibilities and Resources*, pp. 211–212, Brussels: Committee of the Regions.

Davezies, L. (2014) *Vers un retournement historique des inégalités territoriales?* Rapport à l'Institut Caisse des Dépôts pour la Recherche et le PUCA, L'oeil.

Davezies, L. and T. Pech (2014) La nouvelle question territoriale, *Terra Nova*, Note 1/30.

Didelon, C., Y. Richard and G. Van Hamme (2011) *Le territoire européen*, Paris: PUF, coll. Licence.

Dressler, W. (1999) *On Ruins of an Empire: National and Minority Questions in Estonia, Moldova, Kazakhstan and Poland*, Brussels: Bruylant.

Dressler, W. (2005) *La Corse en question*, Ajaccio, Corse: Albiana.

Dressler. W. (2007) *Corse: Le destin d'une île*, Ajaccio, Corse: Albiana.

Dressler, W. (2009) *Eurasia: Myth or Reality*, Brussels: Bruylant.

Europe 2020 Objectives, Working documents, Regions 2020, *Newsletter of the Committee of the regions* 62 (2009), 68 (2010) and 73 (2011).

Foucher, M. and Gonon E. (1993) *Fragments d'Europe*, Paris: Fayard.

Krugman, P. (2000) *La mondialisation n'est pas coupable: Vertus et limites du libre-échange*, Paris: La Découverte.

Krugman, P. (2011) The New Economic Geography, Now Middle-aged, *Regional Studies* 45(1): 1–7.

Lepesant, G. (1997) Dynamique des frontières orientales de l'Union européenne: Le cas des frontières germano-polonaise et germano-tchéque, in M.C. Maurel, *Recomposition de l'Europe médiane*, Paris: Sedes.

Marcou, G. (1999) *La régionalisation en Europe*, Rapport Parlement Européen, Paris: Groupement de Recherches sur l'Administration Locale en Europe.

Maurel, M.C. (ed.) (1997) *Recomposition de l'Europe médiane*, Paris: DIEM-SEDES.

Rosenfeld, B. (2009) Projecting Influence in the Former Soviet Union: Russian Public Views on the Near Abroad, Paper presented at ASN Conference.

Yacoub, J. (1998) *Les minorités dans le monde*, Paris: Desclée de Brouwer.

3. European media policies and the European public sphere

Monika Mokre

Media play a crucial role for a large majority of studies on the European public sphere (EPS). This research preference is based on the premise, evident in Habermas's original work, that citizens in mass societies cannot rely solely on face-to-face interaction, but rather participate in political deliberation and gain the vast majority of their political information from the media (Kunelius and Sparks 2001; Peter 2003). Interestingly, however, media structures and their framing conditions are rarely taken into account within these studies (for exceptions from this general assessment see for example Schlesinger 1997 and Kantner 2004).

For the framework of the Eurosphere project as well as of this publication European media policies can be understood as attempts to create a vertical trans-European space linking national constituencies with the EU. These policies are of special interest, as they go longer back in history than most other activities of EU institutions aiming at constructing or shaping European public spheres. This is due to the fact that media were mainly defined as commercial services, thus falling into EC competence. One could argue, on the other hand, that this focus on economic questions (especially with regard to the free market and possible distortions of it) would mostly exclude considerations on the impact of media and media policies on European public spheres. But a detailed analysis shows that, at least since the 1980s, European media policies did, in fact, not limit themselves to the economic side of media but actively strived for European media, media contents and media networks.

This chapter aims at analysing EC/EU policies out of the perspective of the (lack of a) EPS, thereby asking how media structures and their framing conditions affect the political function of media for European public spheres and, especially, the emergence of agonistic European public spheres not exclusively structured by national cleavages. After a historical overview of EU media policies and an evaluation of their impact on the EPS, the chapter presents empirical results of the Eurosphere project on the preferences of European actors with regard to the EPS. These preferences will be compared with the actual activities of the European Commission. Concluding, the chapter discusses possible future developments of media policies furthering inclusive European public spheres.

1 EUROPEAN MEDIA POLICIES UNTIL THE END OF THE 1970s

> Broadcasting in Europe started as a highly regulated industry, where the primary focus of regulation was decidedly national, the objectives and instruments of these national approaches differed wildly, and where in every case the regulation of broadcasting was treated very differently to that of other sections of the communications sector such as telecommunications or newspapers and publishing. (Levy 1999, quoted in Andjelkovic 2007)

This general trend towards regulation was due to the high costs necessary for starting and operating broadcasting stations. In order to avoid private monopolies on information flows (which would have been very probable owing to these economic framing conditions) public monopolies were introduced. While the freedom of the press was to be warranted by free competition between different private suppliers, freedom of opinion in radio and television should be made possible by public ownership (cf. e.g. Holznagel 1996: 91–96). In this understanding, the state was understood as a neutral mediator of information while, at the same time, the national interest in broadcasting became obvious by the political decision for regulation and played an important role for the further development of public broadcasters.

> Firstly, broadcasting was subordinated to *public service* goals ... Secondly, typical of systems was their *national* character, designed, as they were, to serve audiences and social institutions within the national territory ... expected to protect national language and culture and (however) implicitly to represent the national interest. (Siune and Truetzschler 1992: 9)

However, even in the early period of broadcasting, international regulations became necessary, as frequencies had to be assigned beyond national borders. Thus, in 1925, the International Broadcasting Union was founded in Geneva (Siegordner 2002: 4). The successor of this organization is the European Broadcasting Union (EBU), founded in 1950 by 23 broadcasting stations. Today, EBU has 75 members and 44 associate members (EBU n.d.). EBU sees itself as an interest representation of public broadcasting stations, supporting them technically, and organizing the exchange of contents. Its most renowned production is the Eurovision Song Contest. As will be described later, during the 1980s EBU played an important role in the attempts to launch a European television programme.

While, thus, the *national* character of broadcasting has been contested by the need for international agreements since the outset, the idea of objective *public* broadcasting has increasingly come under critique from the 1970s onwards. Critics of this concept called for a real competition of opinions and ideas and/or of private economic interests. Since then, we have observed a general decline in popular acceptance of the system of public service broadcasting and the transition to dual systems of broadcasting including public and private companies – a transition that took place in most European countries during the 1980s (cf. e.g. Noll 1998: 163–165).

Also, the beginning of EC media policies can be traced back to the early 1970s. Since their outset, these policies have focused exclusively on audiovisual media, as, '[i]n the case of print media, the principle of the free flow of information in EU states has been taken for granted for years and required no joint regulation' (Weidenfeld and Wessels 1998: 170).

Although the Treaty of Rome did not define an EC competence for audiovisual media, this competence has been developed implicitly as part of the freedom of movement and services, above all by the jurisdiction of the European Court of Justice (ECJ). Most important for the further development of EU media politics was the ECJ decision in the Sacchi case of 1974, stating that,

> in the absence of express provision to the contrary in the Treaty, a television signal must, by reason of its nature, be regarded as provision of services … It follows that the transmission of television signals, including those in the nature of advertisements, comes, as such within the rules of the treaty relating to services. (European Court of Justice 1974)

This ruling combines two elements – on the one hand, television is defined as a service and not as a good (whereas media storage devices are defined as goods) and, on the other hand, television is thereby also defined as a commercial activity. However, the ECJ also recognized non-commercial functions of television and, thus, allowed for certain derogations. In this vein, the complaint of Sacchi against the Italian television monopoly RAI was rejected. In the Coditel case of 1980, the ECJ, furthermore, ruled that the provisions of the Treaty can only be applied in the case of transnational provisions of services, thereby allowing the Belgian government to award exclusive licences (European Court of Justice 1980).

Still, the ECJ's ruling that television is, in principle, a commercial service stood in striking contradiction to the understanding of most EC member states. Furthermore, the supranational competence assumed by this ECJ decision was also felt as a threat to the national character of broadcasting.

Thus, the ECJ decisions led to a debate on the character of television – as an economic service or a cultural achievement. As EU competences have been mainly understood as confined to economic questions, two perspectives have constantly overlapped within this debate – the question of the (cultural or economic) function of television and the question of national or supranational competences. The main arguments for understanding television as an economic good are that broadcasting is part of the cultural industries and that trade in cultural productions is of economic relevance. As the internal market warrants free movement of services independently of the content of these services, broadcasting has to be included in the regulations of trade in services.

Those maintaining that television should not be seen as part of the internal market as it is a cultural good have rather stated this quality of television as a fact than arguing it. The issue is then linked to the question of cultural national identities as well as to the question of subsidiarity. The latter question has played a crucial role for Germany, as broadcasting is regulated by the German provinces, the *Länder*, which were not willing to transfer this competence to the European level (cf. e.g. Wiesner 1990).

2 TOWARDS EUROPEAN TELEVISION?

While, within these debates, European institutions confined themselves to interpretations of EC law, in 1980 the European Parliament (EP) discussed two motions on television – one on 'Radio and television broadcasting in the European Community' and one on 'The threat to diversity of opinion posed by commercialisation of news media' (European Parliament 1982: 2). For the first time in the history of European integration, a European institution discussed the political impact of media organization. The first motion led to the funding of a committee and the subsequent adoption of a resolution, dubbed the Hahn Report (European Parliament 1982).

The resolution emphasizes at its very beginning 'the need for all citizens of the Member States to receive authentic information on Community policy and thus to be given a share in the political responsibility', criticizes 'reporting of European Community problems in the past … [as] inadequate and in many cases negative' and also mentions the disappointment of the citizens mirrored in recent opinion polls (European Parliament 1982: 4). Furthermore, the report assumes a strong connection between further integration, European identity and the media:

> European unification will only be achieved if Europeans want it. Europeans will only want it if there is such a thing as a European identity. A European identity will only develop if Europeans are adequately informed … Therefore, if European unification is to be encouraged, Europe must penetrate the media. (European Parliament 1982: 7)

Thus, the Hahn Report proposes the foundation of a European television channel providing 'a full range of programmes, covering news, politics, education, culture, entertainment and sport' and being 'European in origin, transmission range, target audience and subject matter' (European Parliament 1982: 4). This channel should be transmitted by existing national television companies and organized via Eurovision, that is, the European Broadcasting Union (European Parliament 1982: 11–12). The whole programme should be available in all the languages of the member states (European Parliament 1982: 14).

Without any doubt, the focus of the EP on audiovisual media at this point in time was, to a high degree, triggered by new technological developments. The report itself emphasizes the impact of new media, above all satellite and cable transmission, which 'will break down the boundaries of the national television networks and enforce the creation of wide-ranging transmission areas' (European Parliament 1982: 7). In general, one can assess that the high point of EU efforts in the field of audiovisual media 'coincided precisely with the technological revolution that precipitated, especially among the European electronic media, a series of significant developments, such as their liberation from traditional government ownership' (Paraschos 1998, quoted in Andjelkovic 2007: 4).

Still, the interest of the European Parliament in these issues cannot be solely ascribed to technological change. Rather, one can discern a clear political interest of the EP in further developing European integration by fostering a European identity. The first direct elections to the EP in 1979 created considerable political impetus, which led not only to far-reaching concepts for audiovisual policies but also – and more prominently – to the first proposal for a European constitution drafted by Altiero Spinelli from 1982 to 1984 (Pollak 2006: 205).

2.1 Eurikon

The proposal of the EP for a European television programme was implemented in an experimental way in the Eurikon project, which took place during five weeks in 1982. Organized by the European Broadcasting Union, the experiment was carried out by 15 European broadcasters and the European Community. Five of the participating broadcasters (from Austria, Italy, the Netherlands, Germany and the UK) contributed programmes, each of them taking responsibility for one week. Because of copyright issues, the programme was not publicly distributed but only shown to 'invited guests of the participating broadcasters and to panels recruited for the purpose of audience research' (Collins 1993, quoted in Theiler 1999). All programmes were translated into six languages (English, Dutch, French, German, Italian and Spanish), through either multichannel audio or teletext subtitling (Siebenhaar 2002: 3).

The results of this experiment were unsatisfactory in two regards. First, the financial and technological efforts for the translations were enormous. As a full-fledged European programme would produce additional costs for copyrights and satellite space, the experiment raised serious doubts about the feasibility of such an endeavour for economic reasons (Siebenhaar 2002: 3). Second,

> audiences reacted unfavourably to Eurikon's output, finding it hard to comprehend and relate to. In addition to cultural barriers there were linguistic ones as Eurikon's dubbing and subtitling provisions were deemed unsatisfactory. Reactions of this type prevailed throughout the duration of the Eurikon experiment, even though each of the five weeks featured different programming and scheduling formulas. To further complicate matters, while viewers from different countries were united in their dislike for Eurikon's programs, the precise reasons for their dislike tended to diverge along national lines. (Theiler 1999)

2.2 Europa TV

Still, the Eurikon operations group understood the experiment as promising enough to strive for a full-fledged European programme. Furthermore, the proposals of the EP for a European TV programme

> were taken up by the Commission in an interim report to the European Parliament titled *Realities and Tendencies in European Television: Perspectives and Options* (Commission of the EC 1983) … [T]he report … gave 'first

consideration to the practical possibilities of getting a European television programme onto the screen ...'. (Theiler 1999)

The interim report was issued before the final evaluation of Eurikon and took a cautiously optimistic view on the feasibility of a European TV programme. It also emphasized the importance of such a programme as a 'first step towards a more European perception of the prospects and problems of tomorrow', promised 'political and material support' by the Commission for such an endeavour and mentioned a recent 'public opinion poll conducted by the Commission among the citizens of the ten Community countries [which] has shown that a majority (57%) of Europeans are interested in a European television channel' (European Commission 1983: 5–6).

In spite of the fact that the evaluation report on Eurikon was rather negative, the Eurikon Operations Group was able to raise enough enthusiasm among the different parties concerned with a European programme to further develop this plan (Collins 1998: 89). Thus, during the following years, plans for a European television programme were further developed and strongly supported by the European Broadcasting Union – in spite of the fact that none of the major members of EBU actively participated in this endeavour, while some members, above all the BBC, openly opposed it (Collins 1998: 94). In the end, Europa TV was implemented by five EBU members – from Germany, Ireland, Italy, the Netherlands and Portugal. These broadcasting stations as well as the Dutch government and the European Commission financed the project (Theiler 1999).

Europa TV was launched on 5 October 1985. Again, the programme offered 'a public service programme mix of a "wide range of informational, educational and entertainment programmes of high quality" [which should] "contain programmes of interest and relevance to the widest possible audience in the countries of the participating broadcasters"' (Collins 1998: 91).[1]

Furthermore, the programme aimed at a really European perspective. 'Europa TV's mission included the production and transmission of programmes in a non-national format and the reporting of news and current affairs not from a national but from a "European point of view".' Its news team, for instance, 'was carefully structured to avoid the dominance of any single national group' and a 'non-national perspective was encouraged by all available means' (Maggiore 1990: 71). This was aimed at by, among other things, making sure that events were covered by a national of a country other than the one in which they took place

(Theiler 1999). Again, the programme could be received over different language channels as well as with subtitles in different languages.

With regard to the evaluation of its success, Europa TV faced a similar dilemma to Eurikon: the response of audiences was modest, to say the least, while the operators were rather enthusiastic about their endeavour (Collins 1998: 113). Still, this enthusiasm could not prevent the quick end of Europa TV, mainly for financial reasons. Expenditures were much higher than expected and had to be borne by the five original participants, as no further broadcasters were interested in joining the consortium. And, not least because of the lack of interest of audiences, revenues from advertising were much lower than hoped for (Collins 1998: 114). 'Indeed, so low was Europa TV's attractiveness to viewers that even after it had begun to offer commercial slots *free of charge* in an effort to bring itself to the attention of potential advertisers, few made use of the offer' (Negrine and Papathanassopoulos 1990, quoted in Theiler 1999).

After its first year of operations, the channel had already exhausted its initial three-year budget (Zimmer 1989, quoted in Theiler 1999: 6). In the end, even a £720 000 emergency grant by the Commission could not save Europa TV. At the time of its closure, its debts had accumulated to the equivalent of £3.7 million (Negrine and Papathanassopoulos 1990, quoted in Theiler 1999). While all these facts point towards dramatic miscalculations by the operators, it should also be mentioned that Europa 'operate[d] on … a minuscule fraction of the funding that many domestic public service broadcasters use up annually' (Theiler 1999: 6).

In addition to financial problems, Europa faced many administrative problems, which were mainly caused by national interests and mistrust of national partners with regard to the engagement of the European Commission. The dramatic cost overrun, for example, was to a high degree due to the Portuguese claim for Portuguese translations. While legitimated by both the engagement of the Portuguese broadcaster and the high share of Portuguese audience, still these additional translation costs went far beyond the original calculations (Theiler 1999: 6).

Also, the positive interest of the European Commission and its financial support were seen with mistrust by EBU members. 'EBU members believed that an axiom of public service broadcasting, independence of government, was in danger of being compromised by the increasingly close association between the EBU and its pan-European channel, and the Commission of the European Communities and the European Parliament' (Collins 1998: 111).

And, finally, the lack of harmonized legal provisions for television in Europe in combination with the unwillingness of national governments to compromise on their legislation for the sake of Europa TV made the launch of a European programme a nearly impossible task. 'The interdependence between pan-European television service and pan-European politics was apparent in the difficulties presented to pan-European television by the contemporary regulatory regime. The absence of a European "Television without Frontiers" – a single market in broadcasting – profoundly disadvantaged Europa' (Collins 1998: 112).

Thus, Belgium refused to carry Europa TV in its cable network and, thereby, excluded its Dutch community from the use of this programme (Theiler 1999: 6).

> Furthermore, even though Europa TV had its operational headquarters in the Netherlands and received subsidies from the Dutch government, the latter refused to exempt it from a rule prohibiting foreign channels distributed in the Netherlands from carrying subtitles so as to help protect Dutch broadcasters from foreign competition (Zimmer, 1989). This hampered Europa TV's appeal to those Dutch viewers who would have preferred subtitles to (often poorly perceived) dubbing, and thereby lowered its economic viability still further. (Theiler 1999: 6)

In general, even the participating broadcasters were seemingly not willing 'to regard Europa as their own offspring' (European Cultural Foundation and the European Institute for the Media 1988, quoted in Theiler 1999: 7). They neither delegated enough competences to the EBU nor took up responsibility for the new programme – evident 'in their frequent failure to fill the programming slots allocated to them' (Theiler 1999: 7).

Europa TV was abruptly stopped on 26 November 1986; at 8 p.m. its cessation on the very same day was announced. Up to now, this failure has also meant the end for all aspirations for a full-fledged European public service programme.

2.3 Eurosport

Even during the development of Europa TV a plan B for a monothematic sports channel was being launched. After the demise of Europa TV, this plan came again to the fore and was implemented in 1989. The practical reason behind this move can be found in the quasi-monopoly of the EBU on rights for television transmissions of sports events, as no member state had the financial potential to cover the whole sports sector.

Owing to the financial problems of Europa TV, EBU gave a strong priority to cooperation with a commercial partner to launch this new programme (Collins 1998: 121). Thus, EBU entered a partnership with the Murdoch-owned broadcaster News International and thereby

> amplified the uncomfortable inconsistency between the EBU's overt theoretical commitment to a pure vision of public service broadcasting ... and its actual practice of close links with some commercial broadcasters ... eventually even leading the Competition Directorate of the European Commission to suspect European public service broadcasters ... [as] abusing a dominant position under a rhetorical umbrella of public service. (Collins 1998: 121–122)

The cooperation between EBU and News International mainly consisted of the EBU buying transmission rights and News International covering the losses of EBU and thereby reducing its taxable profit. As Collins (1998: 122) correctly describes, this financial arrangement 'enabled the EBU to load a substantial portion of the costs of its sports rights on to the tax payers'. Furthermore, the de facto monopsony of EBU on sports rights disabled competition in this market – a fact critically commented on by the Directorate-General for Competition (Collins 1998: 125). While EBU and the European Commission, thus, acted as partners in the launch of Eurikon and Europa TV, more and more conflict between these two actors developed during the late 1980s and the early 1990s.

These tensions between EBU and the Commission cannot be solely interpreted as conflicts of interest but are also conflicts of values pointing towards different assessments of the role of the market and public broadcasting respectively. However, apart from this interesting normative question, which will be taken up once again towards the end of this chapter, Eurosport seems to play a minor role for questions of the EPS as understood in the Eurosphere project. The interest of the audience for Eurosport lies in its broad coverage of international sports events rather than in a specific European quality of this programme.

2.4 Euronews

Euronews was established in January 1993 by broadcasters from Portugal, Spain, Italy, Greece, France, Belgium, Finland, Monaco, Cyprus and Egypt. While the founding members were mostly public broadcasters, in 1995 a commercial station bought 49 per cent of Euronews (Theiler 1999: 8–9).

Similarly to Eurosport, Euronews focuses exclusively on one theme, namely news, and is thus a much more modest enterprise than Europa TV. Also, its claim for Europeanization is more limited, as national footage is broadcast and accompanied by multilingual channels.

However, at least at the beginning, it was the explicit aim of Euronews to contribute to a European public sphere. In order to do so, Euronews positioned itself in competition to national news programmes, but also to

CNN – Europeanization was understood as a defence against nationalism as well as Americanization (Casero 2001). While this is in itself a very ambitious enterprise, critics of Euronews agree that the way in which the programme distributes news is not adequate to the aim of creating a European identity. In order to spare national feelings, Euronews strives for a very neutral tone, which leads according to Schlesinger (1996, quoted in Casero 2001) to a 'watered-down journalism'. Similarly, Meinhof (2001) describes Euronews as hardly more than a 'collage of bits and pieces from national TV-stations with an added "Euro-text", edited for a pan-European audience and accordingly sallow'.

Thus, the idea of a 'European point of view' represented by Europa TV has been given up in favour of the neutral presentation of national news. In this vein, 'Euronews is more a plurinational than a non-national or denationalized broadcaster' (Theiler 1999: 9). Furthermore, Euronews caters for the needs and interests of European elites rather than for the broad mass of citizens. This becomes evident in the self-description of Euronews (Euronews n.d.): 'Euronews' upmarket audience, composed of high income earners, decision makers, opinion leaders and businessmen'. Summarizing, Euronews can be understood as a particular EPS in itself, but its contribution to a more general European public sphere seems doubtful.

3 REGULATIONS ON AUDIOVISUAL SERVICES

3.1 Television without Frontiers

Parallel to the efforts to establish European television during the 1980s, European institutions developed a regulatory framework for audiovisual activities under the heading 'Television without Frontiers'.

This title was first used for a Green Paper, issued by the Commission in 1984 (European Commission 1984) as a reaction to the motions of the EP from 1980 as well as to several interim activities by the European Parliament. Within this Green Paper, the Commission takes a bold stance on the question of competence for audiovisual services:

> Contrary to what is widely imagined, the EEC Treaty applies not only to economic activities but, as a rule, also to all activities carried out for remuneration, regardless of whether they take place in the economic, social, cultural (including in particular information, creative or artistic activities and entertainment), sporting or any other sphere. (European Commission 1984: 6)

Later in the document, a further specification can be found: 'The concept of remuneration does not necessarily also include the notion of profit or any like intention' (European Commission 1984: 120). Thus, at least in the understanding of the Commission, the debate of the 1970s on the character of television found an end by stating that this character has no impact on the question of supranational competences. The Commission, thereby, also states that public service broadcasting financed by fees or taxes has to adhere to the EC treaties. However, in accordance with the ECJ in the Coditel case of 1980, the Commission sees EC legislation as only applicable in cases of trans-frontier services. As most audiovisual programmes can be received in countries other than the country of origin, this condition applies in many cases (European Commission 1984: 123).

The report, then, emphasizes the technological possibility and normative desirability of cross-border exchange of information and explicitly mentions that

> … all the Community Member States refused to approve the United Nations Resolution of 10 December 1982, which … contains … the requirement that states must seek the prior agreement of countries in which broadcasts might possibly be received before broadcasting any television programmes direct … [as] … [r]equirements of this nature clash with the basic principles of the European democracies. Freedom of information is a prerequisite to the exercise of the right of citizens to elect their parliament. (European Commission 1984: 41)

In its more concrete parts, the Green Paper focuses on cross-border exchanges of national television companies and a European market for audiovisual products in order to develop a European identity and to counter-balance US dominance in this field. It calls for the harmonization of national rules for advertising (European Commission 1984: 268–299) and for youth protection (European Commission 1984: 301–307), and it discusses various solutions for copyright problems due to differing national legislations (European Commission 1984: 328–345). These themes were also mentioned in the Hahn Report, although in a much less prominent form.

Plans for a European television programme (which were very intensely debated at the time the Green Paper was issued) are only mentioned once in the Green Paper. Thus, the Green Paper can be interpreted in two ways. On the one hand, it takes up the need for European regulation, which proved a necessary condition for the implementation of European broadcasting. Therefore, it can be seen as complementary to the efforts to establish such a programme. On the other hand, the Green Paper did not take up the more ambitious and politically motivated concepts for EC audiovisual policies developed by the Parliament and supported in the interim report, and can, in this way, also be understood as a retreat towards less ambitious political measures.

In 1989, the 'Television without Frontiers' Directive (TWFD) was issued, taking up most of the proposals of the Green Paper, but including a quota regulation according to which 'broadcasters [should] reserve for European works … a majority proportion of their transmission time' (European Council 1989). Furthermore, '[b]roadcasters must also reserve at least 10% of their transmission time or 10% of their programming budget for European works from independent producers'.[2] These additions to the Green Paper were strongly supported by France but opposed by many other member states (Donaldson 1996: 98–99).

The directive was revised in 1997 (European Parliament and European Council 1997) clarifying questions of jurisdiction, including regulations on teleshopping, tightening measures for youth protection and allowing free broadcasting of events of major importance for society. A further revision took place in 2007 (European Parliament and European Council 2007) defining audiovisual media services independently of the method of broadcasting (i.e. including the internet). Apart from this important change, the new directive, above all, loosens some rules of the older versions by a stronger focus on self-regulation.

Summarizing, one can state that the general aims and scope of EU policies summarized in the 'Television without Frontiers' Directive have not considerably developed since 1989. This legislation pursues two defensive goals similar to the aims of Euronews described above: the transgression of national borders within the EU and support of European broadcasting against international competition, above all from the US. The latter aim has frequently been criticized as protectionist (see for example Semetko et al. 2000) and, obviously, transcends (or even contradicts) the aim of warranting free competition. However, it can be interpreted as an acknowledgement of the cultural function of television. The aim of EU internal organization of television, on the other hand, is, rather, to reduce cultural differences by unified regulation in accordance with the Single Market. However, this strategy is rather doubted in the academic literature, as arguably television has become commercialized, more uniform in content and format and less informative (see for example Burri-Nenova 2009). While these developments are certainly mainly due to the multiplication of commercial broadcasters, some authors maintain that EC/EU deregulation policies have also played a major role. '[O]ne could suggest that whilst the TVWF has been a "victory for commercial forces", it has done little for the achievement of cultural goals' (Burri-Nenova 2009: 69).

And, clearly, the political impetus of EP activities at the beginning of the 1980s has been abandoned in the debates on Television without Frontiers.

3.2 Public Broadcasting

The political function of media, however, played a role within debates between member states and the European Commission on the role and rights of public broadcasting. The decline in public service broadcasting has not only coincided with deepening European integration but been encouraged by EU politics, as public fees for broadcasting were discussed as distortions of private competition (cf. Semetko et al. 2000). In the end, however, the specific political and cultural role of television led to EC approval of public broadcasting by a protocol to the Treaty of Amsterdam stating that

> considering that the system of public broadcasting in the Member States is directly related to the democratic, social and cultural needs of each society and to the need to preserve media pluralism ...
>
> The provisions of the Treaty establishing the European Community shall be without prejudice to the competence of Member States to provide for the funding of public service broadcasting insofar as such funding is granted to broadcasting organisations for the fulfilment of the public service remit as conferred, defined and organized by each Member State, and insofar as such funding does not affect trading conditions and competition in the Community to an extent which would be contrary to the common interest, while the realisation of the remit of that public service shall be taken into account. (Protocol on the System of Public Broadcasting in the Member States 1997)

These general rules have been operationalized by two communications of the European Commission (European Commission 2001, 2009) ruling, above all, that the appropriateness of state aid for public broadcasting has to be assessed on a case-by-case basis. While, thus, recognizing the political impact of television, legislation and debates on public broadcasting since the Treaty of Amsterdam only deal with questions of market distortion and with national interests; the idea of EU public broadcasting is no longer ventured.

3.3 Financial Support for Media

The most important instrument to support audiovisual industries in the EU is the MEDIA programme, first launched in 1992 and, since 2014, part of the 'Creative Europe' programme[3] 'to promote the production and dissemination of audiovisual works throughout the Union and to protect cultural diversity' (Harrison and Woods 2007: 90). This programme can be understood as a consequence of the 'Television without Frontiers' Directive, as 'some argued that the single European market created by the TWFD would lead to a domination of English-language programming in the Union' (Harrison and Woods 2007: 90) and, therefore, support for cultural diversity in the media was called for. The MEDIA programme has been continued up to now. It provides financial support for quality European films and television programmes. The aims are to boost output and distribution in Europe and to promote European films, other audiovisual works and new digital technologies.[4] Apart from potential underfunding of the programme, MEDIA is generally assessed as a success. For a political EPS, however, MEDIA is probably only of indirect impact.

4 THE EU AND DIGITAL MEDIA

Through its website europa.eu, the European Commission gives access to an abundance of information as well as to various forms of interacting with EU institutions and representatives (public consultations, specific initiatives, blogs, EU sites in social networks) and audiovisual material. Most prominent in the audiovisual part are europarlTV and EUtube.

Specifically, europarlTV is an ambitious project launched in 2008. Nowadays, it features three channels – Parliament News, Young Parliament (consisting of educational material for young people) and Discover Parliament (providing background information). Furthermore, 'Parliament near you' shows EU news of relevance to one's own living place.[5]

While recognizing all these efforts as an important step towards more communication with the citizens, critics doubt the attractiveness and effectiveness of concrete measures:

> [I]ncreasing media does not necessarily generate a more vibrant European public sphere, and due to a number of factors related to both format and content, many of the EU's media pages are fairly ineffective in encouraging Europeanized discourse ... One of the greatest challenges facing EU new media is its simple lack of popularity, as evidenced by low viewing rates and lack of participation on interactive sites. (Atherton 2010: 150–154)

Furthermore, the language problem has not been solved by new media, and many of the mentioned EU contents are only available in English, with others in English, French and German.

5 EU MEDIA POLICIES AND THE PREFERENCES OF EUROPEAN ACTORS

The history of European media policies shows: (1) a clear focus on the removal of market distortions as a general trait; (2) a politicization of these debates understanding media as a precondition of a European identity, a European public sphere and, thus, European democracy in the 1980s; and (3) a considerable loss of ambition since the failure of Europa TV continuing up to now.

Still, the claim that media should further the EPS has remained part and parcel of political and academic debates up to now, while at the same time the problems of Europa TV, especially with regard to cultural and linguistic differences, have not even been solved on a theoretical level. This state of the discussion is also mirrored in the interview data collected in the Eurosphere project. Only a minority of our interviewees see an existing or at least emerging EPS, while its necessity has been claimed by many. Most frequently, respondents confirm the existence of an elite public sphere while deploring the lack of a mass public sphere (see for example Barani and Sciortino 2011: 30; Kutay and Arribas 2011: 28; Selmeczi and Sata 2011: 19). This response can be found among representatives of political parties, NGOs and think tanks, and it corresponds with earlier findings (see for example Schlesinger 1999, quoted in Creutz-Kämppi et al. 2011: 276). And, as in previous research, many respondents see the cause for this lack of a mass public sphere in the lack of European or Europeanized media.

Still, interviews with journalists showed that, in fact, European media cooperate and exchange content (Creutz-Kämppi et al. 2011: 27) so that the question arises of whether Europeanization in the form of European transnational exchange has already incrementally developed owing to individual initiatives:

> For example, in the Norwegian material, three media actors … report that they are engaged in networks of information sharing. Indeed, in reference to one of the above actors, transnational collaborations are reported to be 'mainly journalistic in the sense of buying and selling news items and other journalistic pieces from newspapers with a bigger organization and greater resources than *Klassekampen*. Buying content clearly enriches the newspaper and presents differing perspectives.' Such 'buying content' was common amongst media actors across the countries in our selected sample. Other actors, for example the *Süddeutsche Zeitung* (SZ) and the *Tageszeitung* (taz) in Germany are noted to share content with publications in Europe and the United States. *NRC Handelsblad* notes that its cooperation with *Politiken* (Denmark) 'started in the run-up to the European Parliament elections of 2009

> "with the idea that you can exchange articles and explore the [common European] space"'. (Creutz-Kämppi et al. 2011: 27–28, 33)

In other cases, exchange of content takes place owing to transnational ownership of media (Creutz-Kämppi et al. 2011: 28). Also, a considerable number of interviewed journalists saw it as their task to inform the audience about European affairs (Selmeczi and Sata 2011: 18). Thus, one could argue that, to some degree, national media take up the task to translate European issues and issues from other member states for their audiences, while these audiences remain nationally organized. In the words of a journalist from *Le Figaro*, 'We never think of the European audience, since it is not a criterion for our dissemination policies. The Italians read the Italian newspapers, whereas the French read the French newspapers' (Selmeczi and Sata 2011: 20).

However, especially with regard to EU issues the success of journalistic efforts to adequately inform the citizens seems to be limited, as the Eurosphere project showed in accordance with earlier studies. In this vein, two German journalists 'indicate that present information flows and exchanges on the EU are insufficient, and both claim that informing the public is mainly obstructed because the EU is too complex to explain to a generally disinterested audience' (Selmeczi and Sata 2011: 20).

Apart from 'classical' media, several of our respondents see the internet as a possibility for the development of an EPS (Barani and Sciortino 2011: 32; Creutz-Kämppi et al. 2011: 32, 34). In our material, we can find very optimistic expectations for the 'anarchistic qualities' (Creutz-Kämppi et al. 2011: 34) of this bottom-up medium (Barani and Sciortino 2011: 32) and, thus, some respondents claim freedom for the internet and the absence of political regulation (Kutay and Arribas 2011: 29). However, other respondents understand the internet as a new form of elite public sphere(s) rather than as a mass medium (Creutz-Kämppi et al. 2011: 34).

The Eurosphere project differs from earlier research on the European public sphere by its focus on diversity as well as by the normative hypothesis that diversity could advance rather than hinder the development of an EPS. Our empirical material at least partly supports this thesis; for example, it is striking that those respondents from political parties who hold the most encompassing understanding of diversity are also most interested in the development of European communicative spaces (Sata 2011: 43). Furthermore, several respondents emphasize that an EPS would be important for the empowerment of disadvantaged groups (Selmeczi and Sata 2011: 21, 22). In this vein, it also seems interesting that transnational minorities are most interested in the development of an EPS (van de Beek et al. 2011: 22).

6 CONCLUSIONS

Hitherto EU media policies have proven successful in reducing national barriers for broadcasting and establishing a single European media market, but they did not succeed in providing centralized forms of information distribution and exchange. In the terminology of Scharpf (2003: 219–223), negative integration of the media sector has worked well, while positive integration has not taken place. Negative integration, however, is seemingly doing little for the development of an EPS. Reasons for the failure of positive integration, that is, above all, of European broadcasting programmes, are mainly seen in cultural differences between the member states:

> [I]t was Europa TV's attempt to appeal to an audience as culturally and linguistically fragmented as the West European one which posed a major stumbling block … A good way to illustrate the difficulties inherent to the quest by Eurikon, Europa TV, and their commercial would-be pan-European counterparts to appeal to an audience as culturally and linguistically fragmented as that in Europe is through the often-cited concept of 'cultural discount' … The concept of 'cultural discount' is applied most commonly to cross-national situations, that is, to capture the reduced appeal of audiovisual output produced in one national cultural setting and consumed in another … Yet, in principle, it is equally apt to capture viewers' resistance to programs in a non-national format, a format to which Eurikon, Europa TV, and their commercial pan-European counterparts aspired. To the extent that this non-national format is dissonant with the particular cultural habitus of the viewers in question, its overall attractiveness to those viewers is reduced. (Theiler 1999)

As especially the example of Euronews shows, the problem of cultural discount also applies to the distribution of information. Thus, even Habermas's concept of 'constitutional patriotism' fails when political interest is hampered by cultural differences.

Still, our empirical results have shown a possible way out of this dilemma in transnational exchange of news and the attempts of journalists to include a European dimension in media coverage. Maybe one could speak here of a hidden form of EPS – the audience is addressed as a national audience but shares similar themes and outlooks with other national audiences. In the long run, this could lead to agonistic European public spheres not exclusively structured by national cleavages. For the time being, national sentiments and perspectives still seem to prevail in media audiences, but one can observe a form of Europeanization of public spheres developing independently of – or even in contradiction to – the centralized top-down media policies of the European Commission.

Thus, the question arises as to whether European institutions could enhance transnational exchanges and European points of view in national media. This is a delicate question, as freedom of the media is not only a fundamental democratic principle but also a deeply rooted value in most European societies; thus, interferences by political institutions in the media run the risk of negative reactions. Proposals like the following one are, thus, to be treated with caution:

- Increase funding for PSB [public service broadcasting] programming with EU-related and European-produced content through a fund established by the EU.
- Implement continuing education programs to educate journalists about the European Union and current affairs in Europe.
- The EBU should raise the portion of broadcasting time reserved for European programs to 20%.
- Require commercial television stations to run EU-wide programs.
- Create media fora for newspaper and other media to meet and participate in debates about EU current affairs. Encourage media to participate in these fora. (Allen 2010: 146)

Still, educational efforts towards journalists could prove valuable and, according to our results, would possibly be accepted with interest. With regard to the financing of EU-related coverage, it would be important that this funding was not devoted to show-casing EU successes. Quite on the contrary, it should include critical voices on European integration and, above all, controversial debates on European issues. In order to warrant independence from European institutions, an independent jury would have to decide on the distribution of funding. In this way, agonistic European public spheres can be institutionalized without centralization and standardization.

Similarly, agonistic discourses could be developed by a different use of digital media by European integration:

> A video that clearly outlines EU issues while *also* reviewing the shortcomings of the EU's approach would not weaken the EU's image. Such omissions would show citizens that the institution is willing to acknowledge others' views and explain the logic of its own views to others. It would also highlight the diversity of opinion within the EU – likely even including those MEPs who are fundamentally opposed to the EU's existence – and highlight the political drama of party politics at the supranational level. (Atherton 2010: 159)

Finally, our empirical results suggest that the efforts of European institutions to develop an EPS should not remain limited to national media or the central Europa website. As especially minorities hope for empowerment from an emerging EPS, their media should be considered valuable partners for European integration and, thus, be included in funding schemes.

This holds especially true for transnational minorities and their equally transnational media – 'for example the Turkish *Hürriyet* with its editorial office in Germany, distributed to approximately 20 000 sales points in Germany and 30 000 across Europe' (Creutz-Kämppi et al. 2011: 33). These media are an example for European public spheres which are transnationally organized. In this way, agonistic discourses from below overcome national limitations.

Citizens with multiple or complex ethno-national belongings are, along with migration, a common basis for societal or non-elitist transnational spaces. This phenomenon can strengthen the European public sphere, and the experience of these citizens can give a wider, more positive perspective on diversity. In this vein, it might be a good move for European media policies to put a special focus on transnational groups and citizens with multiple belongings in order to foster an EPS. After all, the diversity of the European Union is at the same time one of its biggest problems and one of its biggest assets. But, irrespective of normative evaluations, 'complex diversity' (Kraus 2012) has to be accepted as a basic condition of a European public sphere.

NOTES

1. The decision for such a broad programme was, however, in no way unanimous – over quite some time a so-called 'Project B' was discussed which would mainly be based on live sports events. Much later, 'Project B' was implemented in the form of 'Eurosport' (Collins 1998: 96).
2. See http://europa.eu/legislation_summaries/audiovisual_and_media/l24101_en.htm (accessed 11 July 2012).
3. See http://ec.europa.eu/programmes/creative-europe/ (accessed 11 July 2012).
4. See http://europa.eu/pol/av/index_en.htm (accessed 11 July 2012).
5. See europarlTV.europa.eu (accessed 12 July 2012).

REFERENCES

Allen, J.M. (2010) Mass Media and the European Public Sphere, in Henry M. Jackson School of International Studies (ed.), *Task Force Policy Report on Democracy in the European Union*, pp. 134–148, Seattle, WA: University of

Washington, https://digital.lib.washington.edu/researchworks/bitstream/handle/1773/15598/TF_SIS495D_2010.pdf?sequence=1#page=157 (accessed 11 July 2012).

Andjelkovic, A. (2007) Regulating Audiovisual Media Services in the European Union: On Theory of Low Intensity Constitutionalism, www.etd.ceu.hu/2007/andjelkovic_aleksa.pdf (accessed 11 July 2012).

Atherton, A. (2010) New Media and the European Public Sphere, in Henry M. Jackson School of International Studies (ed.), *Task Force Policy Report on Democracy in the European Union*, pp. 149–170, Seattle, WA: University of Washington, https://digital.lib.washington.edu/researchworks/bitstream/handle/1773/15598/TF_SIS495D_2010.pdf?sequence=1#page=157 (accessed 11 July 2012).

Barani, L. and G. Sciortino (2011) *The Role of Think Tanks in the Articulation of the European Public Sphere*, Work Package 5.1 Report, Eurosphere Online Working Paper Series, http://eurospheres.org/files/2010/06/WP_5_1_final.pdf (accessed 12 July 2012).

Beek, J.H. van de, F. Vermeulen and M. Lagerspetz (2011) *Minorities, the European Polity and a Nascent European Public Sphere*, Work Package 6.1/2 Report, Eurosphere Online Working Paper Series, http://www.eurosphere.uib.no/files/2010/06/WP_6_1-2.pdf (accessed 12 July 2012).

Burri-Nenova, M. (2009) Cultural Diversity and the EC Audiovisual Media Services Directive: Beyond the Handsome Rhetoric, http://www.tilburguniversity.edu/research/institutes-and-research-groups/tilec/meetingsandevents/conferencesandworkshops/04mediaworkshop/burri.pdf (accessed 11 July 2012).

Casero, A. (2001) European-wide Television and the Construction of European Identity: The Case of Euronews, *Formats* 3, http://www.iua.upf.edu/formats/formats3/cas_a.htm (accessed 1 July 2012).

Collins, R. (1998) *From Satellite to Single Market: New Communication Technology and European Public Service Television*, London: Routledge.

Creutz-Kämppi, K., P. Holley, P.A. Kraus, P. Laine and J. Warius (2011) *Assessing Transnational Spaces*, Work Package 6.3 Report, Eurosphere Online Working Paper Series, http://eurospheres.org/files/2010/06/WP_6_3_final.pdf (accessed 12 July 2012).

Donaldson, J.D. (1996) 'Television without Frontiers': The Continuing Tension between Liberal Free Trade and European Cultural Integrity, *Fordham International Law Journal*, 20(1), 92–180.

EBU (European Broadcasting Union) (n.d.) Who We Are and What We Do, http://www.eurovision.tv/upload/media/EBUcorporate.pdf (accessed 10 July 2012).

Euronews (n.d.) Euronews and Metropolitan Media Ltd, http://metmedia.net/Open_Letter.pdf (accessed 10 July 2012).

European Commission (1983) *Interim Report: Realities and Tendencies in European Television: Perspectives and Options*, http://aei.pitt.edu/6341/1/6341.pdf (accessed 5 July 2012).

European Commission (1984) *Television without Frontiers: Green Paper on the Establishment of the Common Market for Broadcasting, especially by Satellite and Cable*, http://aei.pitt.edu/1150/1/TV_frontiers_gp_table_COM_84_300.pdf;

http://aei.pitt.edu/1151/1/TV_frontiers_gp_pt_1_3.pdf; http://aei.pitt.edu/1152/1/TV_frontiers_gp_pt_4.pdf; http://aei.pitt.edu/1153/1/TV_frontiers_pt_5.pdf; http://aei.pitt.edu/1154/1/TV_frontiers_pt_6.pdf (accessed 05 July 2012).

European Commission (2001) *Communication from the Commission on the Application of State Aid Rules to Public Service Broadcasting*, http://eur-lex.europa.eu/LexUriServ/LexUriServ.do?uri=CELEX:52001XC1115%2801%29:EN:NOT (accessed 11 July 2012).

European Commission (2009) *Communication from the Commission on the Application of State Aid Rules to Public Service Broadcasting*, http://eur-lex.europa.eu/LexUriServ/LexUriServ.do?uri=CELEX:52009XC1027%2801%29:EN:NOT (accessed 11 July 2012).

European Council (1989) Council Directive 89/552/EEC of 3 October 1989 on the Coordination of Certain Provisions Laid Down by Law, Regulation or Administrative Action in Member States Concerning the Pursuit of Television Broadcasting Activities, http://eur-lex.europa.eu/LexUriServ/LexUriServ.do?uri=CELEX:31989L0552:EN:HTML (accessed 11 July 2012).

European Court of Justice (1974) Judgment of the Court of 30 April 1974. – Giuseppe Sacchi. – Reference for a Preliminary Ruling: Tribunale civile e penale di Biella, Italy, Case 155-73, http://eur-lex.europa.eu/LexUriServ/LexUriServ.do?uri=CELEX:61973CJ0155:EN:HTML (accessed 12 July 2012).

European Court of Justice (1980) Judgment of the Court of 18 March 1980. Procureur du Roi v Marc J.V.C. Debauve and Others. Reference for a Preliminary Ruling: Tribunal de première instance de Liège – Belgium. Provision of Services: Cable Diffusion of Television, Case 52/79, http://eur-lex.europa.eu/LexUriServ/LexUriServ.do?uri=CELEX:61979J0052:EN:NOT (accessed 12 July 2012).

European Parliament (1982) *Report on Radio and Television Broadcasting in the European Community* (Hahn Report), Document 1–1013/81, http://aei.pitt.edu/3120/1/3120.pdf (accessed 11 July 2012).

European Parliament and European Council (1997) Directive 97/36/EC of the European Parliament and of the Council of 30 June 1997 Amending Council Directive 89/552/EEC on the Coordination of Certain Provisions Laid Down by Law, Regulation or Administrative Action in Member States Concerning the Pursuit of Television Broadcasting Activities, http://eur-lex.europa.eu/LexUriServ/LexUriServ.do?uri=CELEX:31997L0036:EN:HTML (accessed 11 July 2012).

European Parliament and European Council (2007) Directive 2007/65/EC of the European Parliament and of the Council of 11 December 2007 Amending Council Directive 89/552/EEC on the Coordination of Certain Provisions Laid Down by Law, Regulation or Administrative Action in Member States Concerning the Pursuit of Television Broadcasting Activities, http://eur-lex.europa.eu/LexUriServ/LexUriServ.do?uri=OJ:L:2007:332:0027:01:EN:HTML (accessed 11 July 2012).

Harrison, J. and L. Woods (2007) *European Broadcasting Law and Policy*, http://www.ourpgs.com/books/law/European%20broadcasting%20law.pdf (accessed 11 July 2012).

Holznagel, B. (1996) *Rundfunkrecht in Europa: Auf dem Weg zu einem Gemeinrecht europäischer Rundfunkordnungen*, Tübingen: J.C.B. Mohr (Paul Siebeck).

Kantner, C. (2004) *Kein modernes Babel: Kommunikative Voraussetzungen europäischer Öffentlichkeit*, Wiesbaden: Springer.

Kraus, P. (2012) The Politics of Complex Diversity: A European Perspective, *Ethnicities* 12(1): 3–25.

Kunelius, R. and C. Sparks (2001) Problems with a European Public Sphere: An Introduction, *Javnost – The Public* 8(1): 5–20.

Kutay, A. and A. Arribas (2011) *The Role of SMOs/NGOs in the Articulation of the European Public Sphere*, Work Package 5.3 Report, Eurosphere Online Working Paper Series, http://eurospheres.org/files/2010/06/WP_5_3_final.pdf (accessed 12 July 2012).

Maggiore, M. (1990) *Audiovisual Production and the Single Market*, Luxembourg: Commission of the EC.

Meinhof, U.H. (2001) Auf der Suche nach Euro-news-land: Satellitenfernsehen und die Konstruktion transnationaler Identitäten, in B. Busch, B. Hipfl and K. Robins (eds), *Bewegte Identitäten: Medien in transkulturellen Kontexten*, pp. 111–127, Klagenfurt/Celovec: Drava.

Noll, A.J. (1998) Medienentwicklung – und ihre (un)mögliche rechtliche Bewältigung, *Österreichische Zeitschrift für Politikwissenschaft* 27(2): 157–171.

Peter, J. (2003) *Why European TV News Matters: A Cross-nationally Comparative Analysis of TV News about the European Union and Its Effects*, Amsterdam: University of Amsterdam.

Pollak, J. (2006) *Repräsentation ohne Demokratie: Kollidierende Systeme der Repräsentation in der Europäischen Union*, Wien: Verlag Österreich.

Protocol on the System of Public Broadcasting in the Member States (1997), *Official Journal* C 340, 10 November, http://eur-lex.europa.eu/en/treaties/dat/11997D/htm/11997D.html#0109010012 (accessed 12 July 2012).

Sata, R. (2011) *The Role of Political Parties in the Articulation of the European Public Sphere*, Work Package 5.2 Report, Eurosphere Online Working Paper Series, http://eurospheres.org/files/2010/06/WP_5_2_final.pdf (accessed 12 July 2012).

Scharpf, F.W. (2003) Politische Optionen im vollendeten Binnenmarkt, in M. Jachtenfuchs and B. Kohler-Koch (eds), *Europäische Integration*, Opladen: Leske + Budrich.

Schlesinger, P. (1997) From Cultural Deference to Political Culture: Media, Politics and Collective Identity in the European Union, *Media, Culture and Society* 19(3): 369–391.

Selmeczi, A. and R. Sata (2011) *The Role of Print and Broadcast Media in the Articulation of the European Public Sphere: Comparative Qualitative Analysis of Selected Eurosphere Media Representative Interviews*, Work Package 5.4.1 Report, Eurosphere Online Working Paper Series, http://eurospheres.org/files/2010/06/WP_5_4_1_final.pdf (accessed 12 July 2012).

Semetko, H.A., C.H. de Vreese and J. Peter (2000) Europeanised Politics – Europeanised Media? European Integration and Political Communication, *West European Politics* 23(4): 121–141.

Siebenhaar, H.-P. (2002) Europäisches Fernsehen: Mehrsprachige, grenzüberschreitendes Fernsehen als Instrument des Einigungsprozesses? in H. Haas and W.R. Langenbucher (eds), *Medien- und Kommunikationspolitik*, Vol. 12, pp. 180–190, Wien: Studienbücher zur Publizistik und Kommunikationswissenschaft, http://www.unet.univie.ac.at/~a9807630/STEP4/Siebenhaar.pdf (accessed 5 July 2012).

Siegordner, M. (2002) *Die EBU (European Broadcasting Union): Geschichte und Aufgaben*, Norderstedt: Grin.

Siune, K. and W. Truetzschler (1992) *Dynamics of Media Politics: Broadcast and Electronic Media in Western Europe*, London: Sage.

Theiler, T. (1999) Viewers into Europeans? How the European Union Tried to Europeanize the Audiovisual Sector, and Why It Failed, *Canadian Journal of Communication* 24(2), http://www.cjc-online.ca/index.php/journal/article/view/1126/1035 (accessed 5 July 2012).

Weidenfeld, W. and W. Wessels (1998) *Europe from A to Z*, Brussels: European Commission.

Wiesner, V. (1990) Fernsehen, Kultur und kulturelle Identität in Europa: Ein Interpretationsversuch, in H.J. Kleinsteuber, V. Wiesner and P. Wilke (eds), *EG-Medienpolitik: Fernsehen in Europa zwischen Kultur und Kommerz*, pp. 157–179, Berlin: Vistas.

4. European state building, top-down elite alliances and the national media[1]

Hakan G. Sicakkan

Is European elites' ambition to create a common European citizen identity echoed in European countries' public spheres? If so, what does this mean for different groups of citizens?[2] Who are excluded from and included in different designs of common European citizen identity? Are the new transnational processes of inclusion and exclusion in Europe creating new Others? These are the empirical questions that I strive to answer in this chapter.

My theoretical argument aims to reinvigorate a specific perspective on citizenship in Europe. My point of departure is a constructivist approach that emphasizes the prominence of elite rationality and prudence that is instrumental in construction of collective identities. That is, identities are socially constructed, but the design of the surrounding social edifice is undersigned with the initials of political elites. This idea contests the orientalist-culturalist Weberian understanding of how citizenship emerged in the East and the West. The Weberian approach asserts that not only context-specific material conditions, like mode of production and ownership of production means, the need for equipping and sustaining an army, and the organization of defence, but also cultural features were crucial in the emergence and development of modern citizenship. In this connection, Weber attributed the qualities of demystified life (absence of magic), autonomous individuality, rationality and modernity only to Western cultures. In the West, individual autonomy and citizenship emerged because Western cultures allowed a demystification process which diminished the existing group boundaries that were an obstacle to groups of people identifying with each other, perceiving their common good, and becoming equal citizens pursuing common goals. In Weber's analysis of subjecthood in Egypt, western Asia, India and China, on the other hand, we are told this did not (and could not) happen in the East because the

Eastern cultures did not allow such a boundary-breaking process through demystification, remaining divided as ceremonial communities (Weber 1981 [1923]).

However, Benedict Anderson (1991) showed us how nations were imagined in both the East and the West, and how religious magic and miracles, on the one hand, and ethno-religious rituals, on thc other, were transformed into magical national heroes and national rituals during and after state- and nation-building processes. In contrast to what Weber's culturalist approach would predict regarding today's European citizenship, European elites are not trying to demystify cultures and cultural practices in order to demolish the group boundaries between the 'divided' people of Europe. On the contrary, they are using the already mystified collective identities as the building blocks of a common European identity: 'diversity in unity'. Moreover, collective identities deriving from religions, nations, ethnic groups, territorial belonging and gender are being magnified through the motto of 'unity in diversity'. Thus, the ongoing common citizen identity formation in Europe is not a process of demystification, unlike what the Weberian approach would claim, but a new process of increased mystification wittingly devised by the EU elites and carried out by trans-European elites.

I build my argument on four premises. First, whatever form its political system currently has, or in whatever different forms we may imagine its future, the EU is a state- and nation-building project. Its territorial consolidation and expansion efforts are reminiscent of European nation states' history, although the means and discourses deployed this time are innovatively different. In this connection, I follow an idea inspired by Stein Rokkan (1970, 1975; Rokkan and Urwin 1983): in order to curtail possible resistance from local elites and the people, state-building elites strive to treat everybody in the targeted territories as a potential citizen. Thus, elites select the most encompassing and the most feasible citizen identity, especially in contexts where assimilation is too costly a route (cf. Sicakkan 2005).[3] Further, elites reluctantly share their authority and power with others only when they have to do so in order to preserve their own power and rule.

Second, attempts at new citizen identity formation are more likely to be successful when political elites manage to create sustainable strategic alliances, networks and lines of communication, and common understandings with local elites (Rokkan 1970). With regard to European elites, the principal concern is alliances, communication networks, and understandings between European, trans-European and national elites. Seen through neo-functionalist lenses, European elites' views are to be found in the EU's political and judicial institutions, laws and policies.

Trans-European elites' visions, on the other hand, are discernible in their discourses and activities in trans-European networks and organizations whose primary aim is to constitute an additional, corporate-plural link between individuals and the EU institutions. Likewise, national elite views are observed in their activities and discourses in nation-wide organizations that participate in politics and/or policymaking processes (e.g. political parties, public and corporate interest groups, social movement organizations, research institutes and think tanks, and print and broadcast media actors).

Third, when national and trans-European elites start perceiving their own belongings in similar ways, this is likely to be reflected in media as similar framings of different social groups across different countries. Such mirroring is expected to happen since, among other factors, media owners, editors and journalists with significant influence on public opinion are often part of national elite networks engaging in either collaboration with or resistance against European, trans-European and national elites. Such congruence implies an agreement about who 'us' and 'them' are, which is an essential point of departure for the creation of the new common citizen identity and its 'Others'.

Fourth, it is important to note that the data about views of trans-European and national elites and media framings of citizen identity used here were collected shortly after the current financial crisis hit Europe, that is, from mid-2008 to the first two months of 2009. In times of deep economic crises, state elites often lose their control over construction and maintenance of the common citizen identity. This power fatigue may be partial or total, depending on the resources and support available to political elites compared with the support and resources of opposition. Competing for the same scarce resources, certain social groups often attempt to discriminate against and exclude other groups based on certain human traits that they believe are unalterable (e.g. gender, race, ethnicity, nation, religion, culture). It is usually, though not exclusively, the dominant group that claims ownership of the state's territory and the resources in it. This tendency is often reinforced by political processes in which influential political elites take sides with certain groups and/or new political elites appear and campaign in order to seize power on behalf of their own groups. In the EU context, the competition is between Europeanists, nations, native minorities and immigrant minorities; class strugglers are largely passivized through the massive involvement of the representatives of corporations in EU policymaking, combined with a nearly imperceptible presence of farmers, workers and students' organizations in the supranational policymaking processes.

With a point of departure in the premises outlined above and following the general questions posed at the very beginning, I pose the following questions: Are the views of trans-European elites and national elites, on one hand, and the framings of national media, on the other, similar to each other when it comes to which groups are excluded from and included in the common citizen identity? Is the European state- and nation-building process of our century creating new Others, or just inheriting the Others of its constituent nation states?

First, I delineate and compare the trans-European and national elites' ways of defining the European citizen identity. Next, I present the results from my analysis of media framings of different identities in 15 European countries. Finally, I compare the citizenship visions observed in EU policies and trans-European and national elite discourses with the media framings. These three comparative analyses are meant to examine whether the Eurosphere, the vertical, top-down communicative public space of pro-European elites and citizens in Europe, has succeeded in constituting a European public sphere.

1 THE CITIZEN AND THE OTHER IN TRANS-EUROPEAN AND NATIONAL ELITE DISCOURSES

From a perspective relating the notion of a European public sphere to state formation and nation building, alliances between trans-European and national elites are a central concern. This concerns both the alliance networks that they form and their discourses, attitudes and political preferences. European cases of historical state and nation building show that elites can consolidate and hold on to a territory only with support from local elites (Sicakkan 2005). In collaboration, central and local elites try to generate state-friendly discourses within the population so as to increase the legitimacy of the state. To spread these attitudes, they use any available means of communication – in the case of the European Union this is the national mass media. Concerning the case of the European Union, Chapter 1 in this volume portrayed the mindset and systematic attempts of the European founding generation aiming to generate a European public opinion. These attempts are still continuing with more advanced methods. Chapters 6, 7 and 8 discuss the trans-European elites' ways of establishing alliances and common discourses with national elites. In the following, thus, I compare the preferences of national and trans-European elites to see whether or to what extent discourse conformity has been created at the national level. I do this by comparing the most critical discourses that bring the European and national elites into confrontation: citizenship and diversity.

1.1 Identifying the Elites' Discourses on Citizenship and Diversity

The systematically selected 764 national and trans-European elites in 15 European countries[4] were encouraged to talk about persons and groups that they see as relevant to their own idea of a diverse society. After the interviewees talked about their own preferences, they were asked to consider whether they would like to include other categories, of which they were given a list. The answers were then registered and coded in a common database. Interviews with leaders of national and trans-European-level organizations show there are clear level-wise differences in organizations' approaches to citizen identity. Although the whole spectrum of views is represented at both levels, the set of views that dominate at each level differs.[5]

Table 4.1 presents the results from a principal component analysis of the categories mentioned by the respondents. This is an inductive method that identifies the categories that respondents tie with each other in their statements. The first dimension indicates an inclusive global and transnational understanding of a diverse society. All the variables loading on this dimension concern categories that are unrelated to the notion of a homogeneous nation state, that is, groups and belongings that contest the nation-state citizenship. I labelled this dimension 'Globalist and Transnationalist Orientation to Citizen Identity'. It represents respondents' tendency to include all types of diversity, not only group-based diversity but also individual diversity. This also includes diversity generated by internal mobility within the EU.

The second dimension measures the extent to which a respondent is willing to include gender, disability and sexuality groups, different generations and social classes in his or her definition of citizenship. This dimension has moderate loadings on the categories that can be called 'individualist'. I labelled this dimension 'Bodily and Individualist Orientation to Citizen Identity'. These variables are associated with social class, as the majority of the respondents were concerned that such belonging might affect people's social class or status.

The third dimension gathers the indicators measuring whether the respondents include national, religious and ethnic groups in their definitions of diversity. This dimension is about the inclusion or exclusion of minority groups that were generated by the history of nation states. I labelled this dimension 'Nation-statist Orientation to Citizen Identity'. In

Table 4.1 Groups relevant for definition of the diverse society

Orientation to citizen identity		
Globalist, transnationalist	Bodily and individualist	Nation-statist
Transnational belonging (to more than one country)	Gender groups (men/ women)	Ethnic groups (identification with a specific ethnic group)
Shifting belongings (belongings are under change)	Disability groups (people with physical or mental disadvantages)	Religious groups (identification with a specific religion)
European belongings (identification with the EU)	Sexuality groups (gays, lesbians, transsexuals, homosexuals)	National belonging (identification with a specific nation)
Global belonging groups (identification with humanity)	Generation (children, youth, elderly)	
Multiple belongings (identification with more than one group)	Social class (workers, employers, farmers, rich, poor, etc.)	
Life-style groups (identification with different life-styles)		
Territorial belonging (identification with a region in a country)		
Ideological groups (identification with a specific ideology)		
Migrant groups (people coming from non-European countries)		

this dimension, we measure how inclusive respondents are to group-based diversity created by the nation state itself.

These three discourse dimensions on citizenship and diversity constitute a summary of the discourses we find amongst the trans-European and national elites in Europe. Some of them are more oriented towards an all-inclusive global and transnational identity; some hold views that give primacy to national identity and find acceptable including only minority and majority identities generated by nation states in their notions of citizenship. A third discourse dimension of elites highlights the primacy of individual identities. These three types of citizenship and diversity discourses are often blended in people's minds; that is, we frequently find individuals who combine bodily-individualist and nation-statist discourses.

1.2 Comparing the National and Trans-European Elites' Discourses

By using discriminant analysis, I will now show how the above three discourses are blended in the minds of the elites that we studied. On the other hand, I will also show which discourses dominate in the national and transnational elite circles. Discriminant analysis is used to identify the discourse dimensions that most clearly distinguish between the discourses of national and trans-European elites.

Discriminant analysis of the three scales with the grouping variable 'national versus trans-European organization' gave the results shown in Table 4.2. There were 21.8 per cent of the interviewees from national organizations and 52.9 per cent from trans-European organizations who agree on a globally or transnationally oriented definition of citizenship. Inversely, 78.2 per cent of national and 47.1 per cent of trans-European elites agree on a nation-statist orientation to citizenship. These results show that nationalizing and Europeanizing discourses are spread in both national- and trans-European-level organizations, but nation-state orientation is stronger at the national level, whereas the transnational or global orientation is stronger at the trans-European level.

Table 4.2 National and European elites' orientation to citizenship

National or transnational organization? (N=724)	Orientation to citizenship		Total
	Nationalizing	Europeanizing	
National (%)	78.2	21.8	100.0
Trans-European (%)	47.1	52.9	100.0

Equally important are the details of the contents of these discourses (Table 4.3). I will call the discourse that is dominant in the trans-European umbrella organizations a 'Europeanizing discourse'. The other discourse that characterizes the majority of national elites' views can be labelled a 'nationalizing discourse'. Europeanizing discourses include a broad and inclusive definition of common citizen identity, whereas nationalizing discourses stick to the categories of the nation-state idea. The former see diversity as a normative goal to achieve, whereas the latter regard diversity as a reality that has to be handled or as a means of achieving national goals. Nationalizing discourses want to see the future of the EU, at best, as a de-centralized regulatory entity that allows national autonomy, whereas Europeanizing discourses express a preference for more transnationally integrated polity forms like multilevel governance or a federal European state.

Table 4.3 Contents of the two main elite discourses about European citizen identity

	Europeanizing discourses	Nationalizing discourses
Inclusion of groups that emanate from globalization and Europeanization	Very high	Very low
Inclusion of groups emanating from the historical nation-building processes	High	Very high
Inclusion of gender, class, disability, sexuality, social class	Very high	Medium
Approach to diversity	A normative goal to achieve	Instrumentalist and realist
Desired form of a future EU polity	Multilevel governance or a federal EU polity	De-centralized, regulatory, with autonomous nation states
Preferred communication and networking	Both vertical and horizontal structures of communication with the EU and others	Horizontal structures of communication with other states and organizations

1.3 Is the European Elites' Ambition Mirrored within National Elite Circles?

These findings have several implications in relation to the conceptual framework presented at the beginning. First, as expected, an inclusive and all-encompassing view on common European citizen identity is adopted and spread by the trans-European organizations that the EU has set up and is sponsoring. The degree of this inclusiveness matches quite well with the European territories that are to be consolidated under EU rule. Although allegiance to the nation-state citizen identity is strongly represented among trans-European elites, one-third of national elites are convinced about the trans-European elites' understanding of common citizen identity. Europeanizing views' presence within the national elite contexts is notably high, and the similarity between the views of trans-European and national elites about a common European citizen identity is on the way to becoming encompassing.

Second, the fact that almost half of trans-European elites embrace nationalizing views and more than half hold Europeanizing views implies an ideological, agonistic struggle between Europeanists and nation-statists at the European level. It should be noted that the EU state-building elites have consolidated a significantly large intermediary level of trans-European elites that are meant to function as an intermediary layer between themselves and citizens of the member states. Recent research offers empirical evidence suggesting that the fact that trans-European elites with nationalizing discourses are working through the very structures set up by the EU institutions means that these nationalizing discourses may gradually fade away through adoption and internalization of the EU vocabulary, language and values (Kutay 2012; Perez 2013; Sata 2012; Sicakkan 2012, 2013), which in turn may have a parallel impact on individual citizens' views (Klicperová-Baker and Košťál 2012).

Then, who are becoming the new Others in this process? All-inclusive discourses of trans-European elites do not give solid clues; nationalizing discourses seem to be reinforcing the existing Others. Current research suggests, however, that the EU diversity policies bolster a notion of language as a gate to opportunities – a common-market-oriented policy path which leaves out native minorities who experience language as a social tie (Kraus and Kazlauskaite 2013). Further, the EU's treatment of religious diversity favours majority religions. In contrast to linguistic minorities, majority religions have managed to remain outside the common-market logic (Zanon and Sciortino 2013). Native minority and immigrant religions are either left outside the policy field or dealt with through anti-discrimination measures. Moreover, the EU gender policy is characterized by the 'citizen versus non-citizen' and 'redistribution versus recognition' divisions; that is, immigrant women are excluded at the policy level (Agustin and Siim 2013). As to immigrants, a case study of the European Integration Forum shows the Forum is rather oriented towards implementation of political priorities established at the EU level (Lozano et al. 2013). These are similar to my own findings on the trans-European networks of civil society, think tanks and political parties (Sicakkan 2012).

2 THE CONSTRUCTION OF COMMON EUROPEAN CITIZEN IDENTITY IN EUROPEAN MEDIA

Whose views, then, are mirrored most by the national media? The trans-European elites or the national elites? The political parties, civil society organizations, think tanks and media organizations that were interviewed represent the most visible actors in public debates in each of the 15 countries. Many of them also participate in European-level political communication in different settings. My conceptual frame suggests that, if the EU is a state- and nation-building project, as asserted by the neo-functionalist approach and European federalists, diffusion of European elites' views on common European citizen identity will at least be partly reflected in national public spheres, since media elites are embedded within the national and trans-European lines and networks of communication.

To investigate this claim, I map out how different groups of people are framed in media news in 15 European countries. Five media actors are studied in each country – three newspapers and two television broadcasters, which were selected on the basis of the same selection criteria in all countries.[6] Also, a standard procedure was followed in all countries when selecting news items for content analysis.[7] The time period covered for each of the selected media actors was 9 May to 10 October 2008. With a significant variation between countries, the total number of the news items coded, from both print and broadcast media, was 8458. Although the research also covered 12 053 sources – that is, persons representing themselves or institutions who were cited with direct quotations in the news – they are not analysed here, as the aim is to depict the media's framings.

The analysis is conducted in three steps. First, I briefly show how persons' belongings are tied with different EU-related themes[8] in media news. Second, I illustrate how depictions of belongings[9] are linked with media's different normative framings.[10] These two assessments are based on two independent correspondence analyses. Finally, I present results from a two-step cluster analysis, where I use depictions of belongings, news themes and framing perspectives as clustering variables, in order to identify the main media discourses of inclusion and exclusion.

Figure 4.1 illustrates that media separate two themes (migration policy and minority policy) along with two groups (native minorities and immigrant minorities) from the other themes and groups. The core themes of European integration – that is, EU institutions, Reform Treaty, construction of Europe, free movement and mobility, gender policy, and enlargement – are kept separate from the themes of migration policy and minority policy. Further, these marginalized two policy themes are also kept separate from each other and aligned with depictions of persons not as European citizens, and not as citizens of a nation state, but as, respectively, native and immigrant minorities. Therefore, based on these comprehensive media content data, we can be certain that immigrant and native minorities are made invisible by the media except when the issue at stake is minority and migration policies. On the other hand, native and immigrant minorities are often mentioned very positively, albeit as groups that are outside the core categories and themes that describe 'us'.

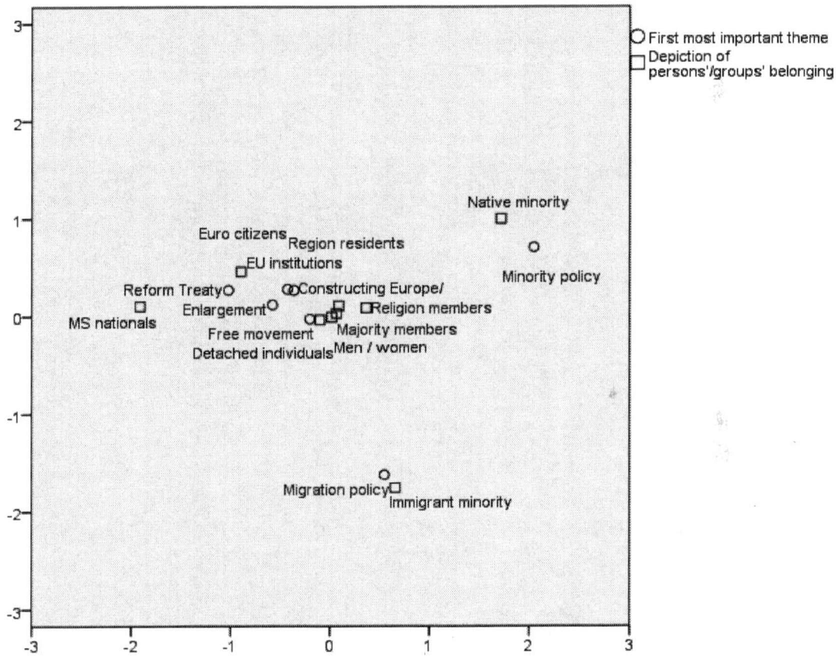

Figure 4.1 Media depictions of persons' belongings with reference to the core themes of news items

Figure 4.2 illustrates how media news shifts between different depictions of people in connection with different framings adopted by the respective news items. A majority of different framings and depictions of belongings are clustered in the middle of the figure, except the three that are placed at a clear distance from this middle group: (1) news pieces that use a Europeanist perspective tend to depict different groups as 'European citizens' no matter what their identity backgrounds; (2) news pieces that adopt a communitarian framing tend to depict people as members of native communities; and (3) news pieces that promote a nation-state framing tend to designate people's belongings as nationals of a country. This is an expected finding.

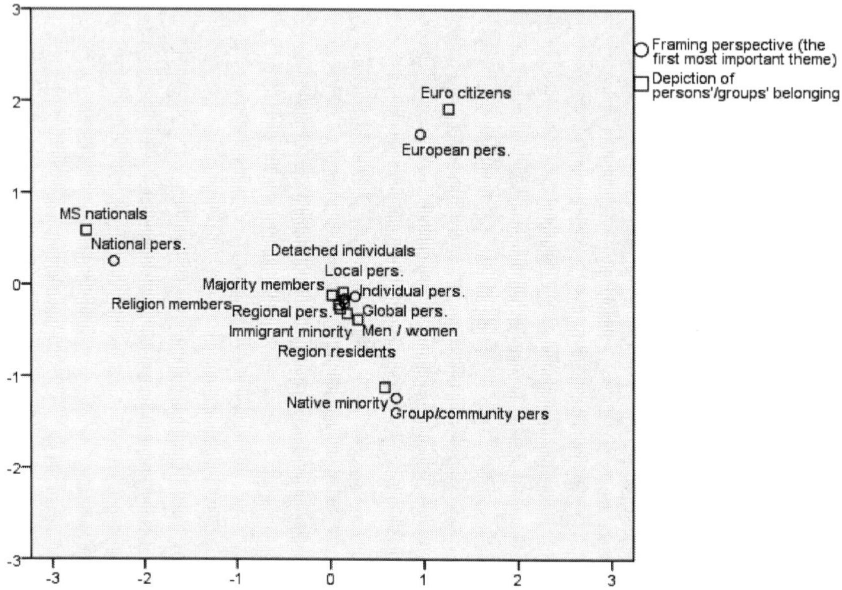

Figure 4.2 Media depictions of persons' belongings with reference to the core framings in news items

What is interesting here, however, is the inclusive middle group of framings that tend to bring together the belonging designations that remain outside the three dominant framings. The configuration in the middle resembles the highly diversity-oriented, all-inclusive 'Europeanizing discourses' of trans-European elites found in the previous section; however, in contrast, this configuration excludes and places the European, the national and the community belongings in separate contexts, that is, within the three dominating and contesting framings: Europeanist, nation-statist and communitarian.

The two correspondence analyses presented in Figures 4.1 and 4.2 imply that, whereas other belonging categories are frequently mentioned together in the news, there are two groups that are excluded from the core

EU-related themes: native minorities and immigrant minorities. Further, there is a body of news items that separates community, national and European belongings from the other belonging categories. This group of news is related to framings of social and territorial sizes that are either smaller (e.g. local society, regions, migrants, individuals) or much larger (e.g. religions, the globe, gender) than communities, nations and Europe.

Bringing the above-mentioned variables together and adding to them reporters' and journalists' political attitudes to the themes in question,[11] three media discourses are identified in Figure 4.3. Table 4.4 briefly describes the contents of the discourses. The first two discourses, nationalizing and Europeanizing, were also identified in the interviews with national and trans-European elites. The third discourse, which I label 'nativizing', is peculiar to media and public opinion,[12] and it did not emerge as a separate discourse in trans-European or national elites' minds. This is with a high probability, because we interviewed only elites leading public interest groups within national and transnational civil society.

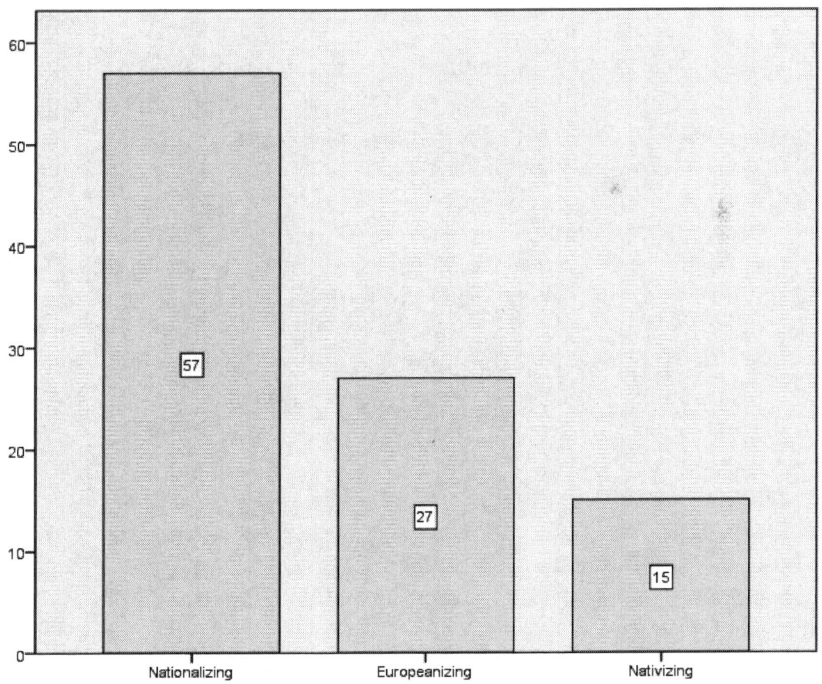

Figure 4.3 Media discourses of citizen identity (percentages rounded to the closest integer)

Table 4.4 Three media discourses on belonging

Discourse	Description
Nation-statist	News is framed with a national perspective. Individuals are viewed primarily as members of nations and secondarily as members of an immigrant minority.
Europeanist	News is framed with a Europeanist perspective. Persons are primarily viewed as European citizens and secondarily as members of their nations.
Nativist	News is framed with a native-community perspective. Persons are primarily viewed as natives or native minorities and secondarily as members of a nation.

3 CONCLUSION

The percentage of national elites with Europeanizing views is 21.8 (see Table 4.5), whereas the percentage of news items with Europeanizing discourses in national media is 27.6. However, whereas the nationalizing elite discourses also contain the nativizing approach to citizen identity, national newspapers and broadcasters separate it from the nationalizing discourse and deploy it as a distinct discourse. The sum of nationalizing and nativizing media discourses is 72.5 per cent, whereas nationalizing elite discourses is 78.2 per cent. It is also important to note that the proportion of nationalizing discourses among the trans-European elites is 47.1 per cent, whereas this figure is 57.4 per cent in the media. In brief, these figures witness in favour of the neo-functionalist and federalist prediction that the attempts of European elites to create a European citizen identity are reflected in the national public spheres. However, the national media seem to better reflect the preferences of the national elites than the trans-European elites. This is because the trans-European elites are more exposed to the values of a truly transnational institution, the European Commission, whereas the European Union's laws and policies are directly affected by the national elites through the Council of Ministers.

Table 4.5 Comparing national and European elites' orientation to citizenship with media framings

	Orientation to citizenship (in percentages)			Total
	Nationalizing	Europeanizing	Nativizing	
National elites (%)	78.2	21.8	n/a	100.0
Trans-European elites (%)	47.1	52.9	n/a	100.0
National media (%)	57.4	27.6	15.0	100.0

European elites' ambition to create a common European citizen identity is mirrored in national public spheres – both in the discourses of national elites and in the framings of national media. As devised by its founding fathers, the European Union seems to be following in the footsteps of its member states when building a European polity. What is peculiar is that, in order to bypass the member states and reach individuals more directly, European elites are establishing nodes of intermediary trans-European elites between the EU institutions and individual citizens of member states. As today's nation states did in their history with local elites, European elites are establishing alliances with key national elites to secure and accelerate the consolidation process. At this stage, nationalizing discourses are still dominant at the national level and significantly present at the trans-European level. However, the EU institutions' socializing attempts seem to be working when it comes to political parties, think tanks, civil society organizations, and media actors that participate in trans-European networks that facilitate direct communication with the European elites.

In this ongoing integration process, European elites are cautious about defining any group as the 'Other'. This is a strategy that was followed by the state- and nation-building elites at the very onset of these processes in Europe's political history. However, the hitherto deployed diversity policies give important clues about who is excluded from the policy field – namely, native minorities and migrants. The exclusionary implications of EU citizenship diversity policies that I briefly mentioned in section 1 above are not discernible in trans-European elite discourses, but highly visible in national media discourses. The once-included native minorities are defined outside the national domain in media framings, if not in elite discourses. On the other hand, although Europeanizing discourses include immigrant minorities in their common citizen identity, national media seem to be reproducing the nation state's excluding approach, which is very similar to what we observe in the EU's diversity policies, if not in its celebration rhetoric about diversity. Thus, currently, native minorities and immigrant minorities seem to be Europe's common others.

In light of these results, it is possible to assert that the Eurosphere, that is, the vertical, top-down communicative space of pro-European elites and citizens, has to some extent created its own projections within both national elite circles and national media.

NOTES

1. This chapter is derived in part from an article of mine (Sicakkan 2012) published in *Javnost – The Public* online on 10 November 2014, available at http://www.tandfonline.com/10.1080/13183222.2012.11009081. This concerns only the quantitative analyses in sections 4.1.1–4.1.3 of the article. Thanks to Routledge, Taylor & Francis Group for granting non-exclusive permission to re-use parts of my article.
2. All the data used in this chapter were collected within the framework of the EU-funded integrated project EUROSPHERE. The project activities lasted from February 2007 until the end of December 2012. EUROSPHERE mobilized approximately 150 researchers in 17 universities and research institutions in 16 European countries (including Turkey). The project was initiated and led by this author on behalf of the coordinating institution, the University of Bergen. EUROSPHERE publications are available at http://eurospheres.org.
3. One common characteristic of the European state- and nation-building attempts in the eighteenth and nineteenth centuries was complementarity between compositions of the populations in the territory that political elites aimed to consolidate, and their designs of citizen identity. Citizen identities constructed or promoted by elites were aimed at maximizing elites' own power and legitimacy, by establishing an identity link between the state and the broadest possible spectrum of ethnic and religious groups. These processes also entailed competition between neighbour states for getting more citizens under their rule. However, the colonial centres in Europe deliberately aimed to exclude the 'citizens' of their colonies from European territories. Almost all European states with high degrees of linguistic diversity developed citizenship laws based on territorial identity, that is, the *jus soli* principle (e.g. the UK, Spain, France and Belgium). This was because basing the common citizen identity on ethnic belonging would weaken the status of the consolidating elites. On the other hand, almost all European states with a high degree of linguistic homogeneity ended up with citizenship laws based on ethnic identity, with *jus sanguinis* as the only criterion of automatic citizenship acquisition (e.g. Germany, Greece and the Nordic countries). In countries with linguistically homogeneous but religiously diverse populations, ethnic identity, here understood as a common language, became even more important for creating a common citizen identity (e.g. Germany). Later, West Germany successfully used its ethnic citizenship ideal as a means for achieving the goal of reunification with the DDR. Exceptions to this pattern of *jus soli* and *jus sanguinis* models systematically derive from countries' colonial pasts. All European countries that were historically involved in colonization processes developed, without a single exception, strict versions of *jus soli* laws in order to exclude the citizens of their colonies and the descendants of their own citizens in mixed marriages from European territories. This includes also the linguistically homogeneous European countries like the Netherlands and Portugal (Sicakkan 2005).
4. Austria, Belgium, Bulgaria, the Czech Republic, Denmark, Estonia, Finland, France, Germany, Hungary, Italy, the Netherlands, Norway, Spain, the United Kingdom.
5. The data material used here covers individual-level data, obtained from in-depth interviews with persons who are in leading positions in the organizations (elite interviews). The

research design focuses specifically on those organizations and elites that have high visibility in public debates – representing the most visible mainstream and alternative discourses and networks. In each of the 15 European countries, I focus on three political parties (the party leading the government, the main opposition party and the most visible maverick party in each context), three non-governmental organizations (NGOs) or social movement organizations (SMOs) – (civil society organizations that are the most visible in their contexts and represent the mainstream or alternative discourses), three think tanks (a policy research organization, an academic think tank and an advocacy think tank in each context), three print media actors (two main-player newspapers and one smaller newspaper that exhibits anti-establishment views in each context) and two broadcast media actors (one public and one commercial TV channel that are main players in each context). In addition, eight trans-European umbrella organizations or networks are included: three European political party federations, three trans-European networks of NGOs or SMOs, and two trans-European networks of think tanks. Owing to concern for representing the actors that are the most visible in the public debates, the final sample includes a larger number of organizations: 242 organizations at member state level (56 political parties, 67 social movement organizations, 46 think tanks, 44 newspapers and 29 TV channels) and eight European umbrella organizations that are the trans-European counterparts of these. In terms of both discourse and networking, these exhibit varying degrees of affiliation with or dissociation from trans-Europeanizing political spaces. Some are contained in national arenas in terms of both discourse and networks; some operate with Europeanizing discourses in trans-European arenas.

6. At the first stage, three main players in print media and two (small) print media actors representing or voicing alternative views, ideologies, discourses and identities beyond the majority and mainstream features were nominated in each country. Concerning broadcast media, two public service news programmes and two commercial news programmes were nominated. That is, a total of nine media actors were nominated in each country. For each country, we finally chose five media actors – three print media and two broadcasters. The final selection was based on a concern for representing the largest possible variation of media types and their approaches to the EU polity. The nominations were based on information in media websites and secondary literature on media's framing of diversity.
7. The media content analysis aimed to analyse all news items in the selected newspapers. For both broadcast and print, we only coded from Monday to Friday. Our content analysis focuses on news stories that have an explicit or implicit 'clear European dimension' and at the same time refer to certain topics. Two main criteria were applied to identify stories with the aforementioned 'European dimension': stories covering EU institutions' affairs, or stories covering issues related to one or more other European states. The stories were analysed if they also addressed one or several of the following topics: (1) EU institutions and/or EU representatives; (2) Reform Treaty; (3) enlargement; (4) minorities or minority policies; (5) immigration or migration policy; (6) free movement or mobility; (7) gender and gender policy; and (8) constructing Europe and the EU: national sovereignty and/or European and national identity or identities.
8. The theme categories into which news items were coded are: (1) EU institutions; (2) Reform Treaty; (3) enlargement; (4) minorities or minority policies; (5) immigration or migration policy; (6) free movement or mobility; (7) gender and gender policy; and (8) constructing Europe and the EU. The average inter-coder reliability of the theme selection variable is 92.4 per cent.
9. The media's depictions of persons' or groups' belongings were coded as depicted: (1) as European citizens; (2) as nationals of a country; (3) as residents of a region; (4) as members of a majority group; (5) as members of an ethno-national minority; (6) as members of a gender group – men or women; and (7) as detached individuals. The average inter-coder reliability for this variable is 79.4 per cent.

10. News items were coded into the following framing perspectives: (1) individual perspective; (2) group or community perspective; (3) local perspective; (4) regional perspective; (5) member state or national perspective; (6) European perspective; and (7) global (justice) perspective.
11. The political preferences of journalists (authors of the news) were coded into the following categories: (1) only positive; (2) more positive than negative; (3) more negative than positive; and (4) only negative. This coding was applied to the eight themes mentioned in note 8.
12. See Klicperová-Baker and Košťál (2013) for the presence of nativizing attitudes to citizen identity in European countries.

REFERENCES

Agustin, L.R. and B. Siim (2013) Gender Diversities – Practising Intersectionality in the European Union, in Peter A. Kraus and Giuseppe Sciortino (eds), *Linking the European Union with the Citizens: Evaluation of EU Diversity Policies Aiming to Create an Inclusive European Public Sphere*, pp. 52–68, Brussels: Eurosphere Consortium.

Anderson, B. (1991) *Imagine Communities*, London: Verso.

Klicperová-Baker, M. and J. Košťál (2012) Ethno-national, Religious, Ideological and Sexual Diversity, *Javnost – The Public* 19(1): 85–102.

Klicperová-Baker, M. and J. Košťál (2013) Citizens, Party Sympathizers and Elites, in Hakan G. Sicakkan (ed.), *Linking the European Union with the Citizens: Evaluation of EU Policies Aiming to Create a Democratic European Public Sphere*, Eurosphere Final Comparative Study, Vol. 1, pp. 216–234, Brussels: Eurosphere Consortium.

Kraus, P.A. and R. Kazlauskaite (2013) Addressing Linguistic Diversity in the European Union: Strategies and Dilemmas, in P.A. Kraus and G. Sciortino (eds), *Linking the European Union with the Citizens: Evaluation of EU Diversity Policies Aiming to Create an Inclusive European Public Sphere*, pp. 6–27, Brussels: Eurosphere Consortium.

Kutay, A. (2012) Europeanization through Civil Society through Sponsored European Publics, *Javnost – The Public* 19(1): 19–33.

Lozano, A.A., N. García-González, L. Sebastiani, A. Álvarez Veinguer and S.G. Araujo (2013) The EU Framework for the Integration of Immigrants: The 'European Integration Forum' and the Technologies of Social Government, in P.A. Kraus and G. Sciortino (eds), *Linking the European Union with the Citizens: Evaluation of EU Diversity Policies Aiming to Create an Inclusive European Public Sphere*, pp. 28–51, Brussels: Eurosphere Consortium.

Perez, M. (2013) Can European Networks Contribute to the Reproduction of Common Views of the European Public Sphere among National Think Tanks?, in H.G. Sicakkan (ed.), *Linking the European Union with the Citizens: Evaluation of EU Policies Aiming to Create a Democratic European Public Sphere*, pp. 111–128, Brussels: Eurosphere Consortium.

Rokkan, S. (1970) Nation Building, Cleavage Formation and the Structuring of Mass Politics, in S. Rokkan (ed.), *Citizens, Elections, Parties*, Oslo: Universitetsforlaget.

Rokkan, S. (1975) Dimensions of State Formation and Nation-building: A Possible Paradigm for Research on Variations within Europe, in C. Tilly (ed.), *The Formation of National States in Western Europe*, pp. 562–600, Princeton, NJ: Princeton University Press.

Rokkan, S. and D.W. Urwin (1983) *Economy, Territory, Identity: Politics of West European Peripheries*, London: Sage.

Sata, R. (2012) Political Parties and the Politics of Diversity in the European Public Sphere, *Javnost – The Public* 19(1): 51–66.

Sicakkan, H.G. (2005) State Formation, Nation Building, and Citizenship in Western Europe, in H.G. Sicakkan and Y.G. Lithman (eds), *Changing the Basis of Citizenship in the Modern State*, Lewiston, NY: Edwin Mellen Press.

Sicakkan, H.G. (2012) Trans-Europeanising Public Spaces in Europe, *Javnost – The Public* 19(1): 5–26.

Sicakkan, H.G. (2013) The Contested European Public Sphere, in H.G. Sicakkan (ed.), *Linking the European Union with the Citizens: Evaluation of EU Policies Aiming to Create a Democratic European Public Sphere*, pp. 252–263, Brussels: Eurosphere Consortium.

Weber, M. (1981 [1923]) *General Economic History*, New York: Cosimo Classics.

Zanon, F. and G. Sciortino (2013) The Newest Diversity Is the Oldest: Religious Pluralism and the EU, in P.A. Kraus and G. Sciortino (eds), *Linking the European Union with the Citizens: Evaluation of EU Diversity Policies Aiming to Create an Inclusive European Public Sphere*, pp. 69–90, Brussels: Eurosphere Consortium.

5. Diversity in the virtual sphere: social media as a platform for transnational encounters*

Deniz Neriman Duru and Hans-Jörg Trenz

Traditional mass media have been institutionalized as complexity reducing mechanisms within the institutional and constitutional framework of national democracies. Mass communication, such as television, was meant to harmonize political culture and to consolidate national identity (Price 1995). New media technologies, in turn, provide new ways to communicate diversity and mediate complexity across spaces (Hampton et al. 2011). While traditional mass media in many ways functioned as assimilation media turning individuals into assimilated members of the public (or citizens), the new media can be said to function as difference media, emphasizing individual self-representation, providing new fluid ways of identification, and constituting new active publics who produce, resist and not just receive information that is provided for them through the one-to-many channels of mass communication. The most distinct manifestation of this shift from the 'means of mass communication' to the 'means of diversity communication' occurs through social networking media.

The rise of the Internet made it possible for people who move to another country to interact with their host societies while also remaining attached to their countries of origin. As a result, a new sense of place, what Castells calls 'space of flow' (Castells 2000), characterized by a constant move, change and exchange of people, cultural goods and information, has emerged. If publics are 'migrating from the bounded, geographical territorialities of the past to the diffuse and immaterial networks of communication and media flows' (Diamandaki 2003: 4), so do migrants themselves increasingly rely on new media technologies to bridge places and to maintain relationships across borders. Social networking media however do not only enable cross-cultural communication across territories; they also support transnational lifestyles and encounters within existing places. This capacity of social networking media to represent cultural spaces of diversity adds a new dimension to our perception of locality, belonging and citizenship. Many social media interactions are not just virtual and mediated but directly experienced and more accurately described as real encounters, recombining the offline and online spaces of community in an innovative way. Digital media practices are employed 'to create mobile and flexible places that span on and offline' (Polson 2015: 630). Complex diversity is in this sense related to a form of cultural pluralism that is not just represented by the media (for instance, the traditional quota system that was used to 'represent' cultural pluralism in the national media sphere), but is as much virtual as real, participatory, activated and experienced.

This chapter discusses the socialization and cultural self-representation of mobile foreign citizens (so-called expats) in Denmark through social networking sites. The mobility experiences of these mobile citizens are, in one way or another, facilitated by the differentiated set of rights granted to them by the Europe of citizenship and free movement. One question related to this is whether these mobility experiences within the Europe of free movement are turning the EU mobiles into a homogeneous group that would populate a distinct European public sphere of mobile elites or whether individuals from different (elite and less privileged) backgrounds engage in shared practices of accommodation to the local sphere.

As will be argued, the social networking media are not only used by established ethnic groups and diaspora communities to affirm their identity and maintain group relationships. The media use of the 'expats' groups rather shifts the frontiers of identities between migrants and locals, and catalyses a new spirit of hybridity and creative 'playing with diversity'. Our informants thus behave differently from 'expatriate' communities which have been described in other settings as a quite homogeneous group of foreigners living abroad for a period of time because of high-skilled and prestigious jobs, but not engaging with the locals (e.g. Europeans living in South-east Asia or in Latin America) (Hannerz 1990). Our group of expats are clearly more inclusive in their circle of friends and networks, by building and maintaining ties with the locals (Danes) and with their own co-nationals, as well as with other foreigners. This process of virtually escaping the ethnic or local spaces of identity and replacing them with a transcendent global (or 'virtual') experience is however still realized within a particular local setting of Copenhagen. Complex or virtual identities of these groups of mobile citizens actually depend in many ways on specifically local ways of managing communication (Panteli and Chiasson 2008: 3). Our analysis will therefore explore the new creative ways through which the virtuality of the online community of mobile citizens is linked back to locality and everyday life experiences.

1 EXPAT COMMUNITIES' MEDIA USE: FROM 'NO SENSE OF PLACE' TO 'NEW SENSE OF PLACE'

The existing literature on migrants' media needs and use has mainly focused on so-called diaspora communities, which make use of new media technologies in an instrumental way to maintain family ties and community relationships by bridging physical spaces across borders and by strengthening migrant community ties in the country of residence (Dekker and Engbersen 2014; Madianou and Miller 2011). With regard to the media experiences of so-called expats, the new media communication tools do much more than simply bridging or mediating physical spaces. They are used primarily for the exchanges of content and meaning across cultures but within a particular demarcated space (i.e. Copenhagen in Denmark). In addition, they do not only 'mediate' content to users from different cultural backgrounds; they are also occupied in innovative ways by the users to 'represent' culture and to communicate their own transnational experiences. The use of social media networking sites thus goes beyond the facilitation of family and community relations. Against this focus in the literature on diaspora media, we wish to highlight here the innovative and complex use of these sites by the transnational communities in Denmark who communicate and network with the primary purpose of 'conquering' the locality and contributing to its dynamic transformation.

Hence, we also explore how social media is used in place-making through which attachments to place and cultural and political activity within place are confined (Glick-Schiller et al. 2011). Globalization, with the growing speed in virtual and physical communications, has led to structural developments that favour the emergence of transnational cosmopolitan communities. Transnational communities are characterized by a transformation in the sense of space, not simply as a binary experience between migrants' societies of origin and settlement, but as multi-stranded social relations that enable 'mobiles' to feel 'at home' in a globalizing environment. Instead of migration as a unique and dramatic experience, mobility keeps transnational communities in flux. We stress the cosmopolitan character of the transnationals in the ways in which they bridge multiple localities (Appiah 2006; Werbner 2008). Cosmopolitanism is meant here as a mind-set of belonging to a transnational community who self-define as 'expats', are young, educated and polyglot, have transferable skills in finding a new job, or work hard to build the necessary skills (e.g. through getting a master's degree, learning Danish, volunteering or working) and hence strive to take profit from the privileges of mobility as granted by the Europe of free movement and rights. We argue that there is a dynamic relationship between processes of de-territorialization and re-territorialization through which social relations are restructured and embedded in a new socialization environment. New communication technologies become an important tool that enables the mobiles to become engaged in practices of place-bridging and place-making, giving way to new conceptions of territory and identity. These hybrid scenarios with less rigid social structures are the perfect terrain for mobile individuals to negotiate alternative ways of belonging and practise citizenship in relation to the local, the national, Europe and the global.

Research on sociality and communicative practices on these social networking sites therefore needs to take into account an increasingly complex relationship between space, community and the needs of the individual users. New media technologies have given migrants access to new opportunities for cultural expression, socialization and interaction, linking host society and different migrant communities in a more dynamic way. The Internet is a virtual space as much as it is turned by the migrants into a place of new encounters (Papacharissi 2002). The Internet fosters what Castells called *socialized communication* (Castells 2007: 240), contributing to the elaboration and diffusion of collective meaning among people who have different cultural backgrounds. This new hybrid media landscape is often seen as a vehicle that foments diversity, adding a new sense of de-territorialization to the exchange of information and encounter among individuals and transcending the importance of place in practising citizenship and claiming people's rights (Fürsich 2010).

The aspects of virtual community building through plural cultural exchanges are at the same time related to life experiences and daily face-to-face encounters among people who claim to belong to the local place. Transnational migrants' media use becomes in this sense a central element of life orientations and experiences of this group of people, not as members of a particular community or as movers between two places, but as creators of culture and community (Baumann 1996) who re-arrange social space. The groups of expats, who engage through social network sites such as Facebook, become thus involved in what is emphatically described as community building. 'Community' is defined through a reference to place (e.g. expats living in Copenhagen) and some degree of interconnectedness of these local expats within that place and their shared relationships to other communities (the Danes) or particular institutions (such as Danish public authorities, sports and cultural associations or commerce). Through their daily online activities, these individuals are involved in processes of self-management that are however closely related to group management in relation to other groups whom they encounter in the online space. The purpose of online network communication is not just closure but also seeing and being seen within the local space. This corresponds, in particular, to the needs of migrants who arrive in new localities and wish to explore social and cultural life by becoming visible themselves in these new localities and contributing to their dynamic development.

This kind of confined interaction in local-cosmopolitan places well suits the lifestyle of the highly mobile group of foreigners who reside outside their country of origin without plans to settle permanently. At the same time, these practices of local-cosmopolitan place-making can also alienate foreigners from native populations with less cosmopolitan attitudes and lifestyles. Especially for EU citizens, freedom of movement is a great facilitator for a new mobile lifestyle and may lead to the formation of a transnational elite community who do not feel obliged to assimilate in the host society, as they are granted rights independently and might not plan to settle there permanently. Even though the non-EU citizens do not have the same rights as facilitators, they build on their social and cultural capital and previous transnational experiences to navigate in their new place. They are therefore not neatly distinguished from the more privileged group of EU mobiles but are found to be in a similar socio-structural position and to develop similar cultural attitudes. The local place is transformed here into 'transition spaces', where the needs and efforts of the expats for integration in their guest societies are diminished (Polson 2015). In such a scenario, assimilationist policies, as they are still underlying the official state approach to immigration in Denmark (Hedetoft 2010), have a difficult time in reaching foreigners who feel safe and comfortable in these spaces with only restricted needs to interact with Danish mainstream society.

In the following, we will first reconstruct the mission and design of these expat sites, which are built to meet the needs and communication demands of a particular community of mobile citizens. In a second step, we will approach the community of expats and describe different strategies that are developed to build community relationships and conquer local space. Finally, we will locate this expat community between the local, the national, the European and the global. The question to be addressed is whether the 'expat bubble' is primarily to be interpreted as a 'cosmopolitan capsule' of a privileged group of people with only limited contacts to the local population, or whether the expats can legitimately claim to 'belong' to the locality, which is transformed and enriched by their experiences.

2 METHODS

Netnography is a method specifically designed to study cultures and communities online. It is participant-observational research based in online fieldwork that uses 'computer-mediated communications as a source of data to arrive at an ethnographic understanding and representation of a cultural or communal phenomenon' (Kozinets 2009: 60). This method has a uniquely adapted set of practices and procedures that set it apart from face-to-face ethnography. We combined netnography (participation in digital communication, responding, sharing Facebook comments, content analysis, distribution of an online survey on Facebook groups) with ethnography (participant observation in events organized by expat websites and Facebook groups and Danish language classes, complemented by casual chats; we conducted face-to-face semi-structured interviews with a sample of respondents who filled in the online survey and also interviewed the organizers of the expat events). We collected data both from the service providers of websites and their administrator as well as from the users of these websites and Facebook groups. Services and information from the providers were collected through mission statements, design of the websites and interviews. The online interactions of expats were collected and analysed via a content analysis of the social media sites over a period of eight weeks in September and October 2014, when traffic on these sites was at a peak. Our systematic content analysis was based on the close readings of entries produced by either providers or users and interactivity linked to these entries. We distributed an online survey over Facebook groups in Denmark and received 1034 completed questionnaires and conducted a further 70 in-depth interviews in the period from August 2014 to February 2015. We transcribed the interviews and used NVivo software to do an open-coding of the qualitative interviews. The type of netnography conducted thus encompasses a guided observation of the providers, the profile of the sites, and the groups' online activities, interactivity and communications through shared content.

3 THE PROVIDERS: MISSION AND DESIGN OF THE EXPAT SOCIAL MEDIA PLATFORMS

The expat Facebook groups under investigation can best be characterized as 'digital emplacement technologies' (Polson 2015: 643). Emplacement of the mobiles occurs through websites, which are specifically designed as a gateway to the locality in which they reside. As such, the websites fulfil an informative and socializing function. They are meant to provide practical guidance but also to interconnect the community of expats and thus help to organize the social life of the migrant. The website further assumes the ethos of the mobile migrant. It expresses solidarity with the foreigner but also provides a cultural representation of the particular lifestyle developed within the expat community.[1] There is thus a value of mobility that is communicated in a specific location and to a specific community. The name of the location (Denmark or Copenhagen) is in fact part of the branding of the Facebook group, making it of immediate relevance to individuals who have whatever relationship to that location (independently of the permanence of their residence).

The mission of the 'providers' – be they public authorities (such as Expat in Denmark) or private (such as Expats Living in Copenhagen) – is best summarized in the motto 'Promoting diversity – experiencing the local'. Such a mission statement is grounded in a cosmopolitan mind-set that is meant to guide practical action. It is similar to the slogan used by the globalization movement: 'Think globally – act locally'. In formulating this cosmopolitan ideology, the providers of the social media platforms are further inspired by the global communication facilities and the possibilities to translate them into new forms of socialization (which, last but not least, can be also turned into profit).

Part of the mission statement of all social media platforms supports the idea of transforming local space, turning Denmark or Copenhagen into a welcoming place for internationals, contributing to the integration of foreigners, promoting diversity and through the contribution of mobiles making Denmark, and especially Copenhagen, a more attractive and fun place for everybody. As the mission statement of 2GOCopenhagen reads:

> With a stylish layout, navigate effortlessly through the website and discover the places that make this the vibrant European capital that it is. Whether you are a Copenhagener or right off the plane, from cocktail bars to nightclubs, discover the hot spots and take your friend out on a night to remember. If you are in town for a frivolous shopping spree, plan your day and hit the famous designer boutiques. Take a break and enjoy a warming coffee by Nyhavn and

> discover the Danish saying of having a 'hyggeligt' [cosy, nice and convivial] time. (https://www.facebook.com/2gocopenhagen/info)

The three social media platforms selected for this survey provide a similar functionality for their users. The timeline is used for posts, either by the providers or by single users, and users are given the opportunity to interact with the proposed content, through liking, sharing or commenting. All the three Facebook groups are further meant to be non-commercial, self-organized and open. They differ however in terms of their status as a group. The Expats Living in Copenhagen group is administered by a member of the expat community, who accepts new members to the group, checks content that is posted by the users, and bans commercial ads and other 'improper' content. 2GOCopenhagen and Expat in Denmark instead rely on content that is produced for their website. Their social media presence is thus linked to start-up initiatives of expats (in the case of 2GOCopenhagen) or to the Confederation of Danish Industries, which administers a website for expats from which content is fed into social media (in the case of Expat in Denmark).

2GOCopenhagen is mainly run by internationals. It is not a membership group and can be followed by anyone on Facebook (in October 2014 it had 1318 followers). The social media platform is designed to facilitate integration and enhance the Copenhagen experience for international students, expats, tourists and locals alike. The major values emphasized in the mission statement are integration, diversity, vibrancy, frivolity, and making Copenhagen a fun and welcoming place for everybody.

Expats Living in Copenhagen goes back to a private user initiative and is an autonomous user-run group on Facebook that does not maintain other organizational ties or rely on any form of funding or business model. The mission statement of Expats Living in Copenhagen (9700 members in October 2014)[2] is stated simply:

> For all internationals living in Copenhagen, Denmark. To help each other whether that be, advice how to search for jobs, information about upcoming events, where to find the best deals, tax help, bank help, help with WHERE to search for apartments, anything where we can help each other as an international community.[3]

Expats Living in Copenhagen was set up as a self-aid group for internationals, and the content that is shared on its site is only accessible for members. The group administrator has the exclusive right to accept members and to control content. Apart from the usual Facebook rules that apply with regard to the sharing of content, the group states that commercial content will not be tolerated.

Expat in Denmark is financed by the Danish Ministry of Business and Growth and the Danish Agency for Labour Retention and International Recruitment and hosted and administered by the Confederation of Danish Industry in cooperation with a range of local and international partners that volunteer to provide various knowledge, services or facilities. Its Facebook profile is open (i.e. not a membership group), and its contents are thus accessible to all web users, who through the liking function can follow the thread on their timeline. In October 2014, the platform had 9041 Facebook followers. Not being so exclusively focused on the area of Copenhagen, the group aspires to extend its mission values nationwide, and states that the ultimate goal is to make Denmark a more attractive place to work, to live and to stay by setting up and maintaining national, regional and local expat networks. The website encourages companies and governmental agencies to be part of these networks, trying to reach out especially to skilled expats.

From this information, we can extract that 2GOCopenhagen's mission puts more emphasis on cultural diversity and integration in the city. The aim is to ease the cultural clash of foreigners by welcoming them into Copenhagen, suppressing the language barriers and showing them the possibilities the city has to offer. In their eyes, participation in city life will trigger further inclusion and contribute to foster diversity. Expats Living in Copenhagen instead is mainly self-organized and spontaneously oriented towards the instrumental needs of expats to exchange goods and information, not necessarily reaching beyond the borders of the community. Expat in Denmark is, in turn, initiated by the public authorities for a better integration of highly skilled migrants in the labour market, focusing on practical needs and putting emphasis on the importance of becoming familiar with Danish rules and systems. It also makes a call to Danish companies to follow a best-practice procedure in the area of integration by developing programmes and engaging further in the promotion of diversity, which is meant to enrich the Danish economy and society.

The language used by all three social media profiles is exclusively English, which sends an important message: Denmark is seen as bilingual or multilingual, and the use of English is seen as more inclusive than the use of the official native language. The predominant use of English as the community language can however turn into a double-edged sword for foreigners. While the dominant use of English as the expats' language helps them to access information and offers opportunities for sociability, it also slows down their attempt to access Danish culture. At the time of writing this chapter, 2GOCopenhagen was thinking of having a Danish version of the website in order to bring the native population closer and include them in the process of integration. At expat events, the organizers ask and joke, 'How many Danes sneaked in today? Put your hands up', and generally one-third of the participants are Danes. One of the event organizers of Expat in Denmark told us in the interview: 'And Danes ... I know that Danes find it funny as well, the things we put up in social media.'

Providers of expat sites in Denmark are thus aware of social media dynamics and creativity. Their initiatives are meant to be self-organized and democratic, public service oriented and non-profit based. They do not wish to patronize the social media sites or groups they create or decide about migrants' lives but rather allow the expats to be protagonists and decide about content and debates. The social media groups and sites are therefore built as autonomous spaces, which turn them into an experimental field for the socialization of the expat community. By shifting in the following from a provider to a user perspective, these dynamics of expat community building in relation to the Danish host society can be further elaborated.

4 THE USERS: THE EXPAT COMMUNITY FINDING A PLACE BETWEEN THE GLOBAL AND THE LOCAL

For reasons of privacy, no systematic demographic user survey could be run as part of this netnographic study. The limited information on users we received from the providers confirms the picture of a group of internationals, with Europeans being clearly overrepresented.[4] According to the same provider, most users are in their early professional years (24–40). The number of likes, followers and members is slowly growing on all three sites.

The term *expats* (an abbreviation of *expatriate*) is chosen by the providers but also by the users themselves to signify a group of persons with high social and cultural capital, who are distinct from the local but also from the traditional migrant, in Polson's term (2015: 642) 'the lone professional migrant'. Usually, expats are part of a highly skilled group of migrants, who move to another country for professional purposes without an explicit desire to settle permanently. The expats are not simply migrants, who come to stay and to integrate, but people who continue to be internationals, who have not necessarily given up mobility, and who develop different, non-assimilationist styles to relate to their host society.

From our survey data with expats, we know that a quarter of our respondents work in privileged and often high-income jobs in the private and public sectors. Many of them were recruited by international firms, which means that Denmark is not their country of choice but only a step on the ladder of their professional career. As a matter of fact, one out of four of our respondents resided in a country other than their home country before they moved to Denmark.[5] They typically move from other cosmopolitan places like London, Berlin or Paris where they have temporarily stayed or studied. This group can be considered elitist. Many of them represent demographically the young, high-skilled professionals who move alone and not with families. They serve the needs of a flexible labour market in Western societies and, especially in the big cities, of global enterprises, which recruit young professionals with 'international experience' and a readiness to move and live abroad.[6] The young, single and temporary migrants see themselves as migrants of choice, who have often been called in, and have not simply asked for admittance (Favell 2008). Many of them also enjoy a high level of protection of rights, often through EU citizenship; they are not precarious but mainly distinguished by multilingual skills, cross-cultural competences and high education. Among our respondents, 80.2 per cent had at least a BA degree. They live a life of permanent mobility and seek to arrange their temporary settlement in Denmark. They further continue to have a highly mobile lifestyle in Denmark, often working for global companies, living in a transnational partnership and being frequent travellers, for work or for tourism. As a consequence of this privileged lifestyle they hardly see themselves as being discriminated-against foreigners but rather self-consciously insist on their rights and privileges.

Other groups of foreigners in our sample can be categorized as 'elites in aspiration'. They typically work in less privileged positions, have lower educational achievements or are still striving to get an education. Especially among the group of recently emigrated Eastern and Southern Europeans we find many inexperienced young people, who migrated to Denmark as they had no prospect back in their home countries. In Duru and Trenz (forthcoming), we in fact explicitly argued that our sample is not a typical one of high-skilled rich people working for JP Morgan, but ordinary citizens. These migrants are often in a waiting position. They aspire to get a better education or to build a professional career. They develop an 'expat habitus' of belonging to a transnational elite, even though their economic position does not (yet) reflect this.

The term *expats* that applies here to an elitist or aspiring-to-be-elite group of transnationals not only allows a positive self-identification but also creates a new public image of the migrant that is more positively embraced by the members of the host society. In a country with an increasingly open and flexible labour market and a tight correlation between offer and demand, expats are portrayed as the desired kind of immigrant that Denmark needs and tries to attract (and eventually keep): educated and highly skilled individuals for those areas of industry open to international workers.

The content that is shared on all these sites reflects in broad terms the mission and values of their providers. Most posts share visual material (pictures and videos) in combination with text. User engagement with content can be expressed through likes, shares and comments. The strength of 2GOCopenhagen's content relies on the promotion of all sorts of events and articles that aim to describe the city from the perspective of the volunteers – mainly international students – who work there. Expats Living in Copenhagen opens a kind of local online market square for exchanging goods, services and practical information. The providers' main occupation is to keep this space free of commercial activities and spam. Expat in Denmark is proud to help users to 'benefit from its influence, a wealth of expertise, business services and events'. Not only does this platform put a lot of emphasis on the cultural content – a major strength in its social media platform – but its website also offers links to governmental pages related to specific administrative information needed by foreigners, something that 2GOCopenhagen still lacks.

All three websites contribute to a form of 'branding' of cultural diversity in Copenhagen and Denmark. Diversity is 'more fun', but also a particular mobile and transnational lifestyle is promoted as an attractive alternative to local, sedentary life: the expats are presented as those who show in an exemplary way how to enjoy what a city like Copenhagen has to offer but also as those who can contribute best to local culture and fun.

The website is further used as a helpful tool for what Urry (1995) has called the 'consumption of places'. Popular pictures that are shared and liked by the users of these websites depict the canals or picturesque streets in Copenhagen, advertising cultural events or leisure activities taking place in the neighbourhood. The users are also consumers in many ways with regard to the services that are put at their disposal through the websites and activities they promote themselves. They are, for instance, part of the shared economy through which services and content are shared in the city of Copenhagen (such as apartments, plumbers and hairdressers). The expats take on an important function in this sharing economy, which is also a way to connect to locals. For instance, the housing market is increasingly based on such sharing-economy services, as in the temporary renting out to tourists and short- or long-term visitors. In similar terms the cultural scene, different leisure institutions or bars and restaurants rely on sharing services through which consumption can be boosted. The websites thus take part in the restructuring of the city as a centre for consumption (Urry 1995). They provide the 'context within which goods and services are compared, evaluated, purchased and used' (Urry 1995: 1).

It is also significant what type of content these routines of sharing do not encompass. The range of shared topics is often restricted to consensual topics that are meant to inform and entertain, but not to express strong opinions or to provoke. This is also reflected in the tone of debate and comment, which is mainly factual, affirmative and responsive, but rarely critical and never insulting. Most of the user posts and comments conform to the mission of the providers, who do not wish to run the website for commercial purposes or for political mobilization. The shared social media content largely excludes politics and religion. Albeit none of the social media sites analysed would explicitly ban political or religious content, it seems that many expats would think it is inappropriate to engage in such debates with other users. This consensual attitude of expat community building is also expressed in the comment threads, which are mainly affirmative, supporting the content of the posts or providing constructive responses but not entering into longer and controversial debates.

Communication on the website is not about extraordinary events; it is also not about international politics; topics like the financial crisis, civic unrest in other countries, the Ukrainian conflict, and news concerning world politics are strikingly absent on the website. Instead, communication evolves around the routines of everyday life: health issues in Copenhagen, challenges with the Danish language, food, restaurants and pubs, and the search for various services. In short, communication is about living locally and managing private life in the local area. It is through these routine communications that online interfaces are used to manage offline interactions in a more efficient way. In other words, social networking media contribute to the formation of the cultural public sphere, where cultural diversity is embraced in the virtual space and consumed in people's daily lives. In line with Jensen (2010: 112), we find that such a cultural public sphere of diversity is often detached from political debates and forms of political activism. These attempts to keep the cultural and political spheres apart are also reflected in the content that is shared on expat social media sites (Table 5.1). Political controversies are seen as potentially harmful to the social cohesion of internationals, and political or ideological statements on the expat websites are often considered inappropriate or, in some instances (such as critiques of Danish or foreign governments), even forbidden.

Table 5.1 Content analysis of social media sites

	2GOCopenhagen	Expat in Denmark	Expats Living in Copenhagen
Shared content			
Culture/events	20	8	9
Work/profession	0	0	2
Language/education	0	0	2
Housing	0	0	6
Leisure	3	1	0
Entertainment	8	11	4
Politics (local, national, international)	0	0	0
Community reference			
Shared cultural activity	8	20	6
Information relevant to community	22	12	13
Promotion of goods/ products	1	0	1
Social events	1	2	0

The relationship of this group of expats to Danish culture is complex. Denmark is generally embraced as a good country to live in, and many values and lifestyles are seen as congruent. At the same time, any assimilationist demand is rejected as inappropriate. The expat groups build identity through distinction. Typical Danishness is often portrayed as something particular, odd or distant, or is even ridiculed. It is commonly accepted both that the Danish language and the cultural particularities are hard to penetrate, but also that it is unnecessary to understand them. Danishness is associated with a kind of tribal attribute, while at the same time the achievements of Danish 'high culture' like film or architecture are recognized and, in fact, regularly consumed by the expats.

In the following, we will take up the suggestion by Polson (2015) to analyse social networking media as place-making processes that take place through hybrid forms of online and offline communication about locality from a mobile person's perspective and the different forms of real encounters linked to it. The social media sites function in this sense as 'mobile emplacement platforms' (Polson 2015: 632) that enable communication about local Denmark (or Copenhagen) from a global perspective. There is, as we shall argue, no reason to assume that the sense of place created through these websites is less real for the users or creates less strong ties and feelings of belonging.

5 'COSMOPOLITAN CAPSULE' OR NEW 'GLOBAL LOCALITY'?

In the literature on online community building, a process of segregation is often emphasized (Papacharissi 2010). Social networking media platforms are often used by like-minded people who share similar experiences or hold similar opinions. From this perspective, the expat websites would reflect a deficit of social integration. Expat sites could be a substitute for other forms of inclusion that are closed to migrants or they could reflect the lack of motivation and initiative of the expats to become engaged with Danish majoritarian society. Such an online seclusion could be explained, for instance, by the difficulties for migrants of participating in Danish social media sites (language barriers), the difficulties of becoming politically engaged (citizenship barriers) or the effects of cultural exclusion (e.g. exclusionary national identity representations) on Danish social media sites. New communication technologies would thus provide substitute or alternative avenues for the representation and civic engagement of migrants (Christensen 2011: 225).

In our case, the expats' social media engagement clearly builds on shared transnational experiences. Expats are distinguished from established groups by having particular skills and mentalities, and these differences in needs and lifestyles are communicated and further developed through social media. Social media networks are primarily meant as a means of socialization but also of distinguishing the expat from the common migrant and from the natives. Expat social media platforms are however not simply a substitute for the lack of integration into Danish host society. Social media are rather used in an instrumental and supplementary way to enhance knowledge about the Danish host society and to offer opportunities for encounters with Danish culture and society. This serves the needs of expats at different stages of mobility: migrants use these sites to collect information about Denmark before departure, collect practical information after arrival, and take advantage of a market for the exchange of goods (like bicycles) or for housing. Expat sites also have an important socializing function for the expat community that reaches beyond the usual contacts with co-nationals. They encourage encounters with internationals and with like-minded Danish people and thus contribute to the building of an open society. The expats develop particular skills as semi-professional cross-cultural communicators, many of them building on their various experiences of living in different places within and outside Europe. From this perspective, social media become a facilitator of integration.

Social media contribute to the building of an international community that understands itself as an integral part of local society, not as secluded from it. Expat sites provide additional, supplementary and not substitute functions; they are multinational and not closed to the communication of particular migrant communities. The intention of the providers is to open them, and not to segregate the migrant groups, but for the users, too, open-mindedness becomes a prerequisite for social media activism. The type of community that is represented by the expat sites is therefore not protective but rather meant as an open cultural space, and one that Danish participants are also invited to join. As such the sites offer a combination of trans-border practices with new forms of territorial anchorage.

The social media expat sites thus help expats to turn a mobile lifestyle into ordinary daily routines and give them back a sense of place and attachment to it (Polson 2015). Online social media engagement can in this sense be analysed as a form of place-making. The website reflects a movement away from disengagement from place to new and creative forms of engagement. As observed also by Polson in her study on expat social networking in Paris, it is precisely the state of frequent travelling that creates 'a pressing need to cultivate connections to the places, in which they temporarily reside' (Polson 2015: 631). De-territorialized lifestyles create a need for forms of communication that create a new sense of place.

These place-making activities explain the intersection of cosmopolitan and capsular social forces found on the social media sites. The expats are in search of a place of encapsulation but at the same time show the ambition to overcome the capsule through networking locally and transnationally. On the one hand, the expats continue to be highly mobile and to live as frequent travellers, but on the other hand they wish to create encounters in the local to exchange their transnational experiences and to open new opportunities for mobility and transnationalism. Typical topics that are exchanged on the websites are travel, food consumption, eating out, cultural events and creativity under conditions of transnationalism. This is linked with very practical needs like housing in Denmark, jobs or dealing with local authorities. On the website, ordinary daily routines and basic information blend with more or less extraordinary experiences, notably transnational cultural encounters and events. Popular stories that are exchanged on the website are the experiences and adventures of expats who have attempted to interact with the local, and the encouraging, frustrating, often ironized and simply funny stories that result from such encounters.

As reported also in our interviews, the group of expats combine two characteristics that are essential for their social networking activities: they are career-minded and adventure seeking (Polson 2015: 630). They develop a lifestyle of what Favell (2008) termed 'Eurostars': free-moving urban professionals, who at the same time attribute high value to city quality of life and lifestyle. This openness to new professional and 'adventurous' experiences explains that the 'cosmopolitan capsule' is rather an inaccurate description of their life. We find many examples of their engagement with rather than disengagement from the local place. In the semi-structured interviews many of our informants depict Danes as more disengaged than the foreigners, leading a more isolated life with their Danish friends from high school, university or work than the expats. In that sense, the expats refer back to the original binary between 'the global' and 'the local' (Hannerz 2004), describing themselves as superior to the 'locals' (in this case Danes), who 'keep their traditions going, watch their boundaries, and largely remain in place' (Hannerz 2004: 69). The expats thus distinguish themselves as a kind of 'urban tribe' (Favell 2008: 122–124), but not by following the cliché of living in the ghetto (e.g. the Sicilians, meeting in the *gelateria*, where they can speak their local dialects and do not need to speak native languages or intermingle with other natives). When we conducted ethnography, participating in events organized by Expat in Denmark, Facebook groups, InterNations and Meetup, we observed that the expats socialize in a network of many local and international friends and with the support of these networks start to occupy the most attractive, prestigious and mixed local places (like Copenhagen hipster-Bohemian neighbourhoods or bars). A Meetup group that also has a Facebook page is called 'Italian Culture and Conversation for Everyone in Copenhagen'. Their title as well as the participants, who meet in a café in the very centre of Copenhagen once a month, include not only Italians but also spouses and partners of Italians, non-Italians who lived in Italy and wanted to practise their rusty Italian, and people who were interested in Italian culture and language and willing to learn the language. Besides the ones who speak Italian, the rest speak English or any other language they happen to have in common. The 'urban tribe' is thus found to be different from the capsule in the sense that tribal behaviour is part of the social and cultural dynamics of cosmopolitan city life, where the expats indeed become a major magnet of city life and culture.

The cosmopolitan attitude, as we described in our ethnographic encounter, adds another complexity to Kraus's (2012) complex diversity, which goes beyond layers of multiple identifications but also socialization, being curious and engaging with the people who come from different backgrounds. Implicit in these social media dynamics of complex networking is the rejection of the official assimilation paradigm as an indicator of successful integration in Denmark. What counts is rather the constant efforts to connect people with different cultural backgrounds online and offline and to interlink the virtual and the real worlds. This emphatic notion of 'networking' is an on-going effort; it is something that continues and that acquires a value of its own, transforming both host society and the ways a new generation of mobile people relate to it. Assimilation into Danish society is thus replaced by something that could be called creative networking and that is seen as more attractive and more profitable. This requires an active user who creates structures instead of simply adapting to them. The capsule can be a useful platform for this creative process, but it is not a purpose in itself and, in fact, is quickly transformed by the dynamics of networking.

6 CONCLUSION

This chapter has explored the new allegiances and the self-understanding of so-called expats as a highly mobile and densely networked group of migrants. The expat social media sites create locally rooted networks for internationals. These sites are not simply meeting places, nor do they stand for the formation of a particular online community (in the emphatic sense of people being collectively engaged in something), but they offer potentialities for being (or becoming) both, but also for being used for many other purposes (such as a market for particular goods or an information carrier). We used mixed methods in blended ethnography and netnography – participant observation in social media platforms and in events organized by these platforms, social media content analysis, a social media online survey, and face-to-face qualitative interviews. We suggested a multidimensional analysis of social networking media as a bridging element between the governmental support, civil society, host society and immigrants, affecting the functioning of migrant networks in particular ways, and helping the migrants build transnational ties, not only family or community ties, but at the same time linking them to the particular city-place where they actually live. These social networking media form a transnational public sphere of a special kind. It is a virtual sphere of place-bridging for transnational mobiles, but it also constitutes a cultural sphere of place-building that is occupied by like-minded people to exchange information about living in Copenhagen and Denmark, to 'consume' diversity of cultural products in the local, and, last but not least, to network, meet face to face and make Copenhagen and Denmark their home. This is not meant in the sense of assimilating to this place but rather interacting within it and contributing dynamically to its transformation. The so-called expats appear not as the subordinated groups who ask for inclusion and integration, but as protagonists of cultural activism and privileged players with power over definition and identification. Mobility and citizenship rights as facilitated by the Europe of free movement do not in this sense lead to the seclusion of a distinct group of privileged EU citizens but contribute to the consolidation of a transnational public sphere in which communicative exchanges and encounters are kept in flow between the well-established group of high-skilled EU (and also non-EU) mobiles and other newly arriving groups of less privileged migrants (e.g. those escaping the economic crisis in Southern Europe, or working migrants in low-skilled jobs from South-eastern Europe).

We were thus able to describe a form of place-making that critically engages with the local space and also often claims to contribute to its dynamic development. More than exiles, the expats then become an important element of the dynamic development of locality; they are a defining element of locality, not outsiders. They are, so to speak, rooted cosmopolitans (Appiah 2006; Werbner 2008) and not the kind of 'footless' and 'rootless' people identified by Hannerz (2004) in an earlier study. Hence, the encapsulation thesis of expat communities was overall rejected by these research findings. Expats' online networking is only insufficiently understood as an isolated enclave or capsule for cosmopolitan-minded people (Jansson 2011). On the one hand, expat social media sites are an important support tool in migrants' endeavour to develop a de-nationalized, mobile lifestyle that links them to particular places, like cities, where they build communities with like-minded internationals (and not necessarily co-nationals). Social media practices reveal in this sense the emergence of an 'international community' that offers stable patterns of identification and belonging. On the other hand, for this group of expats, expanding their networks becomes a novel mode of place-making. Through social media practices and networking, they develop a form of belonging that allows them to relate back to the local without renouncing their mobile lifestyles. Creative place-making takes place through a recombination of online and offline practices. There is a continuing space–communication nexus; spaces produce communication as much as communication produces spaces. Within this evolving social media space, expats are not just media users; they are producers of media content and they draw on rich knowledge and experiences to provide specific information that serves the purpose of the expat community.

One last qualification needs to be made with regard to the dominant non-political character of expats' transnational activism, which mainly contributes to a cultural public sphere that is demarcated by the Europe of free movement and rights but does not actively engage in the struggle for inclusion and expansion of these sets of rights. By adopting a transnational habitus of 'expats', these mobile working migrants can make distinctions based on economic status and rights of citizenship invisible in local everyday life, but these invisibilization strategies might also include latent cleavages between these groups of migrants, cleavages which are often displaced or simply not talked about. The current refugee crisis in Europe is therefore a litmus test for this transnational community of expats and their awareness of taking advantage of the Europe of free movement, which might translate into a political awareness about the need to embrace also different groups of foreigners in need of care and humanitarian protection.

NOTES

* This research was funded by the UCPH Excellence Programme for Interdisciplinary Research.

1. For powerful examples of the development of these mobile denationalized lifestyles in the pre-social media era see Favell (2008).
2. There is a second Facebook group, under the name Expats in Copenhagen, with the same mission statement and approximately 2700 members.
3. See https://www.facebook.com/groups/expats.copenhagen/.
4. 2GOCopenhagen does not have the necessary tools to figure out the nationality of their users, while Expat in Denmark has signalled that Europeans are the most numerous, followed by Americans, Canadians and Chinese.
5. This applied to 266 out of 1034 respondents (25.7 per cent).
6. Recent numbers of so-called OECD expats (migrants from OECD countries temporarily or permanently living and working in another OECD country) can be found at oecd.org/migration/mig/33868740.pdf.

REFERENCES

Appiah, K.A. (2006), *Cosmopolitanism: Ethics in a World of Strangers*, New York: Penguin Books.

Baumann, G. (1996), *Contesting Culture: Discourses of Identity in Multi-ethnic London*, Cambridge: Cambridge University Press.

Castells, M. (2000) An Introduction to the Information Age, in F. Webster, R. Blom, E. Karvonen, H. Melin, K. Nordenstreng and E. Puoskari (eds), *The Information Society Reader*, pp. 138–149, London: Routledge.

Castells, M. (2007) Communication, Power and Counter-power in the Network Society, *International Journal of Communication* 1: 238–266.

Christensen, M. (2011) Online Social Media, Communicative Practice and Complicit Surveillance in Transnational Contexts, in M. Christensen, A. Jansson and C. Christensen (eds), *Online Territories: Globalization, Mediated Practice and Social Space*, pp. 222–238, New York: Peter Lang.

Dekker, R. and G. Engbersen (2014) How Social Media Transform Migrant Networks and Facilitate Migration, *Global Networks* 14(4): 401–418.

Diamandaki, K. (2003) Virtual Ethnicity and Digital Diasporas: Identity Construction in Cyberspace, *Global Media Journal* 2(2), https://www.academia.edu/5102541/Virtual_ethnicity_and_digital_diasporas_Identity_construction_in_cyberspace_Global_Media_Journal_2_2_Spring_2003 (accessed 24 March 2015).

Duru, D.N. and H.-J. Trenz (forthcoming) From Diversity to Conviviality: Intra EU Mobility and International Migration to Denmark in Times of Economic Recession, *Journal of Ethnic and Migration Studies*.

Favell, A. (2008) *Eurostars and Eurocities: Free Moving Urban Professionals in an Integrating Europe*, Oxford: Blackwell.

Fürsich, E. (2010) Media and the Representation of Others, *International Social Science Journal* 61 (199): 113–130.

Glick-Schiller, N., T. Darieva and S. Gruner-Domic (2011) Defining Cosmopolitan Sociability in a Transnational Age: An Introduction, *Ethnic and Racial Studies* 34(3): 339–418.

Hampton, K.N., C. Lee and E.J. Her (2011) How New Media Affords Network Diversity: Direct and Mediated Access to Social Capital through Participation in Local Social Settings, *New Media and Society* 13(7): 1031–1049.

Hannerz, U. (1990) Cosmopolitans and Locals in World Culture, *Theory, Culture, Society* 7: 237–251.

Hannerz, U. (2004) Cosmopolitanism, in D. Nugent and J. Vincent (eds), *A Companion to the Anthropology of Politics*, pp. 69–85, New Malden, MA: Blackwell.

Hedetoft, U. (2010) Denmark versus Multiculturalism, in S. Vertovec and S. Wessendorft (eds), *The Multiculturalism Backlash*, pp. 111–129, Abingdon: Routledge.

Jansson, A. (2011) Cosmopolitan Capsules: Mediated Networking and Social Control in Expatriate Spaces, in M. Christensen, A. Jansson and C. Christensen (eds), *Online Territories: Globalization, Mediated Practice and Social Space*, pp. 239–255, New York: Peter Lang.

Jensen, K.B. (2010) *Media Convergence*, Abingdon: Routledge.

Kozinets, R.V. (2009), *Netnography: Doing Ethnographic Research Online*, London: Sage.

Kraus, P.A. (2012) The Politics of Complex Diversity: A European Perspective, *Ethnicities* 12(1): 3–25.

Madianou, M. and D. Miller (2011) *Migration and New Media: Transnational Families and Polymedia*, London: Routledge.

Panteli, N. and M. Chiasson (2008) *Exploring Virtuality within and beyond Organizations: Social, Global and Local Dimensions*, Basingstoke: Palgrave Macmillan.

Papacharissi, Z. (2002) The Virtual Sphere: The Internet as Public Sphere, *New Media and Society* 4(1): 9–27.

Papacharissi, Z. (2010) *A Private Sphere: Democracy in a Digital Age*, Cambridge: Cambridge University Press.

Polson, E. (2015) A Gateway to the Global City: Mobile Place-making Practices by Expats, *New Media and Society* 17(4): 629–645.

Price, M.E. (1995) *Television, the Public Sphere, and National Identity*, Oxford: Clarendon Press.

Urry, J. (1995) *Consuming Places*, London: Routledge.

Werbner, P. (ed.) (2008) *Anthropology and the New Cosmopolitanism: Rooted Feminist and Vernacular Perspectives*, Oxford: Berg.

6. The contribution of think tanks to the formation of a European public sphere

Marybel Perez

The role of think tanks is usually examined in terms of their contribution to policymaking, that is, in terms of how they are able to contribute to the design, implementation and evaluation of policies. But, in this process of influencing policymaking, think tanks also influence the formation of public opinion. Think tanks contribute to the definition and reproduction of ideas through the dissemination of books and reports, through organizing and participating in seminars and parliamentary hearings, appearing in interviews and media debates and lecturing at educational institutions.

The contribution of think tanks to public opinion formation is frequently described as participation in the 'marketplace of ideas' (e.g. Abelson 2009; Rich 2004; Smith 1991). From this perspective, the focus is on the strategies that think tanks deploy to position their ideas in the market for information. Accordingly, the study of think tanks from the marketplace perspective is designed to show think tanks' capacity to create the 'atmospheric impact' (Stone 2000) which increases their visibility, reputation and policy relevance. Nevertheless, think tanks' strategies to position their ideas in the market for information should in addition be examined as a contribution to the formation of the public sphere. The public sphere refers to the spaces where citizens and policy actors come together to debate the inclusion and exclusion of subjects considered legitimate for discussion and thus find solutions to social problems. Through their work, think tanks create links between different kinds of actors, and through their policy analysis they contribute to the definition and reproduction of discourses in specific contexts that shape the public sphere. Consequently, this chapter discusses the proposition that think tanks – paraphrasing Sicakkan (see Chapter 1 of this book) – contribute to the processes of inclusion and exclusion of actors in the public sphere as well as of supporting or challenging arguments defined and reproduced in the public sphere. Drawing on think tank scholarship, this chapter discusses how think tanks contribute to the moulding of public opinion at transnational and global levels where structures of communication are complex and fragmented. To this end, the analysis focuses on EU think tanks' participation in EU policymaking.

Section 1 briefly introduces the notion of the marketplace of ideas and shows how the work of think tanks has been framed under this approach. It continues by pointing out how the notion of the public sphere can help in better understanding the effect of think tanks on politicians' views and on the moulding of public opinion. Section 2 summarizes the characteristics of the EU system and the strengths and weaknesses of EU think tanks that tailor their contribution to the European public sphere. Section 3 discusses how EU think tanks contribute to the definition of the trans-European public sphere, with a specific focus on their platform function. The discussion in section 4 suggests that, while EU think tanks help to reduce barriers for access to some policy actors through, among other things, their platform function, and to structure debates with their knowledge management capacity, their contribution to the European public sphere is constrained by their resources, their elite orientation and their limited access to EU policymaking.

1 THINK TANKS AND THE MARKETPLACE OF IDEAS

The marketplace of ideas consists of spaces of communication where a wide range of channels are available to disseminate messages in a context dominated by deregulation and competition (Bambauer 2006; Rainey and Rehg 1996). Consequently, the marketplace of ideas is an open space where individuals and organizations can set forth their ideas and strive to gain attention. Accordingly, it is usually assumed that the best ideas and information will gain public acceptance (Bambauer 2006).

In this context, the notion of the marketplace is relevant for think tanks because, as Smith states, 'political ideas have become commodities to be sold, and "experts" [of think tanks] are often those who gain the most routine access to the media' (1991: 201). As a result, Smith states, the marketplace of ideas is a key instrument for think tanks because it helps to disseminate their work and 'sell' the organization (1991: 194; see also Abelson 2009). In this regard, a study by Rich and Weaver has shown that the visibility of think tanks, particularly in the media, assures funding continuity from sponsors, and increases awareness and interest from politicians and the public (2000). Moreover, the high mediatization of a polity tends to make think tanks more visible (Pautz 2012). On the one hand, the media require a permanent flow of information and experts to rely on for their analyses. On the other hand, think tanks are willing to provide attractive policy analysis in order to gain visibility. This has made the relationship between the media and think tanks grow stronger, as Medvetz (2012) and Pautz (2012) have discussed. These trends have been particularly significant during the last few decades with the 24/7 information demand brought about by new technologies (McGann 2007).

Nevertheless, as scholars of the marketplace of ideas contend (Bambauer 2006; Rainey and Rehg 1996), it is questionable whether the deregulated and competitive character of this market is able to lead to the selection of the best ideas and information. Aspects such as information biases and resource structures play a significant role in the dissemination and selection of ideas and information in the marketplace (Bambauer 2006). In other words, as the scholarship of the public sphere contends (see Sicakkan, this volume, Preface and Chapter 1), processes of inclusion and exclusion of actors as well as of alignment and contestation of arguments take place alongside the competition to win the attention of politicians and the public. As a result, accounts for think tanks' competition in the marketplace of ideas have to acknowledge their impact on the public sphere.

Accordingly, the scholarship has shown the effects on think tanks of bias, information asymmetries and resource structures in the marketplace of ideas. For instance, Pautz has found that the increased weight of partisan media in the last few decades in the UK seems especially to attract think tanks focused on partisan policy advice (2012). A similar pattern was identified in the US in the early 2000s by Rich (2004), McGann (2007) and Abelson (2009, also in Canada). In order to capture journalists' attention, think tanks invest considerable resources in providing large amounts of timely analysis and developing close relations with journalists. Nevertheless, as Abelson emphasizes, visibility should not be equated with influence (2014). The fact that think tanks gain exposure does not imply that they mould politicians' ideas and public opinion. Neither should it be assumed that think tanks with little visibility are uninfluential. As Abelson (2009) and Pautz (2012) show, some think tanks are more interested in influencing public opinion, while others prefer to directly persuade politicians.

Moreover, although the media nowadays play a key role in the national public sphere, it should be acknowledged that some think tanks prefer to use different strategies to connect with their publics (Abelson 2009). This is particularly important at transnational and global levels where the media's monopoly to carry information is to a certain extent diluted.

As Fraser puts it, the public sphere at a global level can be described as a 'field divided between corporate global media, restricted niche media and decentred Internet networks' (2007: 18). In this context, alternative means of communication, and significantly networks, become important conduits of information. The flexibility of networks to organize and adapt, to process and disseminate information and, therefore, to contribute to governance processes has increased with recent technological developments (Castells 2013). This is particularly true at a transnational level where unstructured governance dominates (Castells 2008). In this regard, research on think tanks' participation in network governance has shown how discourses are created and reproduced through transnational networks (Ball and Exley 2010; Stone 2014). Networks assume many forms and objectives, but in the following pages we will focus on the knowledge networks (Stone 2002) that EU think tanks organize or join with the purpose of participating in EU politics.

But not only think tanks' resources and media structure shape their position in the public sphere. The position of different administrations regarding policy advice may also make think tanks more or less popular in the marketplace of ideas, as Pautz has shown. Comparing the Thatcher and Major, and Blair and Brown governments, he pointed out that Major and Brown relied less on policy advice than Thatcher and Blair (Pautz 2012). Accordingly, political systems in general (Abelson 2009) and governance dynamics in particular (Perez 2014a) determine the opportunities which think tanks have to affect politics and public opinion. As section 2 will remark, the degree of openness of different stages of policymaking, the informational needs of policy actors, and the relevance of informal spaces for policy debates shape the barriers and opportunities that face think tanks as they try to access policy discussions and influence politicians' thinking and public opinion at national and transnational levels.

The notion of the marketplace of ideas is useful in examining the public sphere because it defines it as a space of competition and conflict. It reveals some of the strategies that think tanks display to direct politicians' and public opinion. It also shows the implications for think tanks' reputation, funding and visibility. However, a comprehensive picture of the public sphere needs to acknowledge the presence of information biases and resource structures. It is also necessary to recognize that the public sphere includes not only mass media but other mechanisms of communication and significantly networks – especially at the transnational level. Finally, the public sphere is also shaped by the organization of politics that affects the rules of the inclusion and exclusion of actors as politically relevant. Accordingly, the purpose of the following sections is to discuss how the organization of EU politics and the development of networks at EU level can shape the trans-European public sphere.

2 EU THINK TANKS AND EU INTEGRATION

Think tanks are non-profit organizations that provide research, analysis and advice on public policy to different policy actors, including policy-makers and the public.[1] From a functional point of view, the impact of think tanks in policy debates and policymaking depends on their capacity to provide timely research, analysis and advice, establish relations with a wide variety of policy actors, and facilitate channels of information and policy debates through which policy discourses are created and disseminated. From the institutional perspective, the degree to which think tanks are relevant policy actors depends on the opportunities set by the policy environment and by think tanks' capacity to perform according to established rules and practices.

The presence of think tanks in politics has been particularly important in the US, the UK and Germany, where these organizations have been operating for decades (Abelson 2014). But nowadays think tanks can be found in virtually every country in the world (McGann and Sabatini 2011).

In the EU, think tanks are a relatively new phenomenon. As Table 6.1 shows, EU think tanks started to appear in the 1970s, but since the EU's governance transformations in the 2000s they have grown significantly. The type of EU think tanks discussed in this chapter are those located in Brussels and having an EU-transnational origin, an interest in EU subjects and the intention to contribute to EU policymaking. There are 27 EU think tanks (Table 6.1), operating along with other national and global think tanks, such as the Bertelsmann Stiftung and the Global Governance Institute, as well as EU agencies, including the recently restructured European Political Strategy Centre[2] (the Commission's think tank).

While EU think tanks emphasize their engagement in generating policy research and analysis similarly to think tanks in other parts of the world (Perez 2014a), in some respects EU think tanks operate differently to think tanks in the US, the UK or Germany. Think tanks' participation in consultation processes of policymaking is frequently used as a mechanism to influence policies and show policy relevance to public opinion. However, research shows that think tank participation in EU policy-making is limited (Perez 2014a) compared with that of other public

Table 6.1 EU think tanks

	Think tank name	Year founded	Signed in the Transparency Register[1]	Think tanks reporting media appearances in websites and annual reports[2]
1	The Trans European Policy Studies Association (TEPSA)	1974	3 January 2014	
2	Groupe de recherche et d'information sur la paix et la sécurité (GRIP)	1979		Reported
3	Centre for European Policy Studies (CEPS)	1983	16 September 2011	Reported
4	Observatoire Social Européen (OSE)	1984		
5	European Institute for Asia Studies (EIAS)	1989		
6	Confrontations Europe	1992	5 October 2011	Reported
7	International Security Information Service (ISIS)	1995		
8	Migration Policy Group (MPG)	1995		
9	European Research Institute for Mediterranean and Euro-Arab Cooperation (MEDEA)	1996	12 December 2012	
10	European Policy Centre (EPC)	1997	22 January 2009	Reported
11	Madariaga – College of Europe Foundation	1998	24 December 2014	Reported
12	Friends of Europe	1999	23 September 2011	Reported
13	Pour la Solidarité	2002	20 December 2012	
14	European Corporate Governance Institute (ECGI)	2002		
15	European Ideas Network	2002		
16	European Policy Institutes Network (EPIN)	2002		
17	Lisbon Council for Economic Competitiveness	2003	5 October 2008	Reported
18	Bruegel	2004	27 September 2011	

Table 6.1 (continued)

	Think tank name	Year founded	Signed in the Transparency Register[1]	Think tanks reporting media appearances in websites and annual reports[2]
19	European Centre for International Political Economy (ECIPE)	2006	6 December 2014	Reported
20	European Liberal Forum (ELF)	2007		
21	Wilfried Martens Centre for European Studies	2007	19 February 2015	
22	Centre Maurits Coppieters (CMC)	2007	15 February 2011	
23	Institute of European Democrats (IED)	2007		
24	Foundation for European Progressive Studies (FEPS)	2008	27 February 2012	Reported
25	Eurodemocracy	2009		
26	New Direction	2010		Reported
27	Eurasian Council on Foreign Affairs	2014		

Notes:
[1] Accessed 28 February 2015.
[2] Collected by 27 April 2015.

Sources: Think tanks' annual reports and websites.

interest groups, such as NGOs (Coen and Katsaitis 2013). In fact, EU think tanks rejected signing the Transparency Register during its first years of operation (Euractiv 2009; Perez 2014b). Nevertheless, it can be seen that their registration has increased in the last few years (Table 6.1). It is difficult to anticipate the motives behind this change of strategy, but it might be connected with the increased role of the European Parliament in policy regulation, with pressures to consult only registered groups in the Parliament (EP 2010) and the feasibility that registration results in de facto accreditation in consultation processes, as some studies have proposed (Greenwood and Halpin 2007).

Yet organizations engaged in policy consultation at EU level need to invest resources to adapt to the specific needs of EU institutions in terms of policy area, the type of information required and the significance of national perspectives (Coen and Katsaitis 2013). In some respects EU think tanks do not always have the features and resources necessary to adapt to the specific needs of EU institutions in order to participate in formal consultation processes. Nevertheless, as Coen and Katsaitis suggest, interest groups that have a negligible impact on EU policymaking play important intermediary roles, which place them at an advantage because their informality makes them harder to control. Our argument (see below) is that features of EU politics as well as of EU think tanks make them more useful actors for the EU system as informal intermediaries (Perez 2014a, 2014b).

Another aspect where EU think tanks operate in a different manner to their counterparts in the US or the UK is their relationship with the mass media. In the US, as explained in the previous section, think tanks frequently use appearance in the media, and particularly the mass media, as a way to show engagement in public opinion formation and the influencing of policymaking. As Abelson (2009, 2014) points out, evidence of think tanks' interest in media appearance lies in their enthusiasm to record the number of appearances in their annual reports and websites. But only a few EU think tanks follow this pattern. Less than two-fifths of EU think tanks show concern for news appearances (see Table 6.1), and those showing some concern are significantly less active than their US or UK counterparts (Perez 2014a). One of the main reasons EU think tanks devote few resources to a mass media profile is the lack of European mass media. This forces them to direct their efforts towards connecting with national mass media. It entails significant effort to establish relations with journalists all over Europe, to rely on a highly multilingual staff and/or to translate their outputs into all 24 official languages.

So how do EU think tanks contribute to the structure of the European public sphere? As will be explained in the following section, EU think tanks seem to invest significant resources in their platform function, whose purpose is to connect different kinds of policy actors. The platform function refers to think tanks' capacity to organize and engage in networks.

3 PLATFORMS OF EU THINK TANKS AND THE TRANS-EUROPEAN PUBLIC SPHERE

While EU think tanks devote limited resources to fulfilling their functions of informing politicians and the public through policy consultation and media dissemination, they assign significant resources to managing knowledge that involves research and policy analysis, as well as to facilitating debates and spaces to connect with policy actors (Perez 2014d). This facilitation task is what we call the platform function. This refers to think tanks serving as a liaison between a wide range of policy actors as a result of their networking capacity. The specific objectives of these platforms are multiple, but basically they seek to exchange and disseminate ideas and further debate.

The two main aspects that make platforms useful for the structure of the European public sphere are a reduction of transaction costs and socialization. First, think tanks reduce informational transaction costs for many policy actors that do not have the same information management capacity as think tanks. The policymaking process at EU level is complex and, for those who have insufficient resources, who are not used to participating in EU politics or who are exploring new policy areas, EU think tanks' information and platforms can constitute valuable sources. EU think tanks reduce informational transaction costs for EU institutions too. These may find difficulties in identifying new stakeholders for the policies they regulate because public and private interest groups jealously guard their insider status (Broscheid and Coen 2007). EU think tanks' platforms constitute a mechanism for EU institutions to identify new stakeholders and look for different informational inputs.

As a result, EU think tanks are transaction cost reducers not only because they help to make economies in information management but also because they contribute towards reducing information asymmetries and mitigate uncertainty (Williamson 1979). Permanent interaction with insiders increases EU institutions' bounded rationality (Simon 1957) – which reduces their legitimacy – and the fact that insiders jealously guard their positions increases the barriers faced by newcomers or weaker actors. Accordingly, in practice EU think tanks are reducers of information asymmetries by connecting these two sets of actors through their platforms. In addition, the intermediary role of EU think tanks makes platform participants avoid opportunistic behaviour (Williamson 1979).

The role of EU think tanks as transaction cost reducers is observed not only in the large number of platform related activities organized by EU think tanks (seminars, workshops and conferences) each year, but also by the variety of actors involved and the significant presence of representatives from EU institutions. Research has shown that, in 2011, 22 of the EU think tanks examined here organized an average of seven platform activities a week (Perez 2014b). That research has shown that the

Commission and the Parliament members are from the two most participative EU institutions, although representatives from the European External Action Service were visible to an extent. Together with EU institutions, the most prominent policy actors participating in EU think tanks' platform activities were national governments, academics and business representatives. These were followed by national think tanks, international institutions and international foundations, associations and NGOs. A similar pattern was found in research examining the transnational 'collaborative and communicative networks' of think tanks in the UK (Pautz 2014). However, the main difference with the Pautz findings is the significant presence of members of the European Parliament, representatives from the business community and from international institutions, and organizations in EU think tanks' platforms. The reasons for these differences are the increased importance of the European Parliament in policymaking, and the relevance of the business sector as EU policy actors and their need to develop political expertise (Coen and Katsaitis 2013). Finally, the research shows that representatives from both the Commission and the Parliament are the participants who most frequently return to think tanks' platform activities (Perez 2014b), which indicates a genuine interest of EU institutions in EU think tanks' platforms.

To summarize, the frequency of EU platform activities, the significant presence of representatives from EU institutions and the wide range of policy actors attending seem to indicate that EU think tanks' platforms are useful mechanisms for both EU institutions and policy actors. Consequently, it is possible to assert that the seminars, workshops and conferences that EU think tanks hold play a role in the exchange and dissemination of ideas and in furthering debate.

Second, EU think tanks are socializers of the EU integration process (Perez 2014c). In some platforms it is possible that the interaction and discussion of specific ideas have an effect on the perceptions and enactment of rules and practices of EU politics. To be sure, the lasting effect of interactions and discussions depends on characteristics of the platforms. As discussions on the study of think tanks' impact have argued, it is a highly difficult task to trace an idea and see how it becomes a policy (Abelson 2009, 2014). As a result, it is difficult to examine the socialization effect of the loose interaction taking place in the EU platforms discussed above (workshops, seminars and conferences). Nevertheless, EU think tanks also rely on more stable platforms to disseminate information, that is, knowledge networks (Stone 2002, 2008). Knowledge networks are groups of actors concerned with a specific set of policy subjects seeking to 'advance, spread and share knowledge' (Stone 2002: 2). Accordingly, research pointing out the increasing relevance of knowledge transfer in processes of Europeanization has shown the important role think tanks play in these processes (Ladi 2005; for a similar argument at global level see Ball and Exley 2010; Stone 2014).

Some EU think tanks are set up as knowledge networks, some are hubs of knowledge networks and some are simply engaged in knowledge networks. The Trans European Policy Studies Association (TEPSA) is an example of an EU think tank network, and the European Policy Institutes Network (EPIN) is an example of an EU think tank network coordinated by another EU think tank, the Centre for European Policy Studies (CEPS). EPIN and TEPSA are networks of national think tanks, and the latter has been operating for just over four decades (see Table 6.1). These two networks have been useful cases to consider regarding EU think tanks' capacity for socialization (Perez 2014d).

In both networks, every country of the EU has a think tank member, and every candidate for EU membership has associated membership. Therefore, EPIN and TEPSA constitute the transnational connection of national think tanks to Brussels politics – and to European politics beyond the national borders. The think tank members are usually ranked among the most influential in their contexts, as an EPIN (2015) description states. From the interviews with national members conducted by Eurosphere, it emerged that the benefits of participating in EPIN and TEPSA are a direct connection with Brussels and other European countries, and the possibility of extending their impact through collaborative efforts.[3] This direct connection with Brussels institutions takes place in different ways. EPIN and TEPSA have participated in the Europe for Citizens Programme of the Commission, EPIN was created with an EU grant for the constitutional convention, and TEPSA has been involved in Framework Programmes of the Commission and organizes the pre-presidency conferences before the change of the presidency of the Council of the European Union. In addition, the membership and coordination role of the CEPS in EPIN is an important asset, since the CEPS is one of the most active EU think tanks (Perez 2014a, 2014b). Moreover, EU institutions have already expressed their interest in think tanks as organizations that observe, analyse and contribute to the debate on European public policy issues (European Parliament 2015) or institutions, 'providing ideas and reflections on European issues, on active European citizenship or on European values and in feeding the debate at European level' (European Commission 2012).

Consequently, on the assumption that EPIN and TEPSA members are keen on learning and debating about EU politics in Brussels and member countries, research has now examined whether EU ideas are socialized through these networks (Perez 2014d). The results indicate that the socialization of EU ideas, such as an interconnected transnational model of the public sphere (discussed in this book), is possible through think tank networks. Specifically, it was observed that two elements are necessary for this kind of socialization. First, think tanks should be actively interested in EU politics. Those think tanks that were not engaged in transnational think tank networks or those that participated in transnational think tank networks without focus in EU politics did not share the same views. Second, it is necessary that EU institutions are present in those networks. It was observed that similar views were shared not only among EPIN and TEPSA members but, generally, among transnational networks concerned with EU politics which had connections in common with EU institutions. These results are in line with other research that has pointed out the importance of EU institutions' presence in policy transfer processes (Ladi 2005), and studies suggesting that at EU level network governance takes place in the shadow of hierarchy (Börzel 2011; *JPP* 2008).

As a result, the EU think tanks' platform function has acquired a certain strength, compared with their counterparts in the US and UK. This strength is the result of four main attributes of the EU system and EU think tanks: (1) their ability to overcome the barriers they encounter to participating in EU policymaking; (2) their contribution to public opinion formation through the mass media; (3) their capacity to manage information and conduct platforms (whether seminars and conferences or knowledge networks); and (4) the apparent interest of EU institutions and other policy actors in meeting and exchanging information in these settings. Consequently, platforms constitute a mechanism not only for EU think tanks to participate in EU politics, but also for the EU system to fulfil its informational and socialization needs.

If EU think tanks' platforms constitute a key element in the dissemination of information and socialization of EU ideas, then how do they contribute to the configuration of the trans-European public sphere? The following section briefly considers the forces of inclusion and exclusion at play in think tanks' platforms as well as the strengths and limitations for EU think tanks' impact on EU integration.

4 EU THINK TANKS AND THE TRANS-EUROPEAN PUBLIC SPHERE

Think tanks can contribute to the configuration of the public sphere by both reproducing discourses and managing interactions. Particularly at EU level, EU think tanks contribute to the trans-European public sphere – as defined by Sicakkan (this volume, Preface and Chapter 1) – by (1) bringing together national, European and international policy actors interested in debating EU politics, and (2) transferring EU ideas and creating common discourses. In this process forces of inclusion and exclusion of interactions in think tanks' platforms, together with the strengths and limitations of EU think tanks, determine the potential of EU think tanks to contribute to EU integration.

Networks are mechanisms for inclusion because they bring together individuals and organizations that in isolation would not be able to participate in governance processes (Stone 2002). Through networks, members increase their capacity to receive, process and reinterpret or adapt information. As observed, members of EU think tanks' knowledge networks consider that the main benefits of their membership are direct connection with Brussels and other European countries, and the possibility of extending their impact through their collaboration. At the same time, the benefits of participation in EU seminars, workshops and conferences were seen as the reduction both of informational costs and of the barriers that make access to EU debates difficult.

Nevertheless, as Castells explains, 'networks work on a binary logic: inclusion/exclusion' (2013: 20). The first factor that creates exclusion is a lack of interest in EU politics. The examination of EU platforms of different kinds shows that this is a key element. In second place, the concentration of politics in Brussels and the use of English and French as the main languages are two particular features of the EU which make access cumbersome. In addition, a characteristic of think tanks is that their platforms are exclusive. Despite think tanks' public orientation and their efforts to provide free access to their material and disseminate their work through websites and social media, their capacity to integrate a wide public in their activities is limited at transnational and national levels (Stone 2002, 2008), and in particular at EU level. Finally, owing to the focus on their know-how and limited resources, think tanks write and speak only to the educated public interested in the subjects of their expertise. As a result, EU think tanks' platforms include a specific kind of public, interested in EU politics and able to speak several languages and understand the EU jargon, with credentials and know-how relevant for different EU policy actors, and with the soft skills necessary to navigate the national, international and EU arenas.

As Stone explains, one of the strengths of think tanks' platform function is that they provide 'discursive, intellectual and scientific structure' to debates in the public sphere (Stone 2008: 32). This strength becomes apparent among EU think tanks' knowledge networks such as EPIN and TEPSA, which are able to reinterpret, reproduce and also socialize members into EU ideas. In addition, EU think tanks are able to socialize policy actors that usually do not have access to EU policymaking.

Nevertheless, the strengths of EU think tanks as intermediaries of the EU system are curbed by their not being the actors of formal EU policymaking. When it comes to influencing policy, the trends seem to indicate that EU policymaking is driven by the informational reliability developed in strong-tie networks of insiders (Chalmers 2013) more than by the need of the new information or stakeholders which EU think tanks provide. Therefore, the platforms of EU think tanks encounter significant competition from public and private interest groups which have developed information management skills and have the status of insiders. Consequently, EU think tank platforms are useful in particular cases where new information or stakeholders are sought.

So far it is established how EU think tanks contribute to the trans-European public sphere by facilitating interactions between actors at national, transnational and EU levels, and by participating in the construction and reproduction of discourses. However, there are still open questions on EU think tanks' scope of contribution and the implications for EU integration. The public sphere, as has been pointed out by Sicakkan (this volume, Preface and Chapter 1), is also a space of contestation. Therefore, it is still necessary to examine and compare the different discourses present in EU think tanks' networks. Two think tank networks with similar discourses, EPIN and TEPSA, were examined in order to determine the socialization capacity of EU think tanks (Perez 2014d). But a comparison with discourses in other think tank networks, such as the European Ideas Network (a network of centre-right think tanks) or the European Corporate Governance Institute, with its specific emphasis on corporate governance, can bring to light contestation.

Regarding the implications for EU think tanks' contribution to EU integration, one of the main aspects to consider is the question of their legitimacy for the EU system. As was argued by Sicakkan (this volume, Preface and Chapter 1), one of the functions of the current public sphere is to grant legitimacy to policy actors, and particularly government institutions. This feature becomes particularly relevant at the transnational level where transparency and democratic procedures adopt complex forms (Stone 2014). This has been the case in the European Union, where debates on the European public sphere came to reflect on the legitimacy of EU institutions. Here it was observed that EU institutions consistently participate in EU think tanks' activities, where they meet with different kinds of policy actors, and interaction with think tanks is seen as part of EU institutions' efforts to improve communication and legitimacy. Nevertheless, the private and elitist character of think tanks' activities shows the challenges of the legitimizing function of the European public sphere. Moreover, the importance of the presence of EU institutions for the socialization of EU ideas poses questions about the processes of inclusion/exclusion and the legitimization of actors taking place in the European public sphere. Consequently, the areas of conflict and the legitimacy of EU think tanks' contribution to the European public sphere should be further examined.

NOTES

1. The definition of the term 'think tank' is a complex and disputable matter, as Medvetz (2012) and Pautz (2012) have discussed. For reasons of length and focus, I adopt here a definition discussed before for the study of EU think tanks (Perez 2014d).
2. Named during the Barroso administration the Bureau of European Policy Advisers.
3. Similar justifications were found by Pautz (2014), questioning UK think tanks' objectives for transnational collaboration.

REFERENCES

Abelson, D.E. (2009) *Do Think Tanks Matter? Assessing the Impact of Public Policy Institutes*, 2nd edn, Montreal: McGill-Queen's University Press.

Abelson, D.E. (2014) Old World, New World: The Evolution and Influence of Foreign Affairs Think-tanks, *International Affairs* 90: 125–142.

Ball, S.J. and S. Exley (2010) Making Policy with 'Good Ideas': Policy Networks and the 'Intellectuals' of New Labour, *Journal of Education Policy* 25(2): 37–41.

Bambauer, D.E. (2006) Shopping Badly: Cognitive Biases, Communications and the Fallacy of the Marketplace of Ideas, *University of Colorado Law Review* 77: 649–709.

Börzel, T.A. (2011) Networks: Reified Metaphor or Governance Panacea? *Public Administration* 89(1): 49–63.

Broscheid, A. and D. Coen (2007) Lobbying Activity and Fora Creation in the EU: Empirically Exploring the Nature of the Policy Good, *Journal of European Public Policy* 14(3): 37–41.

Castells, M. (2008) The New Public Sphere: Global Civil Society, Communication Networks, and Global Governance, *Annals of the American Academy of Political and Social Science* 616(1): 78–93.

Castells, M. (2013) *Communication Power*, 2nd edn, Oxford: Oxford University Press.
Chalmers, A.W. (2013) With a Lot of Help from Their Friends: Explaining the Social Logic of Informational Lobbying in the European Union, *European Union Politics* 14(4): 475–496.
Coen, D. and A. Katsaitis (2013) Chameleon Pluralism in the EU: An Empirical Study of the European Commission Interest Group Density and Diversity across Policy Domains, *Journal of European Public Policy* 20(8): 1104–1119.
EP (European Parliament) (2010) *Parliamentary Questions*, 13 July, http://www.europarl.europa.eu/sides/getDoc.do?type=WQ&language=EN&reference=E-2010–5481 (accessed 26 April 2011).
EPIN (2015) About EPIN, http://www.epin.org/new/about (accessed 27 April 2015).
Euractiv (2009) Lobby Transparency Spotlight Falls on Think-tanks, *Euractiv*, http://www.euractiv.com/en/pa/lobby-transparency-spotlight-falls-think-tanks/article-181404 (accessed 20 April 2009).
European Commission (2012) Europe for Citizens Programme, Action 2 – Active Civil Society in Europe, http://eacea.ec.europa.eu/citizenship/programme/action2_en.php#mesure1 (accessed 20 October 2013).
European Parliament (2015) Political Parties and Foundations, http://www.europarl.europa.eu/contracts-and-grants/en/20150201PVL00101/Political-parties-and-foundations (accessed 29 April 2015).
Fraser, N. (2007) Transnationalizing the Public Sphere: On the Legitimacy and Efficacy of Public Opinion in a Post-Westphalian World, *Theory, Culture and Society* 24(4): 7–30.
Greenwood, J. and D. Halpin (2007) The European Commission and the Public Governance of Interest Groups in the European Union: Seeking a Niche between Accreditation and Laissez-faire, *Perspectives on European Politics and Society* 8(2): 189–210.
JPP (2008) Special Issue: Governance in the Shadow of Hierarchy, *Journal of Public Policy* 28(1).
Ladi, S. (2005) *Globalisation, Policy Transfer and Policy Research Institutes*, Cheltenham, UK and Northampton, MA, USA: Edward Elgar.
McGann, J. (2007) *Think Tanks and Policy Advice in the US: Academics, Advisors and Advocates*, New York: Routledge.
McGann, J. and R. Sabatini (2011) *Global Think Tanks: Policy Networks and Governance*, New York: Routledge.
Medvetz, T. (2012) *Think Tanks in America*, Chicago: University of Chicago Press.
Pautz, H. (2012) *Think-tanks, Social Democracy and Social Policy*, Basingstoke: Palgrave Macmillan.
Pautz, H. (2014) British Think-tanks and Their Collaborative and Communicative Networks, *Politics* 34(4): 345–361.
Perez, M. (2014a) Does EU Policymaking Allow for Skillful Networkers But Limited Knowledge Managers? The Think Tanks' Tale, *International Journal of Politics, Culture, and Society* 27: 323–342.

Perez, M. (2014b) EU Think Tank Fora as Transaction Cost Reducers: A Study of Informal Interest Intermediation in the EU, *Journal of Contemporary European Research* 10(2): 146–165.

Perez, M. (2014c) The EU's Socialising Institutions: The Role of EU Think Tanks in EU Policymaking, Ph.D. dissertation, University of Bergen.

Perez, M. (2014d) What Kind of Public Sphere Shapes the European Educational Research Space? in M. Lawn and N. Romuald (eds), *Shaping of European Education: Interdisciplinary Approaches*, pp. 151–169, New York: Routledge.

Rainey, R. and W. Rehg (1996) The Marketplace of Ideas, the Public Interest and the Regulation of the Electronic Media: Implications of Habermas' Theory of Democracy, *Southern California Law Review* 68: 1923–1987.

Rich, A. (2004) *Think Tanks, Public Policy and Expertise*, Cambridge: Cambridge University Press.

Rich, A. and R.K. Weaver (2000) Think Tanks in the U.S. Media, *Harvard International Journal of Press/Politics* 5(4): 81–103.

Simon, H. (1957) *Models of Man*, New York: Wiley & Sons.

Smith, J.A. (1991) *The Idea Brokers*, New York: Free Press.

Stone, D. (2000) Knowledge, Power and Policy, in D. Stone (ed.), *Banking on Knowledge: The Genesis of the Global Development Network*, pp. 243–260, Florence, NY: Routledge.

Stone, D. (2002) Introduction: Global Knowledge and Advocacy Networks, *Global Networks* 1: 1–11.

Stone, D. (2008) Global Public Policy, Transnational Policy Communities, and Their Networks, *Policy Studies Journal* 36(1): 19–38.

Stone, D. (2014) *Non-governmental Public Action: Knowledge Actors and Transnational Governance*, Basingstoke: Palgrave Macmillan.

Williamson, O.E. (1979) Transaction-cost Economics: The Governance of Contractual Relations, *Journal of Law and Economics* 22(2): 233–261.

7. Protection, participation and legitimacy: the European Union's public consultation system and ethnic and national minorities

Jan H. van de Beek and Floris Vermeulen

The focal point of this chapter is the question of how the wish of ethnic organizations to participate in the policy process interferes with the need of the EU to legitimize itself in the face of a persistent 'democratic deficit'. Are the colour-blind consultation and lobbying channels established by the European Union well suited as a link between ethnic groups and the European Union, or is a more agonistic approach needed in order to address the different needs of these groups that add significantly to the deep diversity in Europe? By ethnic organizations, we mean organizations that identify with ethnic groups in three categories: regional national minorities like the Catalans, national minorities like the Roma who are diffusely spread over member states, and immigrants (third country nationals) like the Turks in Germany. We focus on organizations – like political parties, social movement organizations (SMOs) and non-governmental organizations (NGOs) – which try to influence the policy process on the (inter)national level.

The ongoing development of the European Union has radically changed the possibilities of influencing the policy process, both in member states and internationally. The most obvious change is the development of a new supranational level of governance. A significant share of new legislation in member states is actually made in Brussels. Therefore, political actors like lobby groups, think tanks and political parties have an interest in influencing the European policy process. For small, local or national organizations it may be too large a burden to be present in Brussels, and they may actually lose influence as a result of European integration. But, under some circumstances, similar small organizations that are present in many countries may gain influence by joining forces on the European level in for example an umbrella organization. That applies particularly to organizations that deal with transnational issues such as gender, migration or the environment. In short, the changing opportunity structure brings winners and losers (Koopmans 2007).

An even more fundamental change in the opportunity structure is related to the fact that a nation state-like public sphere is virtually non-existent at the European level. In an ideal-typical picture of representative democracy a demos rules itself by handing over governance to elected representatives. The will of the demos is then formed in a public sphere and communicated to the representatives, who translate it into concrete policy programmes. In turn, those policy programmes are assessed in the public sphere, and the feedback this generates is mediated by the media and absorbed by the representatives. In this way, the representatives stay in touch with the will of the demos and maintain their legitimacy (cf. Schlesinger and Fossum 2007). Hence, in any modern democracy a prerequisite for the legitimacy of the government is the existence of an accessible, inclusive and independent public sphere and media landscape.

However, on the European level, a mature public sphere of the kind that we find in democratic nation states is lacking. In the first place a shared European identity and culture are at best weakly developed, and there is no such thing as a 'European demos'. The underlying reason is the vast ethnic, cultural and linguistic diversity within the EU. More particularly, (linguistic) diversity and the lack of a truly pan-European language are an impediment for the development of pan-European media, which are virtually non-existent or (like *Euronews*) only reach a small, elitist audience. For all those reasons, the first generation of researchers investigating the existence of a European public sphere were quick to point out that such a sphere did not – or even could not – exist (de Vreese 2007). In the last decade or so, there has been ample literature moderating this vision, pointing at a process of 'Europeanization' of national public spheres (Esmark 2007). However, the fact that political decision making is increasingly done at the European level, while public debates are still mostly confined to the national level, can be seen as the core of the democratic deficit of Europe (Koopmans 2007).

One of the effects of the juvenile European public sphere is that it negatively affects those organizations that seek to influence the policy process by attracting media attention with actions or participation in media-covered public debates. This point is well illustrated by the environmental organizations. Environmental issues are by nature international in character, and it seems logical that environmental organizations try to influence EU politics in this field. Moreover, environmental issues were accorded legitimacy by the EU early on and consistently sanctioned and supported by various EU institutions (Marks and McAdam 1996). Nevertheless, environmental organizations do not find much of a stage in Brussels:

> Environmental organizations depend for their legitimacy and their resources upon their ability to command public support, and in the absence of a genuinely European public opinion, it is primarily public opinion at national level to which they must be responsive. Therefore they tend to invest in strengthening their national organizations rather than providing for substantial resources required for collective action at European level. Moreover, action at the EU level is often made disproportionately expensive by the costs of travel, communication and translation, while its effectiveness may be hard to evaluate, since the implementation of policies is still national. (European Parliament 2003)

Hence, for this type of organization, European integration is not a matter of scale, but forces them to change tactics and strategy in order to be influential.

Another effect of the lack of a fully fledged European public sphere is that it increased the relative importance of lobbying as a way of influencing EU policy making. This in the first place applies to the volume of lobby activities in Brussels. EU lobbying has grown considerably over time, and today some 1000 trade associations, the representative bodies of 500 large companies, about 750 NGOs and around 150 offices representing regions are present in Brussels, together with many specialist consultants and law firms (European Parliament 2003: 5). Most of the approximately 5000 accredited interest groups in Brussels are linked to businesses and networks of professionals, but about one-fifth are non-governmental organizations (Coen 2007; Greenwood 2003). All in all, the 15 000 civil servants of the European Commission and the European Parliament face roughly 20 000 lobbyists on a daily basis (Coen 2007; Messer et al. 2011).

Besides, the lack of a nation state-like public sphere and the democratic deficit also have a more subtle effect on lobbying activities. The undemocratic and opaque EU decision making is often parboiled in hardly visible consultative commissions, workgroups and the like for an extensive period of time. During this period, lobbyists may have the opportunity to steer the weeding out of possible policy options in a direction they prefer. This, in combination with the relative high degree of rational ignorance of EU agenda-setting institutions like the European Commission, gives lobbyists a considerable indirect agenda-setting power (Varela 2009).

The democratic deficit shapes the character of EU lobbying in yet another way. In general, there is a strong mutual dependency between EU officials and lobbyists, based on the exchange of expert knowledge and information. Often the juridical and technical complexity of laws and regulations is simply too high, and it is difficult to envision an EU regulation on dangerous chemicals without some involvement of the chemical industry. For actors in for example the industry, financial sector and other corporate branches, the situation is not much different from lobbying on the national level and, for them, European integration is mostly a matter of increasing scale. If we differentiate between consultation and codecision as the two principal legislative procedures (Crombez 2002) this kind of lobbying would be predominantly aimed at codecision.

For lobby organizations like NGOs and SMOs that try to further civic interests, the mutual dependency between EU officials and lobbyists has an extra dimension: legitimacy. The democratic deficit creates an incentive for EU institutions to actively search for sources of legitimacy. This works two ways: for a civic organization, say an NGO, having access to EU institutions adds to its legitimacy with its constituency. Conversely, owing to the democratic deficit of the EU and the resulting lack of legitimacy, EU institutions gain by close cooperation with the NGO because it is a way to gain legitimacy. By consulting NGOs and other civic organizations the EU institutions gain influence and improve their image as responsible political actors (cf. Faist 2004). Since cooperation with NGOs is an alternative source of legitimacy, EU institutions stimulate the formation of for example umbrella organizations of migrant communities in the member states (Geddes 2000; cf. van de Beek et al. 2010). This need of the EU to gain legitimacy has contributed to what is called the EU consultation system. It also has contributed to some specific characteristics of EU lobbying, which in comparison to US lobbying is less aggressive and more geared towards reaching consensus (Woll 2006).

We want to focus the rest of this chapter on the mutual dependency of EU institutions and organizations that identify with ethnic groups. In this, we make a distinction between national minorities and ethnic minorities, where 'national minority'[1] refers to a group that obtained its minority position through the process of (nation) state formation, and 'ethnic minority' refers to a group of people that obtained its minority position through immigration into an existing nation state (cf. Kymlicka 1995: 10–11). For the sake of simplicity we call the latter group 'immigrants', though strictly speaking many second and higher generation individuals of migrant descent never migrated themselves. Among the national minorities we make a further distinction between regional national minorities (like the Catalans and Frisians) and two non-regional national minorities, namely the Jews and the Roma. Among the immigrants, we distinguish between Muslim immigrants and non-religious immigrants.

As said, we are interested in the mutual dependency between those ethnic groups and the EU. First of all, we choose to analyse the structure and degree of institutionalization of the EU consultation system for each of these groups. Furthermore, we want to know what both parties expect to gain by consultation. With regard to the EU we want to look at how consultation feeds into the legislative process and to what degree consultation helps to increase the EU's legitimacy. With regard to the five ethnic groups, we want to know what expectations and preferences they have about the EU. These considerations lead to the following research question:

a. What is the structure of the EU consultation system for each of the five ethnic groups;
b. what do organizations affiliated with these ethnic groups expect from the EU; and
c. to what extent does EU consultation of those groups increase EU legitimacy?

After section 1 on methodology, we will first answer sub-question (a) by sketching the EU consultation system vis-à-vis each of the five ethnic groups (section 2). Then, to answer sub-question (b), we will look into the preferences and expectations each ethnic group has about the EU (section 3). Finally we will tackle sub-question (c) by analysing how consultation affects EU legitimacy and to what extent consultation is congruent with the preferences and expectations of the five groups (section 4).

1 METHODOLOGY, DATA AND ACTOR SELECTION

In order to answer the research question, we make use of data from two different types of sources. Firstly, we make use of secondary literature, EU reports and other sources to sketch the EU consultation system in section 2. For the analysis of the expectations and preferences about the EU of the five ethnic groups, we make use of the Eurosphere project. This project is geared towards understanding the interaction between the development of the European polity, a European public sphere and ethnic and national diversity. For this research, leading figures of organizations in 16 European countries were interviewed on this subject. These were all organizations that somehow influence the policy process: political parties, social movement organizations and think tanks.[2]

From the Eurosphere database we selected a total of 29 organizations that are affiliated with one of the five ethnic groups. The classification of the organizations was done with help of the Eurosphere Country Reports[3] and in consultation with the Eurosphere partners, who revised our initial judgement when necessary. Besides that, we selected 30 political parties that can be seen as 'mainstream'. Those mainstream political parties are used as a control group. For each country several (in most cases two) political parties were selected that belong to the political middle of the country. Again, we used a similar procedure of consultation of Eurosphere partners to reach the final selection of mainstream political parties.

We need to make some remarks on our use of the data. In the first place, the number of respondents per ethnic group is rather limited. To be exact, we have for regional national minorities 26 respondents representing five organizations, for Roma 12 respondents representing four organizations, for Jews 8 respondents representing three organizations, for Muslim immigrants 12 respondents representing seven organizations and for non-religious immigrants 11 respondents representing three organizations. Obviously, this severely limits the validity of our sample. We however feel that the data are suited for illustrating the preferences and expectations about the EU of the five ethnic groups and carefully draw some preliminary conclusions. To reach sufficient validity, more research on a larger sample is needed.

Furthermore, some of the questions of the (structured) interviews we used allow for multiple *overlapping* answer categories. In Figures 7.1 and 7.2, those answers are aggregated. For each answer category we took the fraction of respondents who deemed that answer category applicable to their situation. Then we added all fractions in order to form bar charts. Because a fraction may vary between 0 (=0 per cent) and 1 (=100 per cent), the bars may add up to more than 1 (=100 per cent). Therefore, one should be careful with interpretations, since the length of the bars partly depends on the number of overlapping answer categories. For example, it makes a big difference whether the respondent can only choose 'European polity' or has multiple possible answer categories, one for each institution forming the European polity, as is the case with Eurosphere interview question V5.10 (see Figure 7.1). Also, in those cases where many overlapping answer categories are aggregated, the bars may be rather long, which might give the false impression that no answer category was mentioned often. However, with a high number of answer categories even a score of 1 (=100 per cent) may cover a relatively small part of a bar. Despite those limitations, the data are well suited to comparing the five types of organizations with each other and with the control group of mainstream political parties.

2 THE EU PUBLIC CONSULTATION OF ETHNICALLY AFFILIATED ORGANIZATIONS

As said before, EU lobbying has grown considerably over time. However, the number of lobbyists, lobby organizations and their resources are quite unevenly distributed over the types of actors that want to influence EU politics. Following EU categorization (European Parliament 2003), lobby organizations can be divided into civic and producer organizations. The producer's interests can be subdivided into labour, professions and business, which are all well represented by often resourceful lobby organizations. Likewise, the civic organizations can be further subdivided into four somewhat heterogeneous categories, those representing consumer, environmental, regional, and social and community interests. Though only the latter two are of direct relevance to us, it's insightful to look at the first two as well for comparative purposes.

Consumer lobby organizations are in general well resourced and well organized and in that sense do not deviate much from the producer lobby organizations. As said before, environmental organizations operate in Brussels, but despite their international character and early recognition by EU institutions their influence is curbed owing to the lack of a mature European public sphere. Lobbying by regional organizations is well developed and much institutionalized. This contrasts sharply with the degree of organizations and resourcefulness of organizations that lobby for social and community interests:

> Organisations of women, human rights activists and other societal interests tend to be weaker than their counterparts in the sectors of industry, trade and agriculture and for the most part lag behind in the pace of Europeanisation set by the latter groups. This is even more true of other groups of the population, for instance welfare recipients and pensioners, who lack transnational ties and are widely dispersed – not to mention immigrant workers, minority ethnic groups, and the unemployed. (European Parliament 2003)

As we will see shortly, the degree of self-organization of immigrants and non-regional national minorities indeed falls behind that of the regional national minorities, though the first have been catching up a bit during the last decade. We will now sketch the way EU institutions consult each of the five groups; regional national minorities, Roma, Jews, Muslim immigrants and non-religious immigrants.

2.1 Regional National Minorities

The development of the consultation structure regarding regional national minorities is strongly related to a process of regionalization that started in the 1980s. The meaning of territory to the dispersion of political and economic power has changed dramatically over the past few decades. Some forces like globalization deterritorialize in the sense that they tend to disconnect ties between place and culture. Likewise, European integration weakens the importance of the nation state and its hold on territory. At the same time, European integration makes regionalism a more prominent force in European politics (Keating 1997). Increasingly, cities and industrial regions are lobbying for resources in Brussels (McAleavey and Mitchell 1994). By the end of the 1990s Brussels counted some 150 organizations representing sub-national governments (European Parliament 2003). Furthermore, those organizations combine forces in two overarching organizations: the Council of European Municipalities and Regions (CEMR) and the Assembly of European Regions (AER). The AER – founded in 1985 – is made up of delegates of over 200 regional parliaments who claim to represent 80 per cent[4] of the European population (European Parliament 2003).[5]

The power of the regional organizations varies greatly with the power of the sub-national governments they represent. Some of the more peripheral regions are weak, poor and not well organized, while others like the Belgian region of Flanders, Spanish autonomous communities like Catalonia and the German *Länder* like Bavaria are powerful and relatively independent political entities within their respective states (Hooghe and Marks 1996). In particular the German *Länder* felt they were underrepresented in European politics and lobbied for the creation of a chamber representing the regions in the European polity. This ultimately led to the installation of the Committee of the Regions (CoR), first mentioned in the Maastricht Treaty (Christiansen 1996).

The foundation of the CoR is the culminating point in what Hepburn (2007: 233–235) has coined 'the Rise and Fall of a "Europe of the Regions"' (cf. Elias 2009; Hepburn 2008). In the early 1980s, the attitude of regional politics was characterized by 'nationalist and left-wing animosity to the European project' and a vision of the nation state as a 'giver of autonomy' (Hepburn 2007: 233). Gradually regional parties started to appreciate the decentralization of government in member states and visualized 'an alternative form of autonomy … available to [regional] political parties previously seeking independence, which amounted to a special place in a "Europe of the Regions"' (Hepburn 2007: 233). For some time regional organizations saw the EU as a third way between nation state centralism and full autonomy. Conversely, the EU reached out by founding the Committee of the Regions in 1994 and embedding the principle of subsidiarity in EU treaties. So, to regional actors, the CoR and the idea of a 'Europe of the Regions' seemed a means to 'bypass the nation state' (Keating and Hooghe 2001).

However, rather quickly the Committee of the Regions turned out to have little influence on the EU policy process, and participating parties grew more and more frustrated (Christiansen 1996). One of the reasons was that the EU saw the CoR predominantly as a way to solve its persistent legitimacy problem, without sharing real power with the regional level: 'For the supranational institutions, the creation of such a committee was attractive because it carried the advantage of added legitimacy to European policymaking, while CoR's advisory nature carried little potential for obstructing decision processes' (Christiansen 1996: 95). Furthermore, it turned out that 'influence in EU decision making derive[d] largely from effective coalition building, both with other like-minded actors but also, inevitably in the case of sub-national authorities, with central governments' which contributed to further 'skepticism about the feasibility of a "Europe of the Regions"' (Bomberg and Peterson 1998: 219).

From the mid-1990s onward regional parties began to lose their belief in a Europe of the Regions, mainly because of the continuing weakness of the CoR, but also the unwillingness of the EU to embed regional recognition in the European constitution. Increasingly, they began to see the EU as a threat to regional autonomy, and many regional parties reverted to their original state-centred position, searching for ways to receive protection, recognition and resources not from the EU but from the state (Hepburn 2007: 234). In short, despite the fact that the consultation structure developed in the 1980s and 1990s is still in place and has a high degree of organization, it continues to give regional organizations a more limited say in European politics than they actually want.

2.2 Roma

In recent years, an EU consultation structure has been built around the Roma minority. One of the key players is the European Roma Information Office (ERIO). ERIO – founded in 2003 – works as an interlocutor for EU institutions and links those institutions with an extensive

European network of Roma organizations. 'Moreover, ERIO promotes the participation of Roma communities in decision-making processes at European, national and local levels. ERIO works to sensitize EU institutions to the importance of developing and ensuring the accessibility of equal opportunities for Roma in EU Member States as well as in Candidate Countries.'[6] In 2008, Roma consultation was further institutionalized when the European Commission received a request from the member states 'to organise, initially, an exchange of good practice and experience between the Member States in the sphere of inclusion of the Roma, provide analytical support and stimulate cooperation between all parties concerned by Roma issues, including the organisations representing Roma, in the context of an integrated European platform' (Council of the European Union 2008: 52). This resulted in the so-called Roma Platform, in which Roma representatives and representatives of the EU and national governments meet each other on a regular basis.

A driving force behind this recent development is the eastward expansion of the EU. This resulted in two related problems. In the first place, the accession of countries like Slovakia, Hungary, Romania and Bulgaria with a relatively large Roma population brought a large share of Europe's largest minority (European Commission 2011a) under the shared responsibility of the EU. Many Roma in those countries live in deplorable socio-economic circumstances and face systematic discrimination and exclusion on a daily basis (Maryniak 2004).

In the second place, the freedom of movement within the enlarged EU made it possible for East European Roma to migrate to the West. Countries like Italy and France saw a relatively large influx of Roma seasonal workers and travellers. In many cases, this influx put pressure on local authorities and provoked anti-Roma sentiments among the population. Moreover, the governments of those countries reacted with harsh and sometimes very discriminatory measures. Notorious examples are the Italian 'Roma camps' and the French 'deportations' of unwanted Roma immigrants. Some scholars argue that the old EU countries apply double standards, demanding strict application of minority rights in acceding countries, and simultaneously violating those very rights in the case of the Roma (Johns 2003; Vermeersch 2002).

All in all, the EU saw itself confronted with a very unwanted and difficult situation. Despite the fact that minority rights are securely anchored in the Lisbon Treaty and in directives on racial equality and free movement and residence (European Commission 2011b), both old and new member states behave discriminatorily against the Roma and anti-Roma feelings seem deeply entrenched among their populations. This led to the foundation of the above-mentioned Roma Platform and more recently to the development of an EU Framework for National Roma Integration Strategies up to 2020 (European Commission 2011a, 2011b). All in all, in the case of the Roma, the EU has firmly positioned itself as the protector of minority rights, neglected by many member states.

2.3 Jews

EU institutions do not behave as proactively towards the Jews as in the case of the Roma, though the European Union Agency for Fundamental Rights is for example regularly monitoring trends in anti-Semitism (FRA 2011). On the other hand, during the last two decades, Jews in Europe have founded several organizations aimed at lobbying the EU. For a considerable part, this lobbying is aimed at influencing the foreign policy of the EU regarding the Middle East peace process. In that sense it can be seen as part of the more general phenomenon of Diaspora lobbying (cf. Koinova 2010; Shain 2002). One of the players that tends to side more with Israel is the Centre Européen Juif d'Information (CEJI), founded in 1991.[7] Another much smaller organization, founded in 2002, is the European Jews for a Just Peace (EJJP), which lobbies the EU for a 'just peace' in which both Israel and the Palestinians are treated fairly.[8] Both are umbrella organizations representing many nationally based Jewish organizations. An important recent development is the foundation of the European Jewish Parliament.[9] This Brussels-based parliament represents Jews throughout Europe, both inside and outside the EU. This parliament could have a large influence on the future development of the EU consultation structure vis-à-vis the Jewish minority in Europe.

The identity of the European Jews is rather complex and has a national dimension (in relation to Israel), a religious dimension (to those Jews who are orthodox) and also an ethnic or minority dimension. Therefore, besides lobbying aimed at EU foreign policy, Jewish organizations in Europe deploy many other activities. For example, CEJI is quite active in combating racism in horizontal cooperation with for example organizations fighting racism and discrimination and Muslim organizations (van de Beek et al. 2010). Especially with regard to the religious dimension, Jews increasingly feel threatened by new or proposed laws and regulations that prohibit ritual slaughter or circumcision in some member states.[10] Hence, it is not unlikely that religious matters may play an important role in future EU consultation of the Jewish community. However, so far the religious representation of the Jews in Europe seems limited, with the Conference of European Rabbis as the most important, but a hardly visible, player (Foret and Schlesinger 2007).

2.4 Muslim Immigrants

This last observation is a direct link with the EU consultation of Muslim immigrants. Though the EU is 'certainly not a nation state' (Schmidt 2004) like centralist France, the federal German Bundesrepublik or the US federation, it is nevertheless a state-like structure. In its development, a form of laicité or separation of 'state' and 'church' has always been presupposed. Religion is not seen as an EU competence and left to the national level (Foret 2009; Pastorelli 2009). In general, EU legislative measures make little reference to religion (Steven 2009). In fact, EU institutions are often seen as surprisingly secular (Leustean and Madeley 2009), despite Jacques Delors's action to 'give Europe a soul' (Foret and Schlesinger 2007) and, more recently, the heated debates on the Christian character of the EU in relation to the European constitution (Menéndez 2005).

However, phenomena like Muslim terrorism and the subsequent 'moral panic … about the role of religion in public life' (Leustean and Madeley 2009), a 'growing islamophobia' (van der Brug and van Spanje 2009) and discontent in many member states about Muslim immigrants have pushed the EU towards active consultation of religious minorities. The Lisbon Treaty has a provision stating that the EU shall maintain an open, transparent and regular dialogue with churches, religious associations or communities and also non-confessional organizations in the member states (Houston 2009; Leustean and Madeley 2009). So far religious representations seem to be mainly limited to Christian churches, the Roman Catholic Church in particular. Other denominations are hardly represented in Brussels (Foret and Schlesinger 2007). However, in recent years religious lobbying has increased considerably. This resulted in 'the incorporation of religious communities as partners of dialogue in the EU legislation' (Leustean and Madeley 2009: 13) and 'political mobilisation in the European Parliament' (Foret 2009). Nevertheless 'their lobbying tends to be defensive, aimed at ensuring that established positions at the national level will not be threatened' (Foret 2009: 39).

Conversely, EU institutions actively search for religious dialogue partners (Geddes 2000). Foret (2009) relates this directly to the EU's ongoing quest to increase legitimacy. 'The 2000s have been a period of political decay for the EU', he argues, pointing at the problems with the referenda on the constitution, the eastward enlargement and the euro, and 'that is the reason why the EU has tried – once more – to tackle the legitimisation issue' (Foret 2009: 38). This all being said, one must conclude that Muslim lobbying in the EU is still in an early phase of development and small in comparison to its Christian counterparts, with the Strasbourg-based Muslim Council for Cooperation in Europe as its most prominent organization (Foret and Schlesinger 2007).

2.5 Non-religious Immigrants

With regard to the EU consultation of non-religious immigrants there is a less proactive attitude of EU institutions. Besides, the European Migration Forum (EMF) seems to be the only, somewhat influential NGO lobbying on behalf of immigrants in general, though there are several other organizations that represent minority and immigrant interests in a more general sense, such as the Human Rights Contact Group and United, a European-wide anti-racism network (European Parliament 2003).

3 EXPECTATIONS AND PREFERENCES OF ETHNIC ORGANIZATIONS REGARDING THE EU

The next task at hand is to examine the expectations and preferences of ethnic organizations regarding the EU. First of all, we look at the degree to which each type of organization is geared towards influencing the EU polity. This is done with the help of the answers to a Eurosphere interview question with regard to the actors the organization wants to reach with its actions (see Figure 7.1). In Figure 7.1, we are primarily interested in the relative degree to which the respondents want to reach EU institutions like the European Parliament (EP), the European Commission, the European courts and other institutions that are part of the European polity.[11]

This picture shows three striking trends. Firstly, there is a marked difference between immigrants on the one hand and regional national minorities – Roma and especially Jews – on the other hand. The latter turn out to be aiming most at influencing EU institutions, even more than mainstream political parties. This contrasts sharply with the low tendency to influence EU institutions displayed by the organizations affiliated with immigrants. Secondly, regional national minorities do not show an above-average tendency to influence the Committee of the Regions, which confirms the observation in section 2 that the CoR has little influence and dwindling significance for regionalist actors. Finally, among regional national minorities, Jews and Roma, we see relatively high scores on influencing EU institutions like the European Ombudsman and the European Courts of Justice and of Human Rights. This is an indication that those organization types have an interest in the EU as a

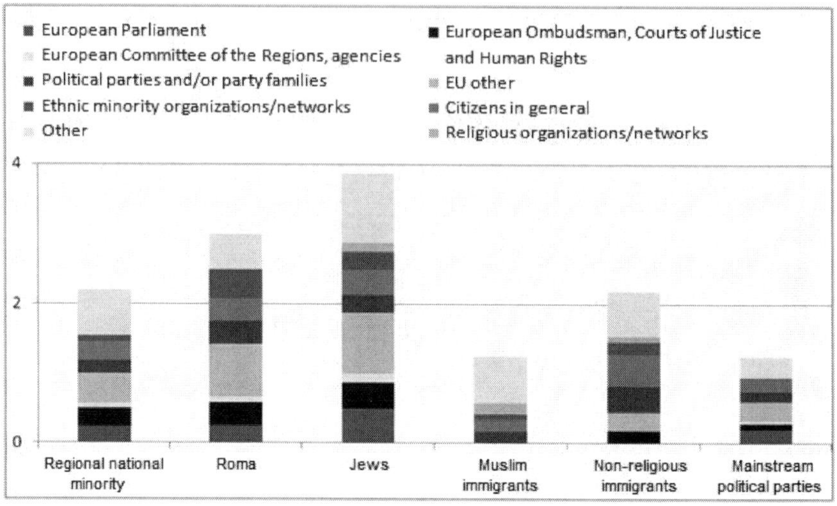

Source: Eurosphere interview database (see van de Beek and Vermeulen 2010, http://eurospheres.org/files/2010/06/WP_6_1-2.pdf, Question V5.10).

Figure 7.1 Which actors on the (inter)national or regional and local level the respondent wants to address with his or her activities

protector of minority rights, next to additional interests like increasing participation for the regions (regional national minorities) or influencing EU foreign policy and securing religious minority rights (Jews).

In order to find out which motive – the EU as protector of minority rights versus regional participation or influencing foreign policy – is more important, we look at another Eurosphere interview question regarding preferences of the ethnically affiliated organizations with regard to shifting power to grant irrevocable minority rights from the member states to the EU level (see Figure 7.2).[12] This question is of importance to all types of ethnically affiliated organizations. Here we see that Roma especially turn out to be strong proponents of a shift of competences regarding minority rights to the EU level, followed by the regional national minorities and non-religious immigrants. Jews and Muslim immigrants are not much in favour of the idea of shifting competences on minority rights to the EU level, with levels comparable to or lower than those of mainstream political parties.

It seems that Roma especially have a lot of confidence in the EU as protector of (their) minority rights. This may well be explained by their negative experiences with national governments – in both Western and Eastern Europe – in combination with the recent efforts by the European

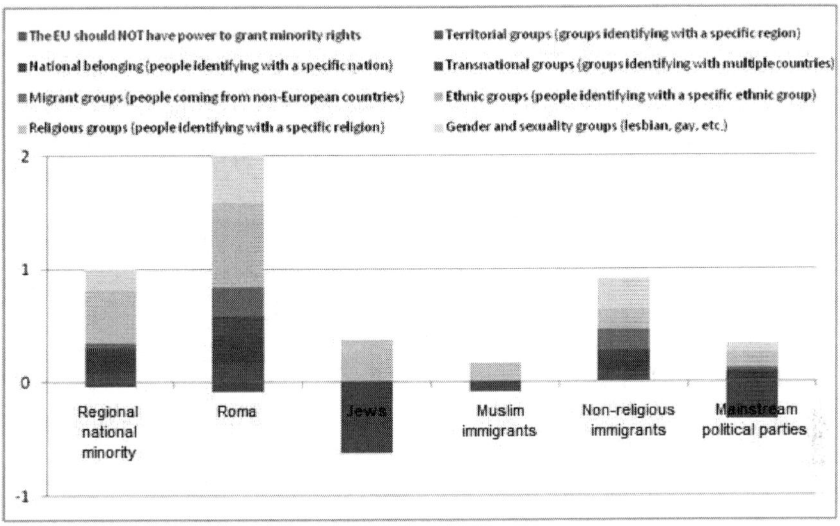

Source: Eurosphere interview database (see van de Beek and Vermeulen 2010, http://eurospheres.org/files/2010/06/WP_6_1-2.pdf, Question V3.5a).

Figure 7.2 To which groups should the EU have power to grant minority rights that cannot be revised by the member states?

Commission to put Roma inclusion firmly on the political agenda (see section 2). Finally, the moderately positive attitude of regional national minorities towards shifting power over minority rights to the EU level may be explained by pointing at the fact that the EU can grant new rights or enforce existing rights, while the costs of such minority rights (bilingual education, conflicts with vested interests) are by and large borne by the member states. However, despite the failure of a Europe of the Regions, gaining regional influence must still be seen as a very important motive for lobbying the EU. Finally, regional national minorities still 'are consistently pro-EU across time, space, and issue area' (Jolly 2007) and can be shown to be much in favour of a federalized Europe in which power is shifted towards the regions at the expense of the member states (van de Beek and Vermeulen 2011).

4 CONCLUSIONS

Remember that we set out to answer the following research question:

a. What is the structure of the EU consultation system for each of the five ethnic groups;
b. what do organizations affiliated with these ethnic groups expect from the EU; and
c. to what extent does EU consultation of those groups increase EU legitimacy?

We will now give an integrated answer to these three sub-questions. The only type of interest in our sample that comes close to the representational success of business and the professions is that of regional organizations and authorities. Moreover, regional interests are (uniquely) entrenched in the EU polity with the installation of the CoR. This has to do with the attempt to create a 'Europe of the Regions'. From the perspective of the EU, this move should by and large be seen as an attempt to increase the legitimacy of the European polity as a panacea for the persistent democratic deficit. One could argue that this approach had two dimensions. Firstly, in a more direct way, the introduction of the Committee of the Regions – founded on the principles of proximity to citizens, partnership between all levels of government, and subsidiarity of legislation and administration – would bring EU decision making much closer to the citizens. Secondly and more indirectly, by 'bypassing the nation state' (Keating and Hooghe 2001) and diminishing its power, the EU could achieve a more state-like image. However, this scheme did not work out very well, and much of its failure may be ascribed to the fact that both the EU and the member states did not really want to share power with the regional level and gave the CoR only an advisory status. As a consequence, the whole idea of the Europe of the Regions did not contribute much to EU legitimacy. Despite this, representatives of the organizations of regional national minorities in our sample are still positive about the idea of a federal European Union, which indicates that the idea of a 'Europe of the Regions' still lives on in some form.

With the Roma, there is a rather clear-cut situation. The Roma are severely discriminated against by 'old' and 'new' member states alike. This constitutes a painful inconsistency for the European Union, because the EU fosters a self-image of being a community based on human rights. For that reason, the EU has taken up the challenge of swift inclusion of the Roma minority. This has led to a moderately institutionalized consultation system for this group, with regular meetings of the so-called

Roma Platform. It seems that the preferences and expectations of the Roma organizations in our sample are rather congruent with this agenda; respondents on average expect much from the EU as a protector of (their) minority rights and are also geared towards influencing EU institutions. However, though EU interference in the case of the Roma will probably increase the EU's image of being a rights-based community, it certainly does not solve the democratic deficit.

The case of the Jews is somewhat different. Firstly, where in the Roma case the European Commission seems to be the proactive actor, for the Jewish case the initiative seems to be coming predominantly from the Jewish community itself. The recent foundation of the Brussels-based European Jewish Parliament illustrates this point. Furthermore, the Jewish case is more complex, in the sense that it is about minority rights, religion and EU foreign policy on the Middle East. Where it is not unlikely that EU institutions consult Jewish interest groups that operate on the European level on matters of religion or minority rights, it would be more difficult to imagine consultation of such groups on the EU's foreign policy towards Israel. So it seems that the balance in this case is less on the side of consultation and more on classic Diaspora lobbying. However, over the past few years, EU institutions have been more actively engaged in finding religious interlocutors, and this together with the interference of several EU member states with religious rituals may make for a changing picture and make consultation relatively more important. The preferences and expectations of the Jewish respondents in our sample seem to be partly congruent with this: they show a strong tendency to influence the EU polity, which is consistent with their Diaspora lobbying, but on the other hand do not have much confidence in the EU as a protector of minority (and religious) rights. Lastly, it is not easy to perceive any improvement of EU legitimacy vis-à-vis the EU population at large related to lobbying or consultation of Jewish organizations in Brussels.

Muslim immigrants are organizationally less articulated then national minorities. This may partly be explained by their shorter presence in the EU and lower socio-economic status. However, in recent years, the role of religion – and the Islamic faith in particular – has increasingly been seen as problematic, and this has put religion on the EU political agenda. Nowadays, a dialogue with religions (and also non-confessional organizations) is entrenched in the Lisbon Treaty. Hence, the EU's more proactive attitude towards religions and increased religious lobbying may result in a much more institutionalized consultation structure for Islam and other religions in the near future. Again, it is difficult to see how the

EU's legitimacy could be substantially improved by opening up opportunities for religious lobbying, because it does not solve fundamental problems like the selection and representativeness of interlocutors and their precise influence in the murky EU policy process (cf. Foret 2009).

The consultation structure vis-à-vis non-religious immigrants seems to be the least organized of those of the five groups at study here. Only a few organizations represent the interests of immigrants in general at Brussels. Also, unlike religious communities, immigrants do not have special provisions in EU treaties that open up lobby opportunities. Lastly, the EU does not seem to act much differently from member states when it comes to excluding third country nationals, for example at its southern borders, and hence it seems unlikely that the EU can gain extra legitimacy by a more proactive and inclusive attitude towards non-religious immigrants.

With regard to sub-question (c), we may conclude that the regional national minorities are best represented in EU consultation and the EU polity partly because of the influence of some very powerful players like Bavaria. On the other hand, the degree of organization varies immensely between regional players. The structure of participation and consultation built around regions must be seen as a first failed attempt of the EU to gain legitimacy. Today, the EU tries to gain legitimacy by Roma protection and by an ordered dialogue with (non-)religious confessions. Though this may increase the EU's image as a protector of minority rights, it is unlikely that it is going to solve the fundamental problems underlying the democratic deficit.

In terms of this book's overall theoretical approach focusing on the agonistic features of the European public sphere, the most important aspects of our findings are:

- the gap that we found between the EU's objective to legitimize itself, the EU consultation system as a tool of legitimacy, and what minority groups expect from the EU;
- the variety of different groups' demands of the European Union concerning minority affairs and protection of minority rights;
- the conflicting and contesting nature of different groups' preferences as to conceiving the European level institutions as a relevant addressee of their demands.

These three aspects may require an agonistic-pluralist policy approach from the EU's side rather than applying a single overall method to link different groups with the EU institutions. Although the regular consultation and lobbying system provides channels of direct vertical communication between the EU and the ethnic organizations that see the EU as a relevant addressee, such a system may increasingly put the EU in a referee position where it has to choose between the conflicting and contesting claims of different groups, specifically regarding the protection of minority rights. The current democratic deficit of the EU makes such choices all the more suspect. A linkage provided by the current consultation system will not be legitimate before such conflicts and contestations have been negotiated horizontally by ethnic organizations and other stakeholders themselves within the confines of an agonistic European public sphere.

NOTES

1. The term 'national minority' is a rather vague term. The International Covenant on Civil and Political Rights speaks of 'ethnic, religious or linguistic minorities' without further specification. The European Convention on Human Rights also uses the term 'national minority' without specifying it. More importantly, even the Framework Convention for the Protection of National Minorities does not define the term 'national minority'; this is left to participating states.
2. Note that different entities play a role in our research: the respondents, the organizations they belong to and the ethnic groups these organizations affiliate with. We want to analyse the differences and similarities of each type of organization, but as a matter of convenience we will often refer to the respondents or the ethnic groups involved.
3. See http://eurospheres.org/publications/country-reports/ (accessed 12 November 2011).
4. The numbers are from the mid-1990s.
5. Another form of cooperation of regional organizations on the European level is the formation of the European Free Alliance, a faction in the European Parliament that represents the interests of many nationally based political parties of regional minorities like the Frisians, Welsh and Catalans.
6. See http://erionet.org/ (accessed 9 November 2011).
7. See http://www.ceji.org/ (accessed 14 November 2011).
8. See http://www.ejjp.org/ (accessed 14 November 2011).
9. See http://www.eju.org/news/europe/european-jewish-parliament-elections-news (accessed 11 November 2011).
10. See for example http://www.ynetnews.com/articles/0,7340,L-4144496,00.html (accessed 11 November 2011).
11. The percentage of respondents per organization type who mentioned a certain answer category in response to the question 'Which actors on the (inter)national or regional and local level do you [the respondent] want to address with your activities?' The fraction of the total number of respondents of a certain organization type who mentioned a particular answer category are aggregated. Because the respondents were allowed to mention more than one answer category, the answer adds up to more than 1 (1 being equal to 100 per cent).
12. The percentage of respondents per organization type who mentioned a certain answer category in response to the question V3.5a, 'To which groups should the EU have power to grant minority rights that cannot be revised by the member states?' The fraction of the total number of respondents of a certain organization type who mentioned a particular answer category are aggregated. The answer category 'The EU should *not* have power to grant any minority rights to any groups' is counted as negative. Because the respondents were allowed to mention more than one answer category, the answer adds up to more than 1 (1 being equal to 100 per cent).

REFERENCES

Beek, J.H. van de and F. Vermeulen (2010) *Minorities, the European Polity and a Nascent European Public Sphere*, Eurosphere Work Group Reports, Work Package 6.1.

Beek, J.H. van de and F.F. Vermeulen (2011) Politieke beïnvloeding door etnisch geaffilieerde organisaties; winnaars en verliezers van Europese integratie en toenemende diversiteit, *Tijdschrift voor Sociologie*, 32(3–4): 387–413.

Beek, J.H. van de, S.A. van de Mortel and S. van Hees (2010) *Diversity and the European Public Sphere: The Case of the Netherlands*, Eurosphere Country Reports, Online Country Report No. 3, http://eurospheres.org/files/2010/06/Netherlands.pdf (accessed 1 September 2011).

Bomberg, E. and J. Peterson (1998) European Union Decision Making: The Role of Sub-national Authorities, *Political Studies* 46: 219–235.

Brug, W. van der and J. van Spanje (2009) Immigration, Europe and the 'New' Cultural Dimension, *European Journal of Political Research* 48: 309–334.

Christiansen, T. (1996) Second Thoughts on Europe's 'Third Level': The European Union's Committee of the Regions, *Publius* 26: 93–116.

Coen, D. (2007) Empirical and Theoretical Studies in EU Lobbying, *Journal of European Public Policy* 14: 333–345.

Council of the European Union (2008) *Press Release, 2914th Council Meeting*, English, 16862/08 (Presse 359), General Affairs and External Relations, Brussels, 8 December.

Crombez, C. (2002) Information, Lobbying and the Legislative Process in the European Union, *European Union Politics* 3: 7–32.

Elias, A. (2009) From Protest to Power: Mapping the Ideological Evolution of Plaid Cymru and the Bloque Nacionalista Galego, *Regional and Federal Studies* 19: 533–557.

Esmark, A. (2007) The Europeanization of Public Spheres, in C. de Vreese and H. Schmitt (eds), *A European Public Sphere: How Much of It Do We Have and How Much Do We Need?* Connex Report Series, Vol. 2, pp. 329–362, Mannheim: Connex.

European Commission (2011a) *An EU Framework for National Roma Integration Strategies up to 2020*, Communication from the Commission to the European Parliament, the Council, the European Economic and Social Committee and the Committee of the Regions, Com (2011) 173/4, Brussels: European Commission.

European Commission (2011b) *Working together for Roma Inclusion: The EU Framework Explained*, Luxembourg: Publications Office of the European Union.

European Parliament (2003) *Lobbying in the European Union: Current Rules and Practices*, Constitutional Affairs Series, Working Paper AFCO 104 EN, 04-2003, Luxembourg: European Parliament, Directorate-General for Research.

Faist, T. (2004) Towards a Political Sociology of Transnationalization: The State of the Art in Migration Research, *European Journal of Sociology* 45: 331–366.

Foret, F.O. (2009) Religion: A Solution or a Problem for the Legitimisation of the European Union? *Religion, State and Society* 37: 37–50.

Foret, F. and P. Schlesinger (2007) Religion and the European Public Sphere, in P. Schlesinger and J.E. Fossum (eds), *The European Union and the Public Sphere: A Communicative Space in the Making?* pp. 187–205, London: Routledge.

FRA (2011) *Anti-semitism: Summary Overview of the Situation in the European Union 2001–2010*, Working paper, April, Vienna: European Union Agency for Fundamental Rights.

Geddes, A. (2000) Lobbying for Migrant Inclusion in the European Union: New Opportunities for Transnational Advocacy? *Journal of European Public Policy* 7: 632–649.

Greenwood, J. (2003) *Interest Representation in the European Union*, Basingstoke: Palgrave Macmillan.

Hepburn, E. (2007) *The New Politics of Autonomy: Territorial Strategies and the Uses of European Integration by Political Parties in Scotland, Bavaria and Sardinia 1979–2005*, EUI Ph.D. theses series, Florence: European University Institute.

Hepburn, E. (2008) The Rise and Fall of a 'Europe of the Regions', *Regional and Federal Studies* 18: 537–555.

Hooghe, L. and G. Marks (1996) 'Europe with the Regions': Channels of Regional Representation in the European Union, *Publius: The Journal of Federalism* 26: 73–92.

Houston, K. (2009) The Logic of Structured Dialogue between Religious Associations and the Institutions of the European Union, *Religion, State and Society* 37: 207–222.

Johns, M. (2003) 'Do as I Say, Not as I Do': The European Union, Eastern Europe and Minority Rights, *East European Politics and Societies* 17: 682–699.

Jolly, S.K. (2007) The Europhile Fringe? Regionalist Party Support for European Integration, *European Union Politics* 8: 109–130.

Keating, M. (1997) The Invention of Regions: Political Restructuring and Territorial Government in Western Europe, *Environment and Planning C: Government and Policy* 15: 383–398.

Keating, M. and L. Hooghe (2001) By-passing the Nation State? Regions and the EU Policy Process, in J.J. Richardson (ed.), *European Union: Power and Policy-making*, pp. 239–255, London: Routledge.

Koinova, M. (2010) Diasporas and International Politics: Utilising the Universalistic Creed of Liberalism for Particularistic and Nationalist Purposes, in R. Bauböck and T. Faist (eds), *Diaspora and Transnationalism: Concepts, Theories and Methods*, IMISCOE Research, pp. 149–166, Amsterdam: Amsterdam University Press.

Koopmans, R. (2007) Who Inhabits the European Public Sphere? Winners and Losers, Supporters and Opponents in Europeanised Political Debates, *European Journal of Political Research* 46: 183–210.

Kymlicka, W. (1995) *Multicultural Citizenship: A Liberal Theory of Minority Rights*, Oxford: Oxford University Press.

Leustean, L.N. and J.T.S. Madeley (2009) Religion, Politics and Law in the European Union: An Introduction, *Religion, State and Society* 37: 3–18.

Marks, G. and D. McAdam (1996) Social Movements and the Changing Structure of Political Opportunity in the European Union, in G. Marks, F.W. Scharpf, P.C. Schmitter and W. Streeck (eds), *Governance in the European Union*, pp. 95–120, London: Sage.

Maryniak, I. (2004) Think Roma, Say Jew – You Won't Get Away with It, *Index on Censorship* 33: 58–63.

McAleavey, P. and J. Mitchell (1994) Industrial Regions and Lobbying in the Structural Funds Reform Process, *JCMS: Journal of Common Market Studies* 32: 237–248.

Menéndez, A.J. (2005) A Christian or a Laïc Europe? Christian Values and European Identity, *Ratio Juris* 18: 179–205.

Messer, A., J. Berkhout and D. Lowery (2011) The Density of the EU Interest System: A Test of the ESA Model, *British Journal of Political Science* 41(01): 161–190.

Pastorelli, S. (2009) The European Union and the New Religious Movements, *Religion, State and Society* 37: 193–206.

Schlesinger, P. and J.E. Fossum (2007) *The European Union and the Public Sphere: A Communicative Space in the Making?* London: Routledge.

Schmidt, V.A. (2004) The European Union: Democratic Legitimacy in a Regional State? *JCMS: Journal of Common Market Studies* 42: 975–997.

Shain, Y. (2002) The Role of Diasporas in Conflict Perpetuation or Resolution, *SAIS Review* XXII: 115–144.

Steven, M. (2009) Religious Lobbies in the European Union: From Dominant Church to Faith-based Organisation? *Religion, State and Society* 37: 181–191.

Varela, D. (2009) Just a Lobbyist? *European Union Politics* 10: 7–34.

Vermeersch, P. (2002) Ethnic Mobilisation and the Political Conditionality of European Union Accession: The Case of the Roma in Slovakia, *Journal of Ethnic and Migration Studies* 28: 83–101.

Vreese, C.H. de (2007) The EU as a Public Sphere, *Living Reviews in European Governance* 2(3).

Woll, C. (2006) Lobbying in the European Union: From Sui Generis to a Comparative Perspective, *Journal of European Public Policy* 13: 456–470.

8. Agonistic politics of the European Parliament: party and party group alignments and voting behavior

Robert Sata

In the ideal case, political parties provide citizens a real choice among competing visions of policy and/or government. They simplify the choices available to voters to enable them to participate in the complex democratic processes that characterize today's world. Parties are accountable to the voters, as parties can be held responsible for government performance at election time. Yet parties often fail to perform their roles: they can limit political competition to specific issues only, grab the benefits of the political system and prevent others from entering the political market. The complexity of the European Union only adds to the importance of understanding what contribution political parties have in this super-structure.

Ever since the Treaty on European Union (1992), political parties have been recognized as important factors for European integration. Most notably, national parties have formed European party groups to compete in the European arena, and access to the European Parliament, the Council or other institutions of the EU is mainly through the channels of party politics. Yet it remains unclear whether European parties managed to create a vertical trans-European public space linking national constituencies with the EU by aggregating political preferences to the European Parliament (EP), as many claim that a democratic deficit (Moravcsik 2002), as well as a cultural deficit (Benz 2006; Majone 1998), plagues the EU and its institutions. Critics claim that European elections fought on non-European issues prove that existing essentializing or nationalizing public spaces resist transnationalizing efforts, and national loyalties are often in conflict and contestation with trans-European discourses of democratization, inclusion and Europeanization.

At the same time, transcending nationalizing publics and public spaces does not need to translate into a demand for a unified European public space to enable citizens "to learn to mutually recognize one another as members of a common political existence beyond national borders" (Habermas 2001: 99). Transnationalization does not have to increase consensus or convergence; in fact new public spaces can be in conflict and contestation with the already existing public spaces that are often closed to new discourses. Agonistic forms of politics (Mouffe 1999), where different conflicts and struggles take a political form of expression, are natural for the sub-national and national publics that constitute European publics and public spaces. In this sense, one can think of the European public space as trans-European publics and public spaces that expand over different levels of the EU and co-exist, interact and contest with the other current public spaces and publics in an arena that is supplied by the democratic process (cf. Sicakkan, this volume, Chapter 1). This chapter investigates whether political parties and European party groups contribute to or hinder the democratic performance of the European Union; more specifically I examine whether a vertical trans-European public sphere of political parties exists and whether national- and EU-level public spheres are in conflict and contestation or rather consensus and convergence.

1 THE EUROPEAN PARLIAMENT AND PARTY GROUPS IN MULTI-LEVEL POLITICS

A rich literature studies European-level politics in order to examine whether the politics of the EU resembles that of the national political system based on party politics, and whether it gives voice to the citizens and transmits their concerns from individuals to national parties to EP party groups. Some note there is a close fit between left–right orientation of candidates and voters in European elections, and political parties do show a tendency to follow changes in their voters' preferences toward integration (Schmitt and Thomassen 2000). Skeptics point out that EU parties are expected to structure electoral choice across Europe; however, transnational cooperation often stops at the level of agreeing on manifestos for European elections, which are often little more than statements of attitude and play very little part in the election campaigns of the national parties subscribing to them (Smith 1996). Coordination among the EU parties is more observable when it comes to allocating offices in the EP and shaping policy outcome on the European level, yet the exact nature of the relationship between intergovernmental bargaining and party politics remains elusive.

Skeptics also argue that European party groups are not genuine parties but are dominated by national party delegations, and European-level politics are often dominated by actors other than political parties, given the Union's multi-level governance system. Accordingly, the EU is a "split-level democracy," where legitimizing mechanisms are split among the different levels of government (Schmidt 2006, 2009), resulting in a "split-level" party system (Lord 2004). Otherwise put, networks of political parties, civil society organizations, think tanks and policy research institutes often constitute a cleavage system of discourses and alliances that conflict and compete with each other not only at the EU level but also at the national level.

The EP, the single directly elected EU institution, has developed a stable European party system: Christian democrats and conservatives, socialists and social democrats, liberals, greens, the far left and the Euroskeptic parties all managed to organize themselves into multinational EP party groups; only the far right was less successful. This by itself is a proof of transnationalization of traditional public spaces. Three party groups are at the core of the EP, holding the majority of the seats: the European People's Party (EPP), the Party of European Socialists (PES) and the European Liberal, Democrat and Reform Party (ELDR). These party groups in the EP fulfill many of the same functions as their national-level counterparts. National parties tend to affiliate with party groups based on policy congruence (McElroy and Benoit 2010) or ideological congruence (Gschwend et al. 2012), although some claimed that Central and Eastern European parties' group affiliation was determined by political rather than ideological reasons and inter-party competition (Delsoldato 2002).

As the EP increased its size and power, its party groups also increased in importance (Chopin and Lepinay 2010). Nevertheless, party groups are not unitary parties but sometimes have very different members within their ranks (McElroy and Benoit 2007). Party group membership is also unstable, parties occasionally switch groups, and new members also join, as was the case with Eastern enlargement, which greatly increased the heterogeneity of the party groups (Hix et al. 2009). New members usually have to officially accept party group policy, but maintaining cohesion is a constant fight for party groups, since the success of their members depends on very diverse domestic political arenas, which might result in very different positions on policy among parties within the same group. Following Kreppel (2002), I perceive European party groups as democratic arenas, coordinators and mediators of the heterogeneous policy interests of their member parties (see similarly Finke and Thiem 2010).

The standard way to evaluate the EP is to examine the policy congruence between party and voter preferences (Schmitt and Thomassen 1999; Thomassen and Schmitt 1997). No incongruence between national party and party group preferences could be expected if the positions of the national parties and the party groups were identical, but this is seldom the case (Thorlakson 2005), as the two act in very different public spaces with very different publics. Studies rely on either national- or EU-level parties (e.g. Mattila and Raunio 2006), but focusing only on the national level disregards the interdependence of national parties within party groups, while emphasis on EU-level dynamics cannot account for national differences in European elections (Katsanidou and Lefkofridi 2011; McElroy and Benoit 2007). In reality, party groups are often heterogeneous, and in most cases there is lack of neat correspondence between EP party group positions and member parties' positions, although the four largest EP party groups and their policy positions correspond to the central tendencies of their constituent parties (Chopin and Lepinay 2010; McElroy and Benoit 2012).

When it comes to explaining voting patterns in the EP, most of the literature uses a principal–agent perspective and argues that MEPs have two principals: their national party (and its voters) and the European party groups. The dilemma is simple: EP legislators are elected as members of their national parties, and the typical voter has no knowledge of his/her MEP's behavior or the European party labels he/she belongs to (McElroy and Benoit 2012). Most MEPs maintain regular links with their domestic party (Scully 1999) and try to balance the achievement of three principal goals – like any other elected politicians: policy, office and re-election (Hix et al. 1999). This dual agent problem of maintaining discipline and cohesion for the EP party groups is well studied in the literature (e.g. Hug 2011; McElroy and Benoit 2012), and it does pose a challenge for any study attempting to decipher whether national ties or EU-level dynamics matter more in determining voting behavior.

While the sanctioning power of the EP party groups remains disputed in the literature (Finke and Thiem 2010; Hug 2011), most scholars claim that EP party groups enforce party discipline over MEPs by controlling the assignment of attractive parliamentary positions like rapporteurships or committee leaderships (Faas 2003; Hix 2002; McElroy 2001). Others claim EP party groups have few sticks and carrots available to discipline MEPs (Thiem 2006) and, if there is a policy conflict between MEPs' two party principals, the MEPs are more likely to vote with their national party and against their EP group if their national party has the ability to punish its MEPs (Hix 2001). Furthermore, with the increase of the powers of the EP, MEPs are increasingly more important for national parties for their potential to advance the party's policy goals (Scully 2001).

Another fact that studies of voting behavior in the EP must account for is that traditionally the EP is characterized by a cooperation of party groups and is often viewed through the lenses of consociational theory (e.g. Steiner 2002), featuring grand coalitions, proportionality and segmented autonomy with mutual veto rights (Settembri 2006). The high majority requirements laid down in the European treaties and the proportionality of both European elections and the distribution of internal offices among the EP party groups support well this approach. Despite the very diverse membership of the EP party groups, studies found high levels of party cohesion even in the first parliaments (Attina 1990; Hix et al. 2005; Raunio 1999). This is important given the limited ability of the EP party groups to discipline members (Hoyland 2006) that we noted earlier.

Furthermore, more recent studies note that voting cohesion has been rising across parliamentary sessions, especially for the three largest political groups (Hix 2002; Hix et al. 2007; Meserve et al. 2009). This increase of cohesion is continuous, notwithstanding the increase of the EP in its size and variety due to enlargement (Hix et al. 2007). While enlargement shifted the political balance in some significant respects, new members being more to the right and less enthusiastic about European integration, most of these effects were absorbed without leaving a lasting impact on the EP (Hagemann 2009; Hix et al. 2011; Hokovský 2012). Transnational federations like PES, EPP and ELDR are more cohesive than the party groups that do not possess these external party organizations (Hix et al. 2002).

2 PARTY AND PARTY GROUP POSITIONING ON EUROPEAN INTEGRATION

To examine what is the nature of the vertical trans-European public sphere of political parties, and whether there is a relationship of conflict and contestation between the national- and the EU-level public spheres, I study whether parties vote in the EP according to their support of Europeanization, whether they vote according to the preferences of their party group or whether national MEPs rebel against their party group to vote along their national preferences. I shall evaluate the workings of the 2004–2009 EP, focusing the analysis on its parties that figure in the

Eurosphere database, complemented by other survey data. The Eurosphere survey was carried out on the higher ranks of political parties in 14 countries of the EU as well as Turkey and Norway. Three to five parties were selected for each country, and for each party up to seven officials were interviewed on questions that inquired about their position towards European integration and the future direction of the EU. Although this is not by far the first attempt to measure party positions on European integration, the study stands out from previous studies because it surveys directly national politicians and not European politicians (EPRG MEP survey data), and it does not rely on experts' party evaluations (Chapel Hill data) or policy document analysis (Euromanifesto data), providing a rich dataset of party preferences on a wide range of EU-level policy issues.

I compile the European integration position for each of our respondents based on two sets of questions. The first question is "In which direction should the EU polity develop in the future?" allowing respondents to choose among multiple answers between more centralization of the EU and the dissolution of the EU. The second battery of questions asked respondents to indicate preferences for policies on free mobility, political rights, living in other EU countries, gender equality, rights of national minorities, laws on citizenship and immigration for both EU and non-EU immigrants, and whether these should be decided nationally, supra-nationally or on a sub-national level. Responses were coded and averaged in mean scores in order to obtain a single cumulative position for each respondent. These were then calculated for each of the parties by averaging its individual respondents' scores. Party scores were then averaged for surveys for a comprehensive score. Since the Eurosphere survey did not inquire about left–right placement, I use an average score on left–right dimension from the other surveys to display the party position on European integration within the same two-dimensional space that all other surveys employ (for details see Sata 2012).

One of the interesting findings of the compiled data is that most of the political parties in our sample support European integration, except for the following parties that end up on the anti-European dimension: on the left – ER, Cons, KSCM and SP; on the right – LN, FPO, DF and NOA. It is interesting to note that both mainstream parties in the UK – Conservatives and Labour – occupy a very similar neutral position on European integration, while the highest levels of support are found in SPD, PD, PP and PSOE, which is all in line with the findings of previous studies of Europeanization. Repeating the exercise for EP party groups' positions, calculated as the mean scores of their member parties, the non-aligned parties are the only ones that are displayed as being

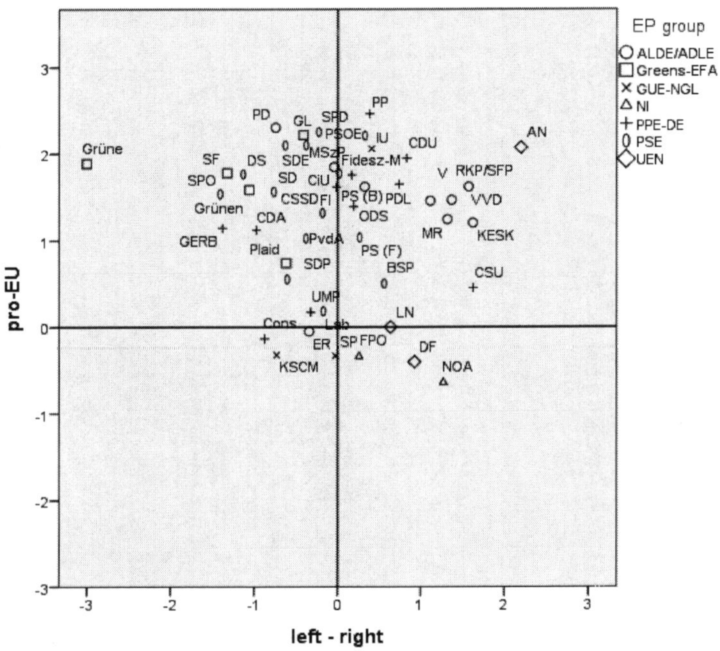

Figure 8.1 *Party positions*

anti-European, while the Greens show the highest levels of support for Europe, closely followed by PSE, PPE-DE and ADLE, while UEN and GUE-NGL display a more moderate support for European integration. Yet these party groups are not uniform, and there could be substantial differences among the different member parties. Unfortunately, there are too few parties in our sample to be able to assess EP party group cohesion, except for the two largest groups, PPE and PSE. Even for these groups we find relatively high deviation among individual members, meaning both groups show very similar levels of group fragmentation.

Aggregating the political parties for each country instead of the EP party groups, one has to note the selection bias in the Eurosphere survey that includes both government and opposition parties that should result in most countries being placed in the middle of the left–right continuum, as ideological differences between the selected parties should cancel out. This means that the left–right continuum should be skewed, though not all center positions for individual countries will be at the same position to reflect the nature of domestic preferences that vary across the European countries. At the same time, our aggregated country scores on the

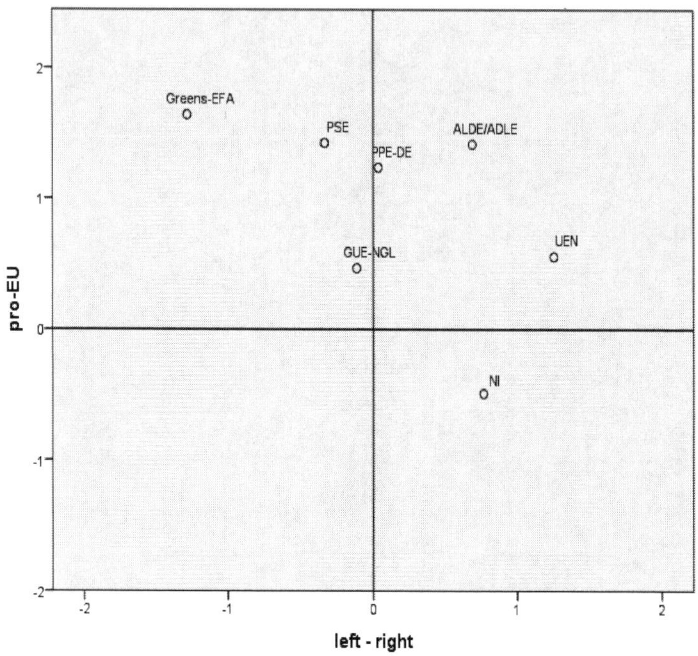

Figure 8.2 EP party group positions based on all surveys averaged

pro-European scale should give a much better prediction of the general attitude towards European integration for every country, as most of the Eurosphere parties are mainstream parties; thus they stand for a large part of the electorate and so display the most important views within each of the countries surveyed.

According to the results, the UK scores by far the lowest score on the European integration scale, as noted by many other studies (e.g. Fligstein et al. 2012), while Spain and Hungary are most in favor. All of the old member states score in about the center of our scale, occupying relatively close positions. On the other hand, new member states are divided: Hungary is at the top, while Estonia, Bulgaria and the Czech Republic score on the lower end of our group of countries. Similarly, there is a marked difference between the two non-member countries: Turkey is a strong supporter of European integration, while Norway is positioned together with most of the new members at the lower end of the pro-integration scale.

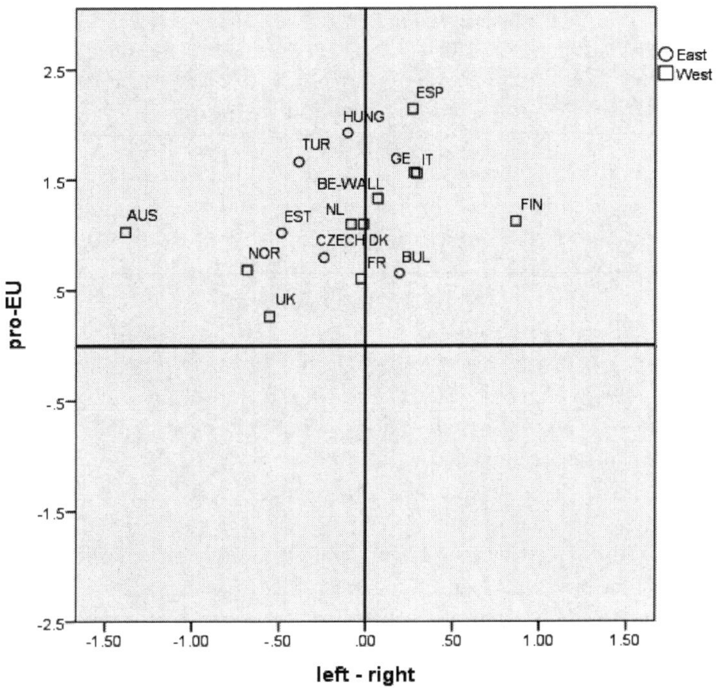

Figure 8.3 Country positions based on all surveys averaged

3 VOTING BEHAVIOR IN THE EP

I examine voting behavior in the EP to see whether MEPs vote according to the preferences on European integration of their own parties, the respective EP party groups or the individual countries. Studies of the relationship between European party groups and national parties usually rely on survey data (e.g. Farrell et al. 2000, 2006; Raunio 2002) and EP roll call votes (RCV) data (e.g. Hix et al. 2005, 2007). For example, Hix et al. find a strong indication for the importance of left–right voting that suggests the EP acts as a national political system. Yet most votes in the European Parliament are either by a show of hands or by "electronic vote" and secret ballot, where how each individual MEP votes is not recorded (Settembri 2006). Only about a third of all EP votes are recorded (Corbett et al. 2000; Hix et al. 2002), and decisions to record the vote are political and strategic acts; thus EP voting data can easily be challenged (Carrubba and Gabel 1999). Furthermore, Carrubba et al. (2004) demonstrate that the RCVs are not random and nor do they represent the legislatively most important votes, assumed to be the most divisive votes, but rather stand for signaling political positions (Thiem 2006). Yet others claim most RCVs in the EP are taken on resolutions, where the opinions of the EP are merely symbolic (Hoyland 2006). Moreover, RCVs are called on an unrepresentative sample of all votes, and disproportionately called more frequently by some of the smaller party groups (Carrubba et al. 2006).

Thus the strategic use of RCVs to enhance cohesion by monitoring or to signal a position relative to other party groups might result in RCV data being biased towards greater cohesion (De Clerck-Sachsse and Kaczyński 2009). Furthermore, the nature of the competences of the EU might affect the nature of the voting in the EP, as vital issues such as taxation, pensions, education or security are not in the genuine focus of EU policies, but rather issues such as consumer protection or healthcare are prominent and enable party groups to follow the logic of compromise in the EP without approving results that are difficult to sell to domestic audiences (Chopin and Lepinay 2010). Yet the adoption of the Single European Act and the increased legislative powers of the EP have led to intensified party competition (Hix et al. 2003; Kreppel 2002). A recent study found 87 percent of RCVs have been cast in line with the left–right dynamic (Hagemann 2009). This was confirmed by others, examining the most controversial issues, such as the Services Directive, where ideology was the main predictor of voting behavior, left–right splits becoming more common than the grand coalition between the two largest EP party groups (Hix and Noury 2009). In fact, any decision of the EP can be the result of a complex interplay between competition and consensus at the different stages (Lord 2006); as observed by Kreppel, real competition can happen at the amendment stage, while adoption of a final text is more frequent through "grand coalitions" (Kreppel 2000).

One should also take into account the high occurrence of near-unanimity votes in the European Parliament, when studying voting cohesion (Hix 2001). While in domestic politics votes are usually divided between government and opposition parties, in the case of the EP, votes stand for the opinion of Parliament as a whole relative to propositions of the Commission or the Council. Coalitions in the Parliament are formed on an issue-by-issue basis, rather than according to pre-arranged coalition agreements between either the political groups or national delegations. MEPs therefore have an incentive to join forces in an attempt to increase the influence of the EP by sheer strength of numbers (Hix et al. 2002). Furthermore, this is the reason why the EP often occupies positions that are more integrationist than those of national governments or parliaments (Scully 1999). This trend of the EP presenting itself as a unitary actor vis-à-vis the other EU institutions (Lord 2006) can counterbalance the emerging left–right spectrum of EP voting dynamics we have noted earlier (De Clerck-Sachsse and Kaczyński 2009). The dilemma for the EP is thus whether to deliver political outcomes acting consensually or to be politically inefficient but loyal to its ideological fragmentation (Settembri 2006).

I use RCV data despite the noted difficulties, since RCV data remain the only reliable and easily available source to researchers. For the purposes of this chapter, I shall examine RCV records for the 2004–2009 EP, made available online at http://www.votewatch.eu. For the 2004–2009 EP, any party group or a group of at least 37 MEPs was able to initiate an RCV (EP Rules of Procedure, Rule 160). There are a total of 6149 votes recorded in this dataset. To examine how pro-European integration attitudes might affect voting behavior in the EP, besides examining overall cohesion, I concentrate on constitutional and inter-institutional affairs votes, a total of 412 votes, and votes on the internal regulations of the EP, a total of 17 votes, as these areas of the EP's legislative action are most directly related to the support of European integration.

I expect that, when it comes to voting in the EP, non-attached political parties will be the most Euroskeptic and thus oppose further integration. Since these parties do not form any party group, one cannot claim in the proper sense of the word that they vote cohesively or not, though one can compare how often all non-attached party members vote together – which will be the measure that I employ in their case to compare vote cohesiveness across the EP groups. At the same time, I have identified the Greens, EPP, PSE and ALDE party groups to be the most supportive of European integration, and therefore I expect a high rate of vote cohesion for these groups in the EP.

Looking at EP party group cohesion rates, I find that all of the party groups vote exactly as predicted by their support of European integration. Accordingly, the Greens and PSE score highest in voting cohesion (both at 0.91), calculated for all the votes on all policy areas of the EP, followed closely by ALDE (0.89) and PPE-DE (0.88), closing the group of primary supporters of Europe. This fits well with the observed survey positions of the EP party groups that showed these groups as the most supportive of the EU and European integration. The same positions would predict a lower rate of voting cohesion for GUE-NGL (0.85), more similar to UEN, which only scores 0.76 on cohesion, while non-attached parties vote together seldom, as expected, their overall cohesion score being 0.44.

Table 8.1 EP party group vote cohesion rates in 2004–2009 EP

Policy area	PPE-DE	PSE	ALDE/ADLE	UEN	Greens/EFA	GUE-NGL	IND/DEM	NI
Overall cohesion rates	**0.88**	**0.91**	**0.89**	**0.76**	**0.91**	**0.85**	**0.47**	**0.44**
Agriculture	0.81	0.83	0.85	0.80	0.87	0.77	0.40	0.49
Budget	0.88	0.93	0.90	0.77	0.94	0.84	0.54	0.45
Budgetary control	0.84	0.94	0.94	0.82	0.94	0.84	0.51	0.25
Civil liberties, justice and home affairs	0.84	0.95	0.88	0.75	0.92	0.86	0.46	0.48
Constitutional and inter-institutional affairs	*0.87*	*0.87*	*0.90*	*0.68*	*0.87*	*0.77*	*0.58*	*0.46*
Culture and education	0.86	0.93	0.93	0.76	0.91	0.74	0.56	0.41
Development	0.85	0.99	0.96	0.85	0.94	0.94	0.45	0.48
Economic and monetary affairs	0.90	0.90	0.91	0.73	0.89	0.84	0.54	0.43
Employment and social affairs	0.86	0.92	0.86	0.75	0.90	0.94	0.47	0.39
Environment and public health	0.88	0.90	0.87	0.77	0.93	0.92	0.43	0.43
Fisheries	0.91	0.89	0.87	0.78	0.89	0.76	0.43	0.49
Foreign and security policy	0.88	0.92	0.88	0.74	0.90	0.82	0.48	0.45
Gender equality	0.81	0.97	0.87	0.72	0.92	0.92	0.44	0.45

Industry, research and energy	0.89	0.90	0.86	0.79	0.92	0.76	0.43	0.44
Internal market and consumer protection	0.90	0.88	0.80	0.75	0.94	0.94	0.45	0.39
Internal regulations of the EP	*0.66*	*0.71*	*0.65*	*0.51*	*0.68*	*0.40*	*0.41*	*0.37*
International trade	0.96	0.92	0.95	0.88	0.93	0.93	0.39	0.38
Juridical affairs	0.92	0.91	0.91	0.83	0.93	0.86	0.37	0.42
Petitions	0.86	0.92	0.88	0.77	0.93	0.91	0.52	0.46
Regional development	0.90	0.92	0.93	0.76	0.93	0.86	0.50	0.40
Transport and tourism	0.88	0.88	0.91	0.80	0.90	0.89	0.45	0.46

Source: VoteWatch Europe, http://www.votewatch.eu/.

Restricting our attention to constitutional affairs, the trend remains similar, only with a minor drop in cohesion rate for the leading groups: the Greens, PSE and PPE-DE each scoring at 0.87. Yet the first place is occupied by ALDE, its cohesion slightly increasing in fact to 0.91. What is more significant is the notable drop in cohesion for GUE-NGL to 0.77 and a further decrease for UEN to 0.68, which in fact much better confirms the prediction of the earlier presented spatial model of pro-Europeanization positions that depicted these two EP party groups showing a lower – or secondary-level – support for Europeanization.

The policy area of internal regulations of the EP seems to be one of the most decisive areas of EP legislative action, as most of the EP party groups display the lowest cohesion rates among all other EP votes in votes related to these types of regulations. Although there is a considerable drop in party group vote cohesion for all of the EP party groups, once again, these findings fit well with the expectations. The results show only minor changes among the forerunners: PSE at 0.71, Greens at 0.68, PPE-DE at 0.66 and ALDE at 0.65, and a clear differentiation between the prime supporters of European integration and those of secondary importance, as UEN scores 0.51 on cohesion, while GUE-NGL stands at 0.40. Non-attached members score only 0.34 on cohesion with other non-attached members.

When it comes to the individual parties, I have previously identified those parties that have the strongest anti-European position and as such are more likely to vote down proposals on European integration. This means that I expect these parties to vote against most European constitutional and inter-institutional propositions and internal regulations of the EP that would target further integration at the EU level. Similarly, the strongest pro-European parties should vote more in favor of such proposals. Using the same logic, based on the country positions presented, I expect that the UK parties will be most likely to vote against European integration, while Spanish and Hungarian parties should be the most consistent supporters of the EU. Notwithstanding this, the other East European countries seem to be less enthusiastic about Europe than most of the old member states, and this should be reflected in their voting behavior as well.

To evaluate how individual political parties vote in the EP, I examine how loyal the individual parties are to their respective EP party groups in EP voting rounds, that is, how closely they follow the voting line of their EP party group. I examine the loyalty of national parties to their respective EP party group for overall EP voting, for voting on constitutional and inter-institutional matters, and for voting on internal regulations of the EP. I have noted that only non-aligned parties were positioned as being clearly anti-European integration, and less inclined to vote together with other parties, including non-aligned parties; therefore we expect a lower voting cohesion rate for individual parties in this group. We also expect lower EP party group loyalty rates for those individual parties that positioned themselves on the anti-European integration scale, since this means a substantial difference between individual and party group preferences, as the latter have all scored on the pro-European integration scale.

Unfortunately, I am unable to calculate party loyalty rates for EP party group voting for some of the parties in the sample, as they have too few MEPs for meaningful calculations. Most importantly, this is the case for some of the parties that we have noted earlier as having a low preference for integration and thus would be primary candidates for low EP party group loyalty rates: FPO (Austria), NOA (Bulgaria) and SP (Netherlands) all have only two MEPs, and DF (Denmark) and ER (Estonia) have one member each in the EP. Furthermore FPO and NOA are non-aligned parties, and thus it is impossible to approximate loyalty rates, while we can check the individual MEPs' voting behavior for SP, DF and ER vis-à-vis their corresponding EP group. As a result of these difficulties, I cannot assess the non-aligned parties – FPO and NOA. However, as I already noted, the non-aligned parties have the lowest overall cohesion rates, which is in line with the predictions of our spatial positioning model of the EP party groups. For SP, DF and ER, I estimate loyalty scores by looking at the individual MEPs' scores, except for SP, where the two MEPs' scores are averaged. In these cases I estimate only overall vote loyalty rates, since there are too few cases on the other dimensions to make meaningful estimations based on the behavior of one or two individual MEPs.

Looking at the overall EP party group loyalty rates, not all of the expectations for low loyalty within the EP party group vote are confirmed. Thus, the single MEP from DF does have the lowest loyalty score among all respondents, yet this is only a very rough estimate that does not allow for generalizing. Only the Conservatives show the expected low loyalty rate consistently across all votes. Nevertheless, ODS scores very similarly, which is a surprise, as the party scored in favor of integration and thus should display higher scores. LN also displays a consistently low loyalty rate, and the two members of SP fare similarly on our estimate for overall loyalty to the EP party group on overall EP votes. The rest of our candidates for outlier positions, KSCM and ER, do not confirm expectations, as their overall loyalty rate is just about the average score observed for all parties in the sample.

Table 8.2 *EP party group loyalty for national parties in 2004–2009 EP*

Country	Party	Party name	EP group	Overall votes (%)	Constitutional and inter-institutional (%)	EP internal regulations (%)
TUR	AKP	Adalet ve Kalkinma Partisi				
IT	AN	Alleanza Nazionale	UEN	85.04	85.83	100
BUL	BSP	Koalicija za Balgarija (BSP)	PES	97.23	100	100
NL	CDA	Christen-Democratisch Appel	EPP-ED	95.90	98.54	92.31
BE-WALL	CDH	Centre Démocrate Humaniste	EPP-ED	94.08	97.82	91.67
GE	CDU	Christlich-Demokratische Union	EPP-ED	97.98	99.27	100
TUR	CHP	Cumhuriyet Halk Partisi				
ESP	CiU	Convergència i Unió	ALDE			
UK	Cons	Conservative Party	EPP-ED	74.24	56.07	76.92
CZECH	CSSD	Ceská strana sociálne demokratická	PES			
GE	CSU	Christlich Soziale Union in Bayern	EPP-ED	97.98	99.27	100
DK	DF	Dansk Folkeparti	UEN	59.91		
NOR	DNA	Det Norske Arbeiderparti				
BUL	DPS	Dviženie za Prava i Svobodi	ALDE	98.55	98.77	100
IT	DS	Democratici di Sinistra	PES	97.07	94.69	100
EST	ER	Eesti Reformierakond	ALDE	96.08		
IT	FI	Forza Italia	EPP-ED	97.77	100	100
HUNG	Fidesz	Fidesz – Magyar Polgári Szövetség	EPP-ED	95.23	99.51	100
AUS	FPO	Freiheitliche Partei Österreichs	NI			
NOR	FrP	Framstegspartiet				
BUL	GERB	Grazhdani za evropeysko razvitie na Balgariya	EPP-ED	98.56	100	100
NL	GL	Groen Links	Greens-EFA			
AUS	Grüne	Die Grünen	Greens-EFA			
GE	Grünen	Bündnis '90 – Die Grünen	Greens-EFA	99.26	99.76	100
NOR	H	Høyre				

ESP	IU	Izquierda Unida	GUE-NGL			
FIN	KESK	Suomen Keskusta	ALDE	95.80	95.39	90.91
CZECH	KSCM	Komunistická strana Cech a Moravy	GUE-NGL	94.13	92.54	76.92
UK	Lab	Labour Party	PES	92.20	91.99	92.31
IT	LN	Lega Nord	UEN	85.04	85.83	100
BE-WALL	MR	Mouvement Réformateur	ALDE	96.72	99.03	92.31
HUNG	MSzP	Magyar Szocialista Párt	PES	97.58	98.54	100
BUL	NOA	Nacionalno Obedinenie Ataka	NI			
CZECH	ODS	Obcanská Demokratická Strana	EPP-ED	77.55	56.55	76.92
IT	PD	Partito Democratico	ALDE	92.82	98.94	100
IT	PDL	Popolo delle Liberta	EPP-ED			
UK	Plaid	Plaid Cymru	Greens-EFA	95.50	83.50	100
ESP	PP	Partido Popular	EPP-ED	96.28	99.76	100
BE-WALL	PS (B)	Parti Socialiste	PES	95.79	92.72	100
FR	PS (F)	Parti Socialiste	PES	95.15	85.83	100
ESP	PSOE	Partido Socialista Obrero Español	PES	97.13	98.30	100
NL	PvdA	Partij van de Arbeid	PES	94.88	95.31	100
FIN	RKP/SFP	Ruotsalainen kansanpuolue/Svenska folkpartiet	ALDE	95.80	95.39	90.91
DK	SD	Socialdemokraterne	PES	92.07	93.35	91.67
EST	SDE	Sotsiaaldemokraatlik Erakond	PES			
FIN	SDP	Suomen Sosialidemokraattinen	PES			
DK	SF	Socialistisk Folkeparti	Greens-EFA			
NL	SP	Socialistische Partij	GUE-NGL	87.64		
NOR	Sp	Senterpartiet				
GE	SPD	Sozialdemokratische Partei Deutschlands	PES	97.70	99.02	99.02
AUS	SPO	Sozialdemokratische Partei Österreichs	PES	96.38	96.81	100
FR	UMP	Union pour un Mouvement Populaire	EPP-ED	92.43	98.62	100
DK	V	Venstre, Danmarks Liberale Parti	ALDE			
NL	VVD	Volkspartij voor Vrijheid en Demokratie	ALDE	94.53	96.60	83.33

Source: Compiled by the author based on figures available at VoteWatch Europe, http://www.votewatch.eu/.

Focusing on the votes on constitutional and inter-institutional affairs, our expectations fail even further, as only the Conservatives display low EP group loyalty rates. While LN also scores below the average, as expected, there are three other parties that have lower loyalty rates in these votes than LN. Moreover, while we expect a low score for KSCM, its results are again very close to the average loyalty rate for all parties. The same can be said about EP party group loyalty rates on internal regulations of the EP, with the exception that KSCM displays here the lowest loyalty, together with the Conservatives, confirming expectations, while the LN has a perfect cohesion rate, contrary to our expectation. Given these results, it is impossible to make definite conclusions on how party support for European integration affects the national parties' loyalty to their respective EP party groups.

Another way to examine whether party vote in the EP is guided by party preferences on European integration rather than their EP party group membership is to look at how parties furthest away from the mean positions of their EP party group behave in the EP. Parties most distant from the position of their respective EP party group will have the most different preferences from the EP party group average and thus will be most likely to rebel against their EP party group, which will affect negatively the voting cohesion rates we observe for the given group. In order to test this hypothesis, I have calculated how many standard deviations away each party's mean score is from its respective EP party group score. Accordingly, the most distant positions on European integration from the respective EP party groups are occupied by ER, Labour, the Conservatives, Plaid, BSP and UMP on the one side, and PP and PD on the other; therefore I expect these parties to have lower loyalty rates in EP votes. Nevertheless, our data strongly confirm this expectation only for the Conservatives, while Labour, UMP and PD do have lower overall loyalty rates than the average party, yet these rates are very close to the average and thus differences are not significant. Furthermore, our expectations for low EP party group loyalty are not confirmed for Plaid, ER, PP and BSP, which each score higher than the average loyalty rate in all the EP votes.

The results do not change if we limit analysis only to constitutional and inter-institutional affairs votes. Expectations for low EP party group loyalty are confirmed only for the Conservatives, Labour and Plaid – all of the UK parties. Similarly, when it comes to voting on internal regulations of the EP, the results display a surprisingly high loyalty rate for the parties, with only Labour and the Conservatives showing low loyalty to their EP party groups. The high loyalty rates observed here in fact can be explained by the overall low cohesion rates of the EP party groups in this domain, meaning that it is only in a few cases that the EP party groups do vote together in a united way, and thus the chances of individual parties voting together with the party group increase, since the calculus only takes into account observations when the EP party group has voted in a unified matter, ignoring all other votes.

I also examine an alternative approach of the relevant literature that argues that the ideological distance on the left–right dimension between individual parties and their respective EP party groups affects their loyalty to the EP party groups during EP votes. Accordingly, parties that should vote most often against their EP party groups are CSU, BSP, DS, GERB, PD, Grüne and SPO, as these display the largest individual differences from the left–right ideology of their respective EP groups. Nevertheless, only PD has a lower loyalty rate in overall EP voting than the average, and even the PD score is very close to the average position, which is contrary to the hypothesis of socio-economic ideological distance. Furthermore, the identified parties vote together with their EP party group more often than the average for both constitutional votes and votes about EP internal regulations, which again contradicts the hypothesis that the left–right divide matters for EP party group loyalty.

I shall evaluate the voting behavior of national delegations by examining how often individual parties from the same country form national coalitions during EP voting, when all the MEPs from the member state vote on a national line rather than on an ideological line, and at least one of the national parties votes against its EP party group. I identified previously those countries that occupy outlier positions with regard to integration that are most likely to vote down EP propositions. According to this hypothesis, building on our earlier findings, UK parties will be most likely to vote against European integration, while Spanish and Hungarian parties should be the most consistent supporters of the EU and have the lowest number of occurrences of national coalitions.

Unfortunately, I cannot compute national alignments for all the countries in the sample, as some countries do not have at least two national party groups, each of at least five MEPs strong, which would enable meaningful averaging of the voting records and calculations of coalitions (e.g. Denmark, Finland and Estonia). As the data show, the EP overall voting scores do not confirm the main expectations: while we expect the UK parties to be most likely to form national coalitions in EP votes, in fact only Germany has fewer national coalitions (given that the number for Bulgaria is only for the period 2007–2009) than the UK, contrary to our hypothesis. Moreover, Hungarian and Spanish parties are also more likely to form national coalitions than their UK counterparts, contrary to what their pro-Europeanization stance suggests.

Table 8.3 Occurrences of national coalitions in 6149 votes of 2004–2009 EP

Member state	Overall number of votes	Constitutional and inter-institutional votes	EP internal regulation votes
Czech Republic	663	91	
Sweden	644	6	1
Greece	439	8	3
Ireland	396	13	3
Italy	315	56	1
Belgium	304	3	
Poland	247	14	
France	241	3	
Austria	218	8	
Hungary	216	2	1
Netherlands	209	5	
Spain	180	1	
Portugal	167	4	1
UK	133	8	
Germany	110	26	
Bulgaria*	82	4	2
Romania*	40		

Note: *Bulgaria and Romania only joined the EU on 1 January 2007.

Source: Compiled by the author based on figures available at VoteWatch Europe, http://www.votewatch.eu/.

Our expectations are only partly fulfilled when we look into voting on constitutional and inter-institutional affairs, as Hungarian and Spanish parties formed only two and one national coalition respectively in votes in this domain. This seems to confirm that the more specific the EP vote, the better the explanatory power of the hypothesis that the pro-Europeanization position of the country can explain the EP vote of the national parties. Yet again, Czech parties form the highest number of national coalitions in this domain as well, totaling 91 coalitions, while UK parties voted together only eight times, contrary to prescriptions. There are a total of only 17 votes cast on internal EP regulations; thus the formation of national coalitions is very unlikely in this domain and therefore it is impossible to interpret the results meaningfully. Yet it is important to note that Bulgarian parties score relatively high in this domain, as we find Bulgarian parties voting together, forming a national coalition twice in this domain. This makes Bulgaria rather skeptical of EU internal regulations, as the number of Bulgarian national coalitions is especially high if we keep in mind that their membership is only for a total of two years vis-à-vis all the other parties' five-year terms.

Another way to test the hypothesis that differentiates among countries' EP votes according to their support for European integration is to examine the cohesion of national delegations in the EP – the extent to which MEPs from the member states vote as a block, irrespective of the EP party group they belong to. Accordingly, the lower the national support for European integration is, the lower cohesion of the national delegation in EP votes that can be expected, as parties will be most divided over European issues. Based on the same logic, one can also check the loyalty of the national parties to their party group, as low support for European integration should also result in low levels of loyalty to the party groups, loyalty decreasing the more pro-European the positioning of the party group is.

Results confirm expectations, as the UK parties score by far the lowest on the cohesion of the national delegation, meaning they seldom can agree on European issues. At the same time, Hungary has the highest, while Spain has the third highest score – well in line with their previously noted positions displaying both countries having the highest support for European integration. The more surprising result is that Czech parties score second lowest, yet this is not against our model, as Czech, French and Bulgarian parties are positioned at the lower end of the support for European integration scale. It is only the magnitude of the Czech cohesion score that is unexpectedly low, but its voting behavior is in line with our hypothesis. Germany and Italy should score relatively higher, based on their higher support of European integration, but notwithstanding this they also confirm the hypothesis. The only country that does not show scores in line with its placement on the pro-European integration axis is Bulgaria, and this is probably due to the fact that, as the latest member of the EU, its voting scores are calculated only for two instead of the five years used for all other parties.

The UK not only has the lowest cohesion score for its national delegation, but also displays the lowest loyalty for both PES and EPP among all other countries in our sample. The Greens enjoy a higher loyalty rate from the British parties, yet still under the average, confirming our expectations. Nevertheless, the hypothesis does not hold for ALDE, as the party group enjoys the second highest loyalty rate among the parties of the member states we have selected from British parties. On the other hand, as expected, Hungary and Spain both display not only very cohesive national delegations but also very high loyalty rates to the same PES and EPP, well above the average loyalty rate showed by our selection of countries.

Table 8.4 Cohesion and group loyalty of national delegations

Country	Cohesion of national delegation	National group loyalty to EP party group					
		PSE	PPE-DE	ALDE	GUE-NGL	Greens-EFA	UEN
UK	55.63	92.20	74.24	97.14		95.50	
CZECH	59.66		77.55		94.13		
FIN	70.90			95.80			
DK	66.02	92.07					
GE	69.58	97.70	97.98	92.65	96.02	99.26	
BE-WALL	66.50	95.79	94.08	96.72			
BUL	73.44	98.41	98.56	98.55			
NL	63.39	94.88	95.90	94.53			
FR	65.61	95.15	96.07	90.04		99.12	
IT	66.02	97.07	97.77	92.82	96.78		90.90
AUS	69.30	96.38	95.11				
ESP	74.72	97.13	96.28				
EST	78.58						
HUNG	79.60	97.58	95.23				

Note: *Bulgaria and Romania only joined the EU on 1 January 2007.

Source: Compiled by the author based on figures available at VoteWatch Europe, http://www.votewatch.eu/EST78.58.

4 DISCUSSION AND CONCLUSIONS

A quick conclusion of the findings is that, although the 2004–2009 EP saw an unprecedented increase in the number of parties whose views had to be accommodated within the different EP party groups, the enlargement of the EU had no effect on voting patterns within the EP. According to vote cohesion figures, Euroskeptic parties have been the most divided within the EP, and all other political parties of the EP largely vote together with their EP party group, though there are cases of national rebellions (see similar results in Hagemann 2009). I also find that differences among the member parties of a given EP party group with regard to positions on European integration and ideology do not affect the loyalty of these parties to the group; even the most distant member parties vote most often in line with the rest of the EP party group. This suggests EU policies – or the EP itself – have indeed managed to create a vertical trans-European public space that integrated national constituencies well into trans-European party groups.

Thus national parties play a role in aggregating citizen preferences on European integration, and EP party groups aggregate national preferences in the EP arena, which in turn play a role in determining voting behavior in the EP. Given the high cohesion of party group votes, one could argue that transnationalization does increase consensus or convergence among the different national political parties, at least at the level of the EU. Moreover, the results show that vote cohesion levels are directly related to the level of support for European integration; thus forerunners of integration support will show consistently higher vote cohesion rates than those EP party groups that only have moderate support for integration. I also found evidence that different issues will bring different party competition into the EP vote, and cohesion figures increase in the case of specific policies related directly to furthering European integration, such as constitutional and inter-institutional affairs or EP internal regulations, again suggesting that vertical integration of the national parties into an EU public space works best for issues that directly concern the EU.

Nevertheless, one should be cautious about the role EP party groups play vis-à-vis the role the national delegations play in determining voting behavior, as most national delegations are too small to have any chance of influencing the group's structure, and parties themselves depend on their participation within the EP party group (Lord 2006). This might distort political action in favor of greater cohesion of the party groups, which in turn might suggest that EP party groups are adequate substitutes for national parties for representing the European electorate, but I argue they are not because the party politics of the EU do not provide much link between European elections and voting in the EP. The legislative outcomes of the EP can be well aligned with the preferences of the EP party groups, but, given the great variety of parties EP party groups must accommodate as members, it is very plausible these outcomes will be far away from the preferences of at least some of the national parties. This will leave ample room for agonistic politics both within the party groups and among the different national parties, underlining that the emerged

European public sphere of political actors is not one of consensus but rather one of contestation.

The most important finding is that political parties in the EP vote according to how supportive towards European integration their country is. Domestic preferences predetermine party choice in the EP, as we have seen that parties of the most Euroskeptic countries display the lowest cohesion of the national delegation and they display correspondingly low loyalty to the EP party groups, while countries supportive of the EU show the highest levels of agreement and high loyalty to EP party groups. If domestic preferences are Euroskeptic, MEPs will often disagree about votes in the EP, while, if domestic public opinion is supportive of the EU, national parties will often vote together in the EP, irrespective of their EP party group membership or ideological differences. This suggests that the trans-European public sphere of political parties is very much linked to existing national public spheres, and the two often compete with each other, underlining the agonistic character of the emerging European public sphere of political parties.

At the same time, we have seen that the level of domestic support for European integration does not determine the likelihood of the formation of national party alignments within the EP. Although one would expect parties of the more Euroskeptic countries to be ready to oppose EP votes by joining forces into a national coalition, the data suggest that this is not the case. This again suggests that national publics and national public spaces are still important sources of cleavages parties will disagree upon, even on a European level. As a result, national loyalties are often in conflict and contestation with the different trans-European discourses, and the formation of national coalition voting is more issue-specific than driven by general attitudes towards the European Union and its policies, as predicted by the agonistic form of the public sphere.

REFERENCES

Attina, F. (1990) The Voting Behaviour of the European Parliament Members and the Problem of Europarties, *European Journal of Political Research* 18: 557–579.

Benz, A. (2006) Policy-making and Accountability in EU Multilevel Governance, in A. Benz and Y. Papadopoulos (eds.), *Governance and Democracy: Comparing National, European and Transnational Experiences*, pp. 99–114, London: Routledge.

Carrubba, C. and M. Gabel (1999) Roll-call Votes and Party Discipline in the European Parliament: Reconsidering MEP Voting Behavior, European Parliament Research Group working paper.

Carrubba, C., M. Gabel, L. Murrah, R. Clough, E. Montgomery and R. Schambach (2004) A Second Look at Legislative Behavior in the European Parliament, Working paper, Institut für Höhere Studien, Wien.

Carrubba, C.J., M. Gabel, L. Murrah, R. Clough, E. Montgomery and R. Schambach (2006) Off the Record: Unrecorded Legislative Votes, Selection Bias and Roll-call Analysis, *British Journal of Political Science* 36(11): 691–704.

Chopin, T. and C. Lepinay (2010) *Political Splits and Compromises in the European Parliament: Voting in Strasbourg*, Fondation Robert Schuman Policy Paper, European Issue Nos 189 and 190, 20 December, http://www.robert-schuman.eu/doc/questions_europe/qe-189-en.pdf.

Corbett, R., M. Shackleton and F. Jacobs (2000) *The European Parliament*, 4th edn, London: Catermill.

De Clerck-Sachsse, J. and P. Kaczyński (2009) *The European Parliament: More Powerful, Less Legitimate?* CEPS Working Document No. 314, Brussels: Centre for European Policy Studies.

Delsoldato, G. (2002) Eastern Enlargement by the European Union and Transnational Parties, *International Political Science Review* 23(3): 269–289.

Faas, T. (2003) To Defect or Not to Defect? National, Institutional and Party Group Pressures on MEPs and Their Consequences for Party Group Cohesion in the European Parliament, *European Journal of Political Research* 42: 841–866.

Farrell, D., S. Hix and R. Scully (2000) EPRG MEP Survey Dataset 2000, http://www2.lse.ac.uk/government/research/resgroups/EPRG/MEPsurveyData.aspx.

Farrell, D., S. Hix and R. Scully (2006) EPRG MEP Survey Dataset 2006, http://www2.lse.ac.uk/government/research/resgroups/EPRG/MEPsurveyData.aspx.

Finke, D. and J. Thiem (2010) Two Principals, Two Motives: The Amendment Process and Roll Call Votes in the European Parliament, Paper prepared for presentation at the Fifth Pan-European Conference on EU Politics, Porto, Portugal, 23–26 June.

Fligstein, N., A. Polyakova and W. Sandholtz (2012) European Integration, Nationalism, and European Identity, *Journal of Common Market Studies* 50: 106–122.

Gschwend, T., J. Lo and S. Proksch (2012) A Common Left–Right Scale for Voters and Parties in Europe, Paper presented at the University of Mannheim, 7 April.

Habermas, J. (2001) *The Postnational Constellation: Political Essays*, Cambridge, MA: MIT Press.

Hagemann, S. (2009) *Strength in Numbers? An Evaluation of the 2004–2009 European Parliament*, EPC Issue No. 58, Brussels: European Policy Centre.

Hix, S. (2001) *How Electoral Institutions Shape Legislative Behavior: Explaining Voting-defection in the European Parliament*, EPRG Working Paper No. 10, London: European Parliament Research Group.

Hix, S. (2002) Parliamentary Behavior with Two Principals: Preferences, Parties and Voting in the European Parliament, *American Journal of Political Science* 46(3): 688–698.

Hix, S. and A. Noury (2009) After Enlargement: Voting Patterns in the Sixth European Parliament, *Legislative Studies Quarterly* 34(2): 159–174.

Hix, S., T. Raunio and R. Scully (1999) *An Institutional Theory of Behaviour in the European Parliament*, EPRG Working Paper Series 1/99, London: European Parliament Research Group.

Hix, S., A. Noury and G. Roland (2002) *A "Normal" Parliament? Party Cohesion and Competition in the European Parliament, 1979–2001*, EPRG Working Paper No. 9, London: European Parliament Research Group.

Hix, S., A. Kreppel and A. Noury (2003) The Party System in the European Parliament: Collusive or Competitive? *Journal of Common Market Studies* 41(2): 309–331.

Hix, S., A. Noury and G. Roland (2005) Power to the Parties: Cohesion and Competition in the European Parliament, 1979–2001, *British Journal of Political Science* 35: 209–234.

Hix, S., A. Noury and G. Roland (2007) *Democratic Politics in the European Parliament*, Cambridge: Cambridge University Press.

Hix, S., A. Noury and G. Roland (2009) Voting Patterns and Alliance Formation in the European Parliament, *Philosophical Transactions of the Royal Society* 364: 821–831.

Hix, S., R. Scully and D. Farrell (2011) National or European Parliamentarians? Evidence from a New Survey of the Members of the European Parliament, APSA 2010 Annual Meeting paper.

Hokovský, R. (2012) The Integration of MEPs from Central and Eastern Europe into the European Parliament, *Central European Political Studies Review*, Part 1, XIV.

Hoyland, B. (2006) Left–Right and Institutional Preferences? EP Roll-call Votes in the Codecision Procedure, Paper prepared for the 3rd Pan-European Conference on EU Politics, Istanbul, 20–23 September.

Hug, S. (2011) Roll Call Votes in the European Parliament, Paper prepared for the ECPR General Conference, University of Iceland, Reykjavik, 25–27 August.

Katsanidou, A. and Z. Lefkofridi (2011) Asymmetrical Representation? Policy Congruence Gaps in the 2009 European Parliament Election, 1st European Conference on Comparative Electoral Research, Sofia, Bulgaria, 1–3 December.

Kreppel, A. (2000) Rules, Ideology and Coalition Formation in the European Parliament: Past, Present and Future, *European Union Politics* 1(3): 340–362.

Kreppel, A. (2002) *The European Parliament and Supranational Party System: A Study in Institutional Development*, New York: Cambridge University Press.

Lord, C. (2004) *A Democratic Audit of the European Union*, London: Macmillan.

Lord, C. (2006) The Aggregating Function of Political Parties in EU Decision-making, *Living Reviews in European Governance* 1, http://www.livingreviews.org/lreg-2006-2.

Majone, G. (1998) Europe's "Democratic Deficit": The Question of Standards, *European Law Journal* 4(1): 5–28.

Mattila, M. and T. Raunio (2006) Cautious Voters and Supportive Parties: Opinion Congruence between Voters and Parties on the EU Dimension, *European Union Politics* 7(4): 427–449.

McElroy, G. (2001) *Committees and Party Cohesion in the European Parliament*, EPRG Working Paper No. 8, London: European Parliament Research Group, http://www.lse.ac.uk/collections/EPRG/working-papers.htm (accessed 9 September 2010).
McElroy, G. and K. Benoit (2007) Party Groups and Policy Positions in the European Parliament, *Party Politics* 13(1): 5–28.
McElroy, G. and K. Benoit (2010) Party Policy and Group Affiliation in the European Parliament, *British Journal of Political Science* 40: 377–398.
McElroy, G. and K. Benoit (2012) Policy Positioning in the European Parliament, *European Union Politics* 13(1): 150–167.
Meserve, S., D. Pemstein and W. Bernhard (2009) Political Ambition and Legislative Behavior in the European Parliament, *Journal of Politics* 71(3): 1015–1032.
Moravcsik, A. (2002) In Defense of the "Democratic Deficit": Reassessing the Legitimacy of the European Union, *Journal of Common Market Studies* 40(4): 603–634.
Mouffe, C. (1999) Deliberative Democracy or Agonistic Pluralism? *Social Research* 66(3): 745–758.
Raunio, T. (1999) The Challenge of Diversity: Party Cohesion in the European Parliament, in S. Bowler, R. Farrell and R. Katz (eds.), *Party Discipline and Parliamentary Government*, pp. 3–22, Columbus: Ohio State University Press.
Raunio, T. (2002) Why European Integration Increases Leadership Autonomy within National Parties, *Party Politics* 8(4): 405–422.
Sata, R. (2012) *Party and EP Party Group Alignments on European Integration and Voting Behavior in the EP*, Eurosphere Final Comparative Study, http://eurospheres.org/files/2010/07/Eurosphere_WP8.1_Final_scientific-deliverable 2.pdf.
Schmidt, V.A. (2006) *Democracy in Europe: The EU and National Polities*, Oxford: Oxford University Press.
Schmidt, V.A. (2009) Re-envisioning the European Union: Identity, Democracy, Economy, *Journal of Common Market Studies* 47: 17–42.
Schmitt, H. and J. Thomassen (1999) *Political Representation and Legitimacy in the European Union*, Oxford: Oxford University Press.
Schmitt, H. and J. Thomassen (2000) Dynamic Representation: The Case of the European Union, *European Union Politics* 21(3): 318–339.
Scully, R. (1999) *Between Nation, Party and Identity: A Study of European Parliamentarians*, EPRG Working Paper No. 5, London: European Parliament Research Group.
Scully, R. (2001) *National Parties and European Parliamentarians: Developing and Testing an Institutionalist Theory*, EPRG Working Paper No. 6, London: European Parliament Research Group.
Settembri, P. (2006) Is the European Parliament Competitive or Consensual … "and Why Bother"? Federal Trust Workshop on the European Parliament and the European Political Space, 30 March.
Smith, J. (1996) How European are European Elections? in J. Gaffney (ed.), *Political Parties and the European Union*, pp. 275–290, London: Routledge.
Steiner, J. (2002) Preface, *Acta Politica* 37: 7–10.

Thiem, J. (2006) *Explaining Roll Call Vote Request in the European Parliament*, Working Paper No. 90, Mannheim: Mannheimer Zentrum für Europäische Sozialforschung.

Thomassen, J. and H. Schmitt (1997) Policy Representation, *European Journal of Political Research* 32(2): 165–184.

Thorlakson, L. (2005) Federalism and the European Party System, *Journal of European Public Policy* 12(3): 468–487.

9. Toward empirical assessment of the European demos and public sphere: comparing democratic value orientations of citizens and elites*

Martina Klicperová-Baker and Jaroslav Košťál

There is an intensive academic debate as to what degree the citizenry of Europe is a united or fragmented public and whether it deserves a label of *European demos*[1] (e.g. Lacey 2014; Risse 2014). The maximalists require real Europeans to manifest not just democratic spirit but also common identity and a European public sphere. Many feel that the fulfillment of all these requirements appears too strict for the EU. Also, the literature on the "European demos" typically treats it as if it were a binary phenomenon, a "yes" or "no" attribute of the European people: as if a demos either was or was not there. We counter this opinion by a quantitative empirical analysis: The European demos is operationalized in terms of democratic spirit, tolerance and civility; the public sphere is assessed by analysis of ideologies.

Democracies are conflict resolution systems; they are defined by constructive solution of multiple natural political cleavages. The purpose of this chapter is to assess the existence (or even degree of existence) of the European demos in the sense of a public that recognizes its shared conflicts and contestations and chooses to solve them in a civil manner. The prevalence of the attitudes and values of democrats should not be in a destructive, antagonistic clash but, instead, in an agonistic, benign competition. The purpose of this chapter is to assess the existence (or even degree of existence) of the European demos in the sense of a unified public or a fragmented public that is kept together by shared conflicts and contestations.

1 THE EUROPEAN DEMOS AND ITS CRITERIA

A rich discourse has developed concerning whether the citizens of Europe qualify at all as Europeans: Cederman (2000) paraphrases the words of Masimo d'Azeglio: "We have made Europe, now we have to make Europeans" (2000: 3); discussion continues as to whether the citizens of Europe possibly constitute a European demos – "a political community that facilitates democratic governance" (Gabel and Anderson 2001: 3). Some lament an obvious democratic deficit in Europe; for example, Scharpf (1999: 187) points out the triple deficit manifested by the lack of pre-existing collective identity, of Europe-wide political discourses and of a Europe-wide institutional infrastructure. Others hold a less alarmed view; e.g. Risse (2010: 15) argues that "the much-talked-about 'democratic deficit' of the EU does not refer to the lack of a sense of community among Europeans" but rather to the shortcomings of the disconnected European Union policymakers. In Risse's words:

> the complaints about the lack of a European demos are largely exaggerated. A European polity that the European peoples consider legitimate does not require a strong sense of collective identification. Multiple identities suffice, as long as the European project respects the heterogeneity and diversity of local as well as national communities. (Risse 2010: 8)

We concur with Risse that it is the respect for heterogeneity which is key for European democratic coexistence and for the ability to live within a supranational structure. Our search for a European demos then will focus on the manifestation of democratic prerequisites across Europe.

1.1 The European Demos as a Civic rather than Ethnic Characteristic

Is the palpable sense of collective identification important for Europeans? Are not social psychological prerequisites for democracy and civic-mindedness more essential for modern Europeans than appreciation of unique distinct characteristics of an exclusive, European identity? This is not to doubt that the feeling of a common identity, a conscious Europeanism, is significant. To the contrary, it may be so natural that Europeans do not even reflect on it, as Václav Havel (2000: 1) attested:

> When I ask myself: "To what extent do I feel European, and what links me with Europe?," my first thought is a mild astonishment at the fact that it is only now, under the pressure of certain political issues, or tasks of the day, that I begin to ponder this question. Why didn't I think of it long ago, in those

> times when I began to discover the world; to dwell upon it; and, to dwell upon myself? Was it because I regarded my belonging to Europe as a merely surface matter of little significance that was not worth troubling over, or even thinking about? Or did I see my European linkage simply as taken for granted, and therefore meriting no query, examination, or even articulation? More likely, the latter was true: *My entire background was probably so self-evidently European that it never occurred to me to think of it that way*, nor did I deem it important to call it European, or to probe into whether my thoughts are to be associated with the name of a continent. And, not only that – I have a feeling that I would have looked, to myself in my youth, somewhat ridiculous if I had written or declared that I was European, felt European, and thought so; or, in fact, if I had professed a European orientation in any explicit fashion. *Such manifestations would have appeared to me then to be very pathetic and pompous*, and I would have regarded them merely as a different, still haughtier version of the kind of patriotism that I have always disliked from national patriots. (Emphasis added)

Are not modern Europeans constituted by their open-minded civic spirit and respect rather than by an exclusive "strong sense of collective identification" which may be imbedded in them unconsciously? A non-dogmatic and non-fundamentalist, tolerant mentality is crucial for democratic citizenship and European integration. This is so because democracy is built on conflict, negotiation and perpetual compromise (Klicperová-Baker et al. 2007). Hence, civility (respect for others and tolerance to diversity) constitutes the necessary buffer which softens the inevitable democratic conflicts and disagreements. It may have the capacity to soften antagonistic conflicts (i.e. conflicts between enemies) into the benign conflicts which Mouffe (2009) calls agonistic conflicts (conflicts between adversaries).[2] Agonistic approaches see the notion of a public as a diversity of identities, ideologies, conflicts and contestations that work together as a glue to form a cohesive public.

Mutual tolerance and respect are essential particularly for the coexistence of peoples, many of whom have waged wars with each other just recently. (Let us leave aside at this point how tolerance and a sense of equality play into coexistence with immigrants from non-European countries and cultures.) Civic citizenship, civic nationalism and constitutional nationalism (Habermas 1992; Müller 2006; Sternberger 1979) are essential for the citizens of the EU, in a similar way to how they were for the citizens of other constitutional cultures such as the U.S.A., Switzerland or West Germany in the past.

1.2 The European Demos as Democratic Citizenship

Most of the relevant literature comes from political science and philosophy. Our intent is to complement it with a stronger accent on political psychology and its key concepts of attitudes and values. The democratic character is best illustrated by social psychological characteristics and predispositions to democracy (Feierabend and Klicperová-Baker 2015; Klicperová-Baker 1999; Klicperová-Baker et al. 2007). These include: *civility* (the ethos of a democratic society, which is a necessary precondition for a peaceful coexistence); *civic political culture* (political attitudes as specified in the theory of Almond and Verba 1989) and, as mentioned above, *civic, constitutional nationalism.* We tend to call this trinity of necessary social psychological preconditions of democracy the *Feierabend triad*, in recognition of the Czech-American political scientist who pioneered the field (Klicperová-Baker 1999: 10).

Hence, we address the European demos from the social psychological perspective of democratic citizenship. Our objective is to analyze the *constellations of democratic values and attitudes* expressed in the most recent data of the European Values Study and to determine to what degree European citizens and their elites qualify as democrats and deserve the "European demos" epithet.

Our research has both a horizontal dimension (analyzing geographic, international differences) and a vertical dimension (comparing the citizenry, parties and elites).

2 METHOD: MENTALITIES AND CLUSTERS

So far, most research and secondary analyses of the European Values Study (EVS) data[3] focused on comparison of populations (or their subsets) or on comparisons between countries. However, in this chapter we want to focus on coherent and representative constellations of opinions and values of citizens, and on identification of various types of political and moral schemata which reflect group mentalities or group characters across Europe.

Our approach has been trailblazed by studies of political personality, political character and political mentalities. Political personality can be defined as "the enduring, organized, dynamic response sets habitually aroused by political stimuli" (Lane 1972: 5), building on the knowledge of classic works by Lasswell, Riesman, Fromm, Adorno and Lane, who developed a typology of political characters (Lane 1972: 20–22).

The modern approach of mentalities was intensely elaborated by a team of the Institute of Sociology, Academy of Sciences of the Czech Republic, in publications by Černý (2002), Havelka (2002) and Černý et al. (2004). Group mentalities were defined as "relatively stable characteristics of group behavior, group evaluations and group orientations" (Černý et al. 2004: 8). Černý (2002) used the mentality approach as he studied attitudes to various marital lifestyles; he employed cluster analysis across nations, generations and education groups and compared various national and group mentalities. We used a similar method (Q-factor analysis) to identify various types of civic political culture and civility in the past (Klicperová-Baker 1999; Klicperová-Baker et al. 2003, 2007).

Our aim in this particular chapter was to extract prevalent constellations of attitudes and values based on the EVS and to identify similarities and differences among the mentalities of Europeans. The secondary aim was to consider the compatibility of the mentalities found with democratic citizenship – the European demos.

Analyses included European Values Study data (EVS 2011b) from 44 European countries [N = 63 281 respondents] gathered during Wave 4 in the period 2008–2010. Multiple statistical methods were used, including multivariate and bivariate methods: cluster analyses (k-means and hierarchical cluster analyses), multinomial regression to explore cluster interactions beyond mere bivariate level, factor analyses, ANOVA, post-hoc tests, and bivariate tests for contingency tables. Our analysis called for an insight into the relationships between a wide array of value orientations and in the second study also their relationship with political inclinations and political party preferences. In the effort to employ a single explanatory framework for a maximum of value orientations and opinions of European respondents, we applied cluster analysis as a very suitable method of classification which manages simultaneously to process variables with different formats if standardized, that is, converted to a Z score (Field 2000).

Cluster analyses were performed with 73 variables selected from the EVS data with respect to the underlying theory of the democratic European demos. The variables included especially: (1) measures of tolerance and benevolence, namely religious tolerance, tolerance of minorities, diverse neighbors and immigrants, tolerance of modern lifestyles (feminism, gays, divorce, abortions), benevolence to others, and identification with the underprivileged and the whole of humankind; (2) religiousness and traditionalism; and (3) democratic spirit and civic engagement (membership of civic organizations, voting, activism). Additional variables were used ex post for analysis of the resulting clusters (they were socio-demographic variables, opinions on public issues, political leaning of respondents and such country indicators as the Human Development or Corruption Index).

3 IDENTIFYING THE EUROPEAN MENTALITIES: AN EMPIRICAL TYPOLOGY

The k-means cluster analysis of European citizens' attitudes, values and behavioral tendencies (all provided by the EVS database) yielded a typology of five mentalities. For brevity, in Table 9.1 we provide only a sample of typical items which help to define the clusters. The interested reader can find a more detailed description of the methodology and technical details of analyses in a separate study (Klicperová-Baker and Košťál 2015), where we provide a more complete list of variables along with their means broken down by citizen clusters and with statistical significance of differences. The focus of this study is elsewhere, primarily on a description of the diversity and commonality of European mentalities.

The 63 281 respondents were subjected to k-means cluster analysis according to their 73 attitudes, with five resulting stable clusters.[4] Based on expressed attitudes and relevant demographics (illustrated by Table 9.1) we characterized the clusters as (a) secularized democrats, (b) religious democrats, (c) non-democratic skeptics, (d) intolerant economically deprived traditionalists, and (e) authoritarian (anti-democratic) religious radicals. The first two clusters reveal two distinct types of democrats. The third cluster appears a-democratic, as if its respondents were almost ostentatiously withdrawn from democracy. The last two clusters stand out by a strong but not necessarily tolerant traditional religiousness. The low tolerance of ethnic, racial, religious and sexual diversity shows them as problematic with respect to European integration and the European demos.

3.1 Secularized Democrats

This was the most secular of all clusters (only 38 percent believing in God). They expressed the strongest faith in democracy and also the highest willingness to express their views by voting, petitions and demonstrations; they were also the most frequent members of various civic organizations. Secularized democrats were more than other groups confident in labor unions, the Parliament and the environmental protection movement and least confident in the Church, the armed forces, the

Table 9.1 *Five main clusters of European citizens with exemplary European Values Study variables*

Exemplary (selected from 73) EVS questionnaire items	Clusters of citizens based on their attitudes and opinions, with values for each cluster						
	Secularized democrats	Tolerant religious democrats	Non-democratic skeptics	Intolerant economically deprived traditionalists	Authoritarian religious radicals	Average value	Eta
Attitudinal items							
Having a democratic political system is good	3.62 a	3.48 b	3.00 e	3.17 d	3.21 c	3.29	0.309
Political action: signing a petition	2.73 a	2.26 c	1.76 d	1.46 e	2.45 b	2.04	0.572
Political action: attending lawful or peaceful demonstrations	2.35 a	1.74 c	1.46 d	1.30 e	2.31 b	1.73	0.558
Justifiable: divorce	8.01 a	5.18 c	6.07 b	3.55 e	4.72 d	5.35	0.489
Justifiable: prostitution	4.56 a	2.37 c	2.83 b	1.48 e	2.22 d	2.57	0.418
Abortion if not wanting more children	0.83 a	0.31 d	0.71 b	0.27 e	0.49 c	0.50	0.449
Membership in associations	0.70 a	0.59 b	0.24 d	0.17 e	0.35 c	0.38	0.423
Most people can be trusted	0.63 a	0.46 b	0.18 c	0.14 d	0.18 c	0.30	0.405
Concerned about humankind	3.08 a	2.92 b	2.27 d	2.87 c	2.88 c	2.78	0.254
Satisfaction with your life	7.83 b	8.22 a	6.52 c	6.37 d	6.55 c	7.06	0.344
Most people try to be helpful	5.49 b	5.72 a	4.09 c	3.84 d	4.06 c	4.60	0.324
Believe in: life after death	0.30 d	0.74 a	0.23 e	0.71 b	0.66 c	0.54	0.445
Confidence: NATO	2.40 b	2.63 a	2.06 e	2.26 d	2.30 c	2.32	0.212
Would you vote at a general election tomorrow?	2.78 a	2.75 c	2.41 e	2.61 d	2.61 b	2.62	0.205
Believing in God (%)	38% d	96% b	56% c	99% a	95% b	80%	0.601
Concerned about sick and disabled people	3.66 d	3.78 c	3.36 e	4.01 a	3.83 b	3.73	0.237
Gays undesirable neighbors (%)	5% e	17% d	36% c	63% a	51% b	36%	0.447

Table 9.1 (continued)

Exemplary (selected from 73) EVS questionnaire items	Clusters of citizens based on their attitudes and opinions, with values for each cluster						
	Secularized democrats	Tolerant religious democrats	Non-democratic skeptics	Intolerant economically deprived traditionalists	Authoritarian religious radicals	Average value	Eta
People of a different race undesirable neighbors (%)	4% e	7% d	15% c	26% a	20% b	15%	0.237
Work should come first even if it means less spare time	2.68 e	3.32 c	3.16 d	3.80 a	3.46 b	3.33	0.311
Desirability of a strong leader	1.56 d	1.91 c	2.25 b	2.56 a	2.52 a	2.17	0.357
Desirability of army rule	1.15 e	1.35 d	1.49 c	1.89 b	1.94 a	1.56	0.376
Political action: joining unofficial strikes	1.65 b	1.12 c	1.13 c	1.03 d	1.95 a	1.29	0.596
Political action: occupying buildings or factories	1.35 b	1.04 c	1.05 c	1.01 d	1.68 a	1.16	0.533
Demographics (not clustered)							
Age in years	42.78 d	48.09 b	44.79 c	52.16 a	42.84 d	46.90	0.207
Educational level of respondent: ISCED (Q110)	6.50 a	5.58 b	5.40 c	4.21 d	5.52 b	5.31	0.342
Monthly household income (1 ≤ €150 … 12 ≥ €10 000)	7.21 a	5.83 b	4.24 c	3.07 e	3.69 d	4.66	0.561
Employed (%)	72% a	55% bc	57% b	30% d	54% c	0.51	0.285

Notes:
Significance of differences marked by indices, the highest (or lowest) mean value highlighted by shading.
Indices a, b, c, d, e mark statistical difference or similarity among values in the same row; values marked with the same letter are statistically similar; values marked by different letters are statistically different using multiple t-tests (post-hoc tests) with Scheffe procedure ($p = 0.05$).

Source: European Values Study, Wave 4 (EVS 2011b).

government and major corporations; they also had rather low confidence in the EU and the UN. With respect to nationalism, secularized democrats seem to best represent the concept of constitutional patriotism: what mattered for them was respect for the country's political institutions and laws and the ability to speak the local language; conversely, they had less pride in their nationality, ancestry, or length of stay (or being born) in the country.

The secularized democrats expressed the most decisive tolerance to diversity (e.g. to diverse neighbors) as well as tolerance to various modern lifestyles (they were most willing to justify divorce, prostitution and abortion). They also voiced high general benevolence and trust in others and a humanistic concern for all humankind. Politically, they had stronger than usual preferences for social democracy, the new left and other small or new emerging parties (as rated by experts).[5] With respect to educational goals, this group was particularly inclined to foster tolerance and respect rather than faith in children.

The secularized democrats turned out to be most affluent, most educated and most employed (73 percent), and contained the highest proportion of people of the "productive age." They were the most healthy and generally satisfied with life. In general, the secularized democrats tend to live in countries with the highest Human Development Index (HDI) and most favorable Corruption Perception Index (CPI). Approximately 50 percent or more of respondents from each of Sweden, Norway, Iceland and Denmark were in this category.

3.2 Religious Democrats

This group stood out by their benevolent religiosity. Their high trust in God (96 percent) was in harmony with the highest manifestation of satisfaction with life, with the most frequent trust in life after death (74 percent) and with the emphasis on religious faith as an education target for children. At the same time, they saw their fellow humans as most helpful and also expressed the highest levels of confidence in established institutions, such as the national educational system or NATO. They manifested a high democratic spirit; however, most likely because of their higher age, they showed less involvement than secular democrats. As a result of their religious belief, they expressed only reluctant tolerance of modern and alternative lifestyles; however, their tolerance of ethnic and sexual diversity was relatively high, second only to the secularized democrats. Religious democrats politically tend to lean to the center right, to established liberal or conservative parties (expert rating), or they are indecisive (the DK/NA responses). Very much like secular democrats, religious democrats tend to lean more toward constitutional patriotism than to ethnic nationalism.

In general, religious democrats tend to draw an upper middle income and live in countries with the second highest Human Development Index (HDI) and Corruption Perception Index (CPI) after secular democrats. Religious democrats can be found frequently among respondents from Ireland (and Northern Ireland), Malta and Switzerland, but a relatively high proportion are also present in many other countries (except Scandinavia, where secular democrats are most prevalent); they are less represented (in single percentage digits) in Turkey, the Czech Republic, ex-communist Balkan countries, Moldova and Ukraine.

3.3 Non-democratic Skeptics

This group manifested striking skepticism toward democracy: they showed little interest in politics, very little confidence in political parties and the educational system and the least interest in voting in elections (along with the highest skepticism regarding life after death). Their political preferences lean statistically more often toward the center and radical left (rated by expert rating) – as a probable result of their life in a communist or post-communist country – or they lean toward new or small parties or have no party preference. They tend to blame democracies for their failure to maintain order.

Non-democratic skeptics expressed very little concern about people in their neighborhood, the sick and disabled, and humanity in general, as well as about the environment. Consistently, religious faith, tolerance and respect for others are rarely among their educational goals for children. Reluctant to organize much in civil society, they also expressed low enthusiasm for participation in politics and little confidence in the Church, in the government and in the Parliament. Conversely, they had a relatively strong respect for major corporations. Although they expressed a distinct preference for state paternalism, at the same time they admitted the strongest tendencies to cheat on taxes. Overall, their style of nationalism contrasted with the constitutional patriotism of secularized and religious democrats: Skeptics showed relatively little respect for the country's political institutions and laws, yet they had pride in their ancestry and in the fact that they were born in the country.

The non-democratic skeptics expressed ambivalence about religion (46 percent with a religious denomination, 56 percent believing in God). This group was of average economic means and relatively tolerant of such phenomena as divorce, abortion and prostitution, fairly tolerant of gays in the neighborhood, but less tolerant of Roma. In general, the non-democratic skeptics tend to live in countries with high corruption (a low CPI), in the post-communist region, and represented a majority in Hungary, the Czech Republic, Estonia and Latvia.

3.4 Intolerant Economically Deprived Traditionalists

The people in this group manifested the highest level of religiousness (99 percent believers) and at the same time the highest political and social passivity (extremely low activism, and low participation in elections and in civic associations), both of which may be a result of their higher age, the highest of all the groups. Rather than appreciation of democracy, these respondents expressed a preference for a strong leader, for army rule or for religious leadership. They tend to have the highest confidence of all in the Church, the UN and the armed forces, and they have relatively low confidence in the police. Democracy tends to be viewed critically as a regime that fails to maintain order. With respect to the upbringing of children, the values emphasized are religious faith and hard work rather than tolerance and respect for others. Their religiousness is an obvious obstacle toward justification of abortion, prostitution, divorce or a gay lifestyle; their traditionalism is a ground for suspicion of novelty, for example diversity in the neighborhood. Still, it should be noted that these respondents do show a considerable concern and benevolence toward their immediate neighbors and toward other under-privileged groups (the sick and disabled).

This cluster tends to unify respondents who are economically challenged, yet they profess a strong work ethic (12 percent are homemakers, 11 percent are unemployed, others are self-employed or in small businesses). Politically, they manifest higher than statistically expected preferences for radical (left or right) political parties (rated by experts) or have no party preference. In general, the traditionalists tend to live in countries with the highest corruption (lowest CPI). Most respondents from Turkey, Romania, Northern Cyprus and Moldova were in this category.

3.5 Authoritarian (Anti-democratic) Religious Radicals

The individuals in this group are mostly religious (96 percent) (only slightly less than the previous cluster) and also little tolerant of such phenomena as divorce, prostitution and gays; however, in contrast to the former cluster, these radicals are significantly younger and more politically active (they also include a relatively high percentage of students and the unemployed). They are more likely than any other group to engage in the most radical political activities, such as taking part in an unofficial strike or occupation of buildings. These respondents reported a high dissatisfaction with the way democracy had developed in their country (blaming it, similarly to the traditionalists, for failing to maintain order and to foster the economy), and often intimated distinctly anti-democratic attitudes and a preference for army rule or a strong leader instead of a democratic political system. The authoritarian religious radicals tend to have the lowest confidence of all in the police and the justice system and relatively high confidence in labor unions. Their nationalist pride is very much related to their ancestry and to their birth or a long stay in the country, and less to language or the country's political institutions and laws. Their political preferences mostly include the right center, radical right and regional minorities (expert rating).

This value orientation is typically represented in higher numbers in countries with the lowest Human Development Index (HDI), in countries with very high corruption (low CPI) and in the Balkan region of former Yugoslavia: Macedonia (with over 48 percent respondents in this cluster), Kosovo, Bosnia and Herzegovina, Croatia, Serbia, Montenegro, Northern Cyprus and Poland.

4 SIMILARITY AND DIVERSITY OF THE EUROPEAN MENTALITIES

This cluster analysis revealed attitudes which both unite and divide Europeans. Five different clusters of mentalities were identified, the incidence of which significantly differed both across the countries and with respect to the social status of the respondents.

4.1 The Horizontal Perspective: National Differences

Although all nations shared the five mentalities, we found varying frequency of their international occurrence. As Table 9.2 attests, the secular democrats are concentrated mostly in the Scandinavian North-west, and religious democrats prevail in Western Europe from Ireland to Spain. Nevertheless, these secular and religious democrats were identified in all the other countries in Europe as well, although in smaller numbers. The democrats constitute an international mentality which can be viewed as the European demos, a socio-psychological basis of European integration and also a basis for democratic peace (Pax democratica – Feierabend and Klicperová-Baker 2015).

Table 9.2 Incidence of social-political mentalities across European countries and territories

	Secularized democrats	Religious democrats	Non-democratic skeptics	Intolerant economically deprived traditionalists	Authoritarian (anti-democratic) religious radicals
Albania	1.6%	11.3%	29.6%	41.8%	15.7%
Austria	21.0%	32.6%	25.5%	12.4%	8.5%
Belarus	2.7%	18.4%	36.7%	36.3%	5.9%
Belgium	34.6%	29.5%	22.7%	7.9%	5.3%
Bosnia and Herzegovina	0.9%	8.4%	17.5%	33.9%	39.4%
Bulgaria	3.0%	6.6%	38.9%	35.7%	15.8%
Croatia	8.5%	15.6%	20.2%	23.9%	31.7%
Cyprus	1.3%	31.6%	4.7%	54.7%	7.6%
Northern Cyprus	1.0%	15.2%	7.6%	54.5%	21.7%
Czech Republic	19.2%	9.9%	56.2%	8.4%	6.3%
Denmark	63.3%	31.8%	2.5%	0.9%	1.4%
Estonia	11.7%	13.7%	57.1%	12.4%	5.1%
Finland	41.1%	31.3%	20.1%	3.6%	3.8%
France	46.1%	16.4%	22.7%	4.6%	10.2%
Germany	28.7%	37.7%	20.5%	8.0%	5.2%
Great Britain	24.1%	32.6%	31.0%	6.1%	6.1%
Greece	10.2%	23.3%	11.5%	39.1%	16.0%
Hungary	4.0%	10.8%	56.5%	25.2%	3.5%
Iceland	48.7%	38.6%	7.2%	1.7%	3.8%
Ireland	11.5%	56.8%	10.9%	11.4%	9.4%
Italy	16.0%	31.6%	12.3%	25.4%	14.7%
Kosovo	0.5%	22.2%	2.6%	35.4%	39.2%
Latvia	4.0%	12.6%	55.5%	17.5%	10.4%
Lithuania	3.4%	11.3%	41.5%	27.8%	16.0%
Luxembourg	34.4%	38.4%	14.3%	6.9%	6.0%
Macedonia	4.1%	12.5%	7.0%	29.6%	46.8%
Malta	2.0%	46.9%	4.7%	32.3%	14.2%
Moldova	0.6%	6.0%	8.4%	64.6%	20.4%
Montenegro	3.5%	11.6%	25.2%	37.2%	22.5%
Netherlands	48.3%	34.4%	12.4%	3.1%	1.8%

Table 9.2 (continued)

	Secularized democrats	Religious democrats	Non-democratic skeptics	Intolerant economically deprived traditionalists	Authoritarian (anti-democratic) religious radicals
Northern Ireland	8.9%	48.2%	20.3%	11.4%	11.2%
Norway	48.0%	42.5%	6.8%	1.1%	1.8%
Poland	4.5%	24.2%	13.1%	38.4%	19.8%
Portugal	7.8%	23.9%	24.9%	26.3%	17.3%
Romania	0.6%	16.9%	14.2%	57.4%	10.9%
Russian Federation	2.8%	10.2%	44.5%	33.3%	9.2%
Serbia	3.6%	5.8%	28.0%	33.4%	29.3%
Slovakia	7.4%	27.8%	28.9%	30.4%	5.5%
Slovenia	22.5%	22.1%	29.6%	15.4%	10.4%
Spain	32.2%	24.9%	20.0%	15.4%	7.5%
Sweden	63.2%	17.3%	14.5%	1.3%	3.7%
Switzerland	36.7%	45.5%	9.0%	4.9%	4.0%
Turkey	0.5%	5.6%	0.9%	80.2%	12.7%
Ukraine	1.5%	6.5%	32.4%	44.0%	15.5%
Total	16.9%	20.9%	24.9%	26.8%	10.5%

Note: Shaded cells highlight results of the sign test, sig. <0.01; CHI^2=323590.670, df=172, sig. <0.001, and Cramer's V=0.356. Weighted by population size.

Source: European Values Study, Wave 4 (EVS 2011b).

4.2 The Vertical Perspective: Social Status Differences (Elite versus Non-elite)

The diversity in attitudes was also identified with respect to the social status of respondents. The respondents with the highest socio-economic status, the higher professionals, top managers and politicians were clearly identified in the EVS study by the International Standard Classification of Occupations (ISCO). Table 9.3 shows that, among the elite, democrats significantly prevailed and formed the majority. Coincidentally, secular and religious democrats were represented in the same proportion. In contrast, non-democratic skepticism and intolerant traditionalism were underrepresented among the elite. Anti-democratic religious radicalism turned out to be the only mentality which did not seem to differ in occurrence between elites and non-elites.

Table 9.3 Mentalities broken down by the social status of respondents

Participants	Mentalities: clusters based on their EVS attitudes, opinions and behavior				
	Secularized democrats	Religious democrats	Non-democratic skeptics	Intolerant economically deprived traditionalists	Authoritarian (anti-democratic) religious radicals
Elites	**27.1%**	**25.9%**	20.7%	16.6%	9.7%
Others	14.5%	19.7%	**25.9%**	**29.2%**	10.7%
Total	16.9%	20.9%	24.9%	26.8%	10.5%

Note: Differences were tested by Student's t-test of percentages; significant differences are highlighted. Chi square was significant at the level <0.000. Bold values denote higher than expected frequency counts based on a sign test ($p \leq 0.01$). Percentages were weighted by population size.

The EVS study is based on a solid methodological basis, yet elites do not seem to be ideally represented among the respondents in all countries. (Some countries lacked interviews with politicians; other countries had top elites overrepresented. Thus, elites in Germany seemed to get fewer opportunities, while elites from Turkey, Greece and Macedonia were overrepresented.) For that reason we refrain from listing exact percentages of democratic elites in every country and, instead, present an illustration in Figure 9.1 which demonstrates that elites express democratic attitudes (secular or religious) more often that the rest of the citizenry in every nation across Europe.

Democrats (secular or religious) appear to constitute only a minority of the general population, approximately 38 percent. However, the impact of democrats is higher, as the democrats are prevalent amongst the elites; that is, they constitute a distinct majority among managers, professionals and politicians. The democrats constitute at least a 53 percent majority among the elites, even among many post-communist states which have a long recent history of having been dominated by anti-democratic top elites.

The elites are close to power and tend to be decision-makers, negotiators and mediators. They have the opportunity to use democratic attitudes, tolerance and benevolence in their public conduct. And many do so, even if the top politicians use their influence in a different manner.

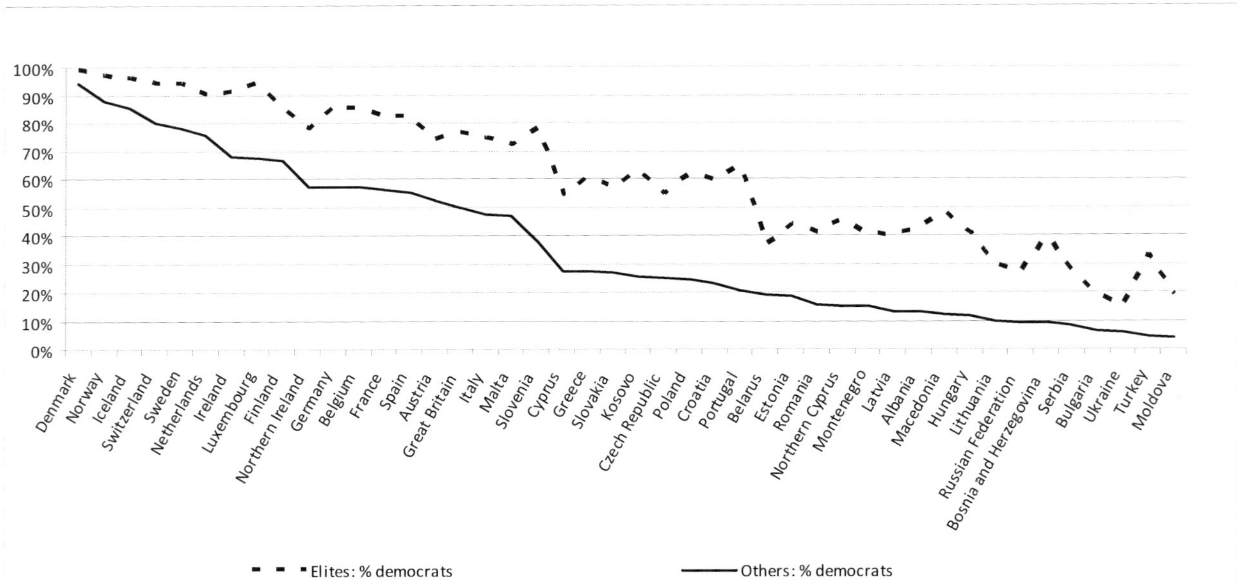

Figure 9.1 *Democrats (secular and religious democrats combined) among the elite and non-elite across European countries*

5 IN SEARCH OF THE EUROPEAN PUBLIC

Tolerant and benevolent democratic attitudes manifested by a substantial portion of Europeans represent a disposition not just for democracy in their respective countries but also for democracy across the region. Theoretically speaking, the shared democratic mentality across Europe allows us to speak of a European demos and European public.

Our analysis of various European socio-political mentalities was complemented by a search for shared political ideologies. The assumption was that across Europe there might be a nascent shared network, for example of social democrats, liberals, apoliticals and so on. After all, like-minded politicians group together in the European Parliament, and right-wing radicals also tend to reach out across national borders.

We subjected the same respondents and same variables to an additional analysis: This time our unit was not an individual citizen but a representative partisan or, more precisely, a representative of a characteristic electoral case. Those electoral cases were altogether 302, as for every nation they included: a typical sympathizer of every major political party; a typical voter of other parties; a typical respondent who liked no party; and an average DK/NA respondent. The number of electoral prototypes was only 302, which allowed us to use hierarchical cluster analysis. (The detailed methodology is described in the study by Košťál and Klicperová-Baker 2015.)

While the analyses of individual citizens' mentalities (described above) showed both national specificities and pan-European international similarities, the analysis of partisan ideologies yielded a different picture. The cluster analysis of partisan (along with non-partisan) ideologies identified three distinct regional types of democracy: active, moderate and passive democracy, corresponding to (a) Northwestern Europe, (b) Central and Southwestern Europe, and (c) Southeastern Europe.

We failed to find pan-European ideologies which would cross national and regional borders the way individual mentalities did. In general, partisan ideologies stayed confined within national borders or the borders of one of the three above-listed European regions. Thus, the ideologies very much equaled the stereotypes of (a) a robust bloc of affluent and civilly active democracies of Northwestern Europe, (b) a bloc of somewhat larger size which unites mid-rich, post-totalitarian and often frustrating moderate democracies, and (c) a small bloc of poor and strongly religious passive democracies (see Košťál and Klicperová-Baker 2015). The only marginal exceptions appeared when sympathizers of extreme "vanguard or laggard" parties crossed into the neighboring region. Thus, some Czech and Slovak party ideologies "progressed" from their region of moderate democracy to a more democratically advanced region, to the active democracy region of Northwestern Europe. Conversely, in one case the ideology of an ethnic minority geographically belonging to the region of moderate democracy "regressed" to the ideological region of their ethnic origin in a more traditional area (to the region of passive democracy of Southeastern Europe). Other than that, ideologies stayed generally confined within their countries and the three ideological blocs; we have not found any ideology transgressing across Europe the way the mentalities (democratic or not) did. We failed to observe a proof of pan-European ideology, such as a possible trans-regional social democratic party. It seems that ethnic and economic partition of Europe is reflected in its ideological partition. In contrast, citizen mentalities seem to be more diverse and more accommodating of diverse electoral choices; for example, secular democrats leaned not just to a social democratic party but also to new left and small emerging democratic parties (the electoral choices are mentioned with each of the five mentalities' characteristics above).

6 DISCUSSION

To study the preconditions for a European demos and European public, we analyzed constellations of European democratic values and attitudes from the EVS data by two different cluster analytic approaches. We focused primarily on the diversity of typically manifested socio-political mentalities, and the occurrence of a democratic European demos and a shared ideological public sphere.

The preconditions for the European demos were assessed by k-means cluster analysis of citizens' attitudes, and the five resulting mentalities, which can be viewed as democratic, non-democratic or anti-democratic:

1. Two mentalities were distinctly *tolerant and democratic*, in harmony with the spirit of the European demos. These tolerant democratic clusters – secular democrats and religious democrats – represented nearly 17 percent and 21 percent of Europeans respectively.
2. Two other clusters, intolerant economically deprived traditionalists and non-democratic skeptics, were associated with a rather inert and uninvolved mentality and selective intolerance to others. These two clusters represented almost a half of the European population (about 27 percent and 25 percent respectively).

3. A particular challenge for democracy seems to be associated with the group of authoritarian religious radicals (anti-democratic rebels). Although least numerous (constituting only 10.5 percent of respondents), this mentality signals activism and preparedness to get involved even in very confrontational anti-democratic actions.

A different approach was used in the study of ideologies: the hierarchical cluster analysis of mean values of political party (non-)sympathizers. This analysis failed to reveal signs of a European ideological public sphere; identified ideologies were contained within their countries and cultural regions.

It may appear rather disappointing that, (a) with respect to the demos (democratic mentalities), the democratic character accounted for only a minority of Europeans, concentrating mostly in the European Northwest; (b) with respect to the European ideological public sphere, we failed to reveal signs of a unified European transnational public.

Still, there are also encouraging signs in our findings: Democratic mentalities (secularized or religious) were identified in a significant number in all European countries, and they can be considered a basis for the European demos. Elites in particular appear to be democratic (see Klicperová-Baker and Košťál 2015), thus increasing the impact of European democrats and absorbing the effects of free-loaders and non-democratic radicals.[6] Perhaps a further analysis of ideologies of the elites may provide new insights into the nascent European public.

Another source of optimism may appear if we define the public sphere not ideologically but culturally. Instead of seeing the public sphere as an overreaching arena "that would act as a *transnational discursive space* uniting various communication fluxes and actors from all strata of society" (Nitoiu 2013: 26, emphasis added), it can be defined in cultural terms: Compare Farte (2009: 22) and his elaboration of the *culture-based public sphere* where the "public sphere could be defined as a unique world, characterized by consensus and cooperation."

We detected a majority (over 50 percent within each country) of democrats in Austria, Denmark, Finland, France, Germany, Iceland, Ireland, Luxembourg, the Netherlands, Norway, Spain, Sweden, Switzerland, Great Britain and Northern Ireland. In Denmark and Norway democratic mentalities constituted as many as 90 percent or even more. Although the social desirability of the responses has to be taken into account, these above-mentioned countries may be considered the democratic core in which the European demos – in the sense of robust democratic character – cannot be disputed, and with it also a culture-based public sphere. The European Northwest is generally found to be the bastion of democracy; compare also the findings by Makarovič and his coworkers, who point out Denmark, the Netherlands and Sweden as "active democracies" before we did (Makarovič 2008; Makarovič et al. 2007).

Our data confirm that the elites expressed democratic attitudes significantly more often than the general public did. This also suggests that the elites are better disposed to uniting on the democratic platform than the rest of the population. There may be exceptions to this general rule, such as anti-democratic top elites in countries which used to be governed by authoritarian elites: Tudoroiu (2010) documented the anti-democratic and anti-EU conduct of the ultra-nationalist government in Slovakia under Mečiar and the neo-communist regime in Romania under Iliescu. Thus, we repeat that in our study we consider as elites not just the top government politicians but also much wider strata of managers and higher professionals, who represented over 20 percent of the sample.

We observed elite versus non-elite difference in democratic values and opinions, which is in congruence with the generally recognized notion of the "elite–mass divide" and a growing gap between populism and elitism (see Teney and Helbing 2014). Elites notably tend to differ from citizens in such aspects as sympathies to the EU and in openness to the public European sphere. (Compare studies derived from Eurobarometer, and works by Lasch 1996, Nissen 2003, Lengyel 2011 and others.)

Flockhart explains that within each country there are two radically different "we-concepts": "'state' and 'society' can be conceptualized as two differently constructed social groups; one located at the state level and consisting of the elite, and one located at the nation level and consisting of 'the people,' traditionally described as the mass" (Flockhart 2006: 98–99). Tudoroiu (2010) complements this observation by examples of countries where either elites or masses were more prominent during the democratization process before accession to the EU.[7]

Our findings are also in concord with literature which indicates that the elites tend to be more congruent in their attitudes than the rest of the citizens and that the elites often tend to reach over borders in their transnational efforts. Thus, for example, Miller et al. (1995) observed a remarkable agreement in attitudes on democracy, reforms and market between Russian and Ukrainian elites (although they clashed over views on nationalism, with the exception of nationalism Russian elites were very close to the Russian masses; Miller et al. 1995: 14). Lengyel (2011: 1036) described "significant divergence between elites and the population as regards European attachment: over one-third of members of the elites (two-fifths of Western elites) are strongly attached while the corresponding rate among the population is less than a quarter."

The transnational outreach of the elites appears significant whether they reach over borders to pressure the EU candidate members (the EU's democratic conditionality) or are activists spontaneously uniting internationally, for example for environmental causes (Nicholson 1987, among others).

Our study has some limitations. The EVS, although designed for cross-cultural comparisons, is not free from a possible pro-Western bias and, like most surveys, it is not immune to social desirability. To increase validity and to control for random and non-random measurement errors, we used multiple items for assessing the respective features (democratic spirit, tolerance, etc.), as also recommended by Ariely and Davidov (2011); however, in this case we have not tested cross-national invariance, which they also recommend; that will be a subject of our future study.

CONCLUSION

Our objective was to verify to what degree the citizenry of Europe deserves the label of a European demos and to probe for the existence of a European public. Our concept of European demos stresses its pro-democratic character, particularly respect and tolerance of diversity, which are inevitable for European integration as well as for perpetual negotiations in a democratic system. Conflicts are a natural substance of democracy (Klicperová-Baker et al. 2007). Benevolence and civic-mindedness are necessary in Europe, a continent of diverse cultures and violent history.

This study confirmed that, despite global convergence, post-communist democratization and EU unification pressures, inhabitants of Europe embody a heterogeneous populace with diverse values and political attitudes. Cluster analysis proved to be a useful method sensitive both to the diversity and the international similarities in European thought. In contrast to a notion that nations differ by their distinct national characters, we counter that (a) there is more than one (typically several) representative socio-political mentality in each nation; (b) individual mentalities span internationally, nations share them and they may be unifying, which may be said of a cosmopolitan democratic character as well as of intolerant xenophobic traditionalism; (c) finally, we have observed diversity also within the democratic mentalities – we observed not just one but two distinct types of democratic mentalities: a secularized and a religious form.

Our analyses revealed two widely spread democratic mentalities compatible with the European demos; thus we can infer the existence of a precondition of the European demos and with it also a palpable precondition for a public sphere, unless it is defined ideologically. Yet at the same time we also observed a wide incidence of neutral mentalities or mentalities ill suited for democracy. In some regions, particularly in the European Northwest, the democratic mentality was absolutely prevalent; in Denmark and in Norway democratic mentalities constituted over 90 percent of the population. Still, the democratic mentality, the demos, appeared scarce in other regions. Almost two-thirds (62.2 percent) of the European general public seemed to lean to skeptically non-democratic or anti-democratic mentalities.

The democratic character appeared in a minority in the post-communist region, in the post-Soviet countries and in Southeastern Europe. There, non-democratic mentalities (non-democratic skeptics) or anti-democratic tendencies (intolerant economically deprived traditionalists and authoritarian religious radicals) were significantly overrepresented. Still, the vertical (elite) perspective reassures us that the democratic spirit seems to significantly and reliably prevail (or at least hold plurality) among the European elites and hence may have a stronger influence than sheer numbers suggest.

The democratic citizens and elites reliably demonstrated their democratic "habits of the heart," democratic activism, a high level of participation in civil society (membership in societies) and hence their readiness to be engaged in the public sphere, especially if the public sphere is defined in terms of democratic culture rather than in political or ideological terms. After all, our findings did not confirm the existence of a widespread ideological public sphere based on political (non-) partisanship, but we have observed indications of the pan-European occurrence of democratic socio-political mentalities. (Admittedly, we also observed the pan-European occurrence of anti-democratic mentalities.) Thus, although a pan-European public sphere was not explicitly revealed, the international spread of democratic culture suggests that, if there is not a functional public sphere already, there is a viable potential for it, even if only the culture-based kind of public sphere. Perhaps, if the reader can kindly tolerate a crude parallel, the public sphere is not unlike a system of public facilities: one may not use them constantly, but the civic community knows about them and will use them whenever need be.

In conclusion, we believe that now the challenge is not, in Cederman's paraphrase, that "We have made Europe, now we have to make Europeans" (2000: 3). After all, Václav Havel (2000) poignantly showed that Europeanness may be within us without its open revelation. Instead, one may need to paraphrase the words which the first Czechoslovak president, Thomas Masaryk, used about democracy: Just as "Democracy is accomplished by democrats and better democracy by better democrats," "Europe is constituted by Europeans and better Europe by better Europeans." The core of "better" appears to be in the cultivation of a European demos and public spirit and in connecting the national and regional public spheres.

NOTES

* In addition to the Eurosphere funding from the European Commission, this study was also supported by the Grant Agency of the Czech Republic, grant 15-11062S, 'Psychosocial Analysis of non-democratic character in a post-communist society' and by RVO 68081740 as a part of the research programme of Czech Academy of Sciences 'Strategy AV21'.

1. Let us leave aside the issue of whether "demos" is a flattering epithet in the first place. After all, Aristotle himself is known to have looked down on the rule of demos (and with it also on democracy as direct rule of the mob and the needy). Instead, he was in favor of aristocracy (the rule of the best) or rule by an enlightened monarch.
2. Agonism according to Mouffe is a type of antagonism which involves relations not between enemies but between "adversaries." Adversaries are defined paradoxically as "friendly enemies," that is, "persons who are friends because they share a common symbolic space but also enemies because they want to organize this common symbolic space in a different way" (Mouffe 2009: 13).
3. Publications related to EVS (2011a) can be found at http://evs.place.pukurin.uvt.nl/.
4. Stability (reordered and split-half) for the selected five clusters was at 90–91 percent, with a satisfactory check by the Sokal–Michener Confusion Index. (We also found stable solutions for three and four clusters, but those had a weaker differentiating power.) Clusters were then subjected to ANOVA and post-hoc testing.
5. Expert ratings of parties from country reports on the EVS website.
6. In an adjacent analysis we compared EVS elites' views on diversity (tolerance of diverse neighbors) with Eurosphere data examining elites' opinion on the relevance of diverse groups in the current society. The results suggest that, while elites generally manifest more embracing and tolerant attitudes to diversity than the general public, at the same time they express a heightened awareness of relevant social problems (see also Klicperová-Baker and Košťál 2012).
7. "In Poland, Hungary or the Czech Republic, elites responded positively and the rapid democratization that ensued made the society level less visible. But the cases of Slovakia and Romania show that the socialization of this latter level also took place and was strong enough to override the elite's resistance to externally-induced democratization. Therefore, the democratization process was a complex interaction between Western international organizations and states and each of the two levels" (Tudoroiu 2010: 92).

REFERENCES

Almond, G. and S. Verba (1989) *The Civic Culture*, London: Sage.

Ariely, G. and E. Davidov (2011) Can We Rate Public Support for Democracy in a Comparable Way? Cross-national Equivalence of Democratic Attitudes in the World Value Survey, *Social Indicators Research* 104(2): 271–286.

Cederman, L.-E. (2000) *Nationalism and Bounded Integration: What It Would Take to Construct a European Demos*, European Forum Series, EUI Working Papers No. 34, Florence: European University Institute, Robert Schuman Center for Advanced Studies, http://www.eui.eu/RSCAS/WP-Texts/00_34.pdf (accessed 28 April 2015).

Černý, J. (2002) Vliv skupinových mentalit na postoje k manželství [The influence of group mentalities on attitudes to marriage], in J. Havelka, M. Tuček, J. Černý, J. Česal and M. Hudema (eds.), *Skupinové mentality* [Group mentalities], Sociological Papers, pp. 51–63, Prague: Academy of Sciences of the Czech Republic, Institute of Sociology.

Černý, J., M. Sedláčková and M. Tuček (2004) *The Formation of Group Mentalities in the Czech Republic after 1989*, Prague: Academy of Sciences of the Czech Republic, Institute of Sociology.

EVS (2011a) Citation Archives, http://evs.place.pukurin.uvt.nl/ (accessed 6 December 2011).

EVS (2011b), European Values Study 1981–2008 Longitudinal Data File, GESIS Data Archive, Cologne, Germany, ZA4804 Data File Version 1.0.0 (2011-04-30), doi:10.4232/1.4804.

Farte, G.-I. (2009) Mass Media and the European Cultural Citizenship, *Cultura – International Journal of Philosophy of Culture and Axiology* 6(1): 22–33.

Feierabend, I.K. and M. Klicperová-Baker (2015) Freedom and Psychological Proximity as Preconditions of Nonviolence: The Social Psychology of Democratic Peace, *South African Journal of Psychology* 45(4): 564–577.

Field, A.P. (2000) *Discovering Statistics Using SPSS for Windows: Advanced Techniques for the Beginner*, London: Sage.

Flockhart, T. (2006) "Complex Socialization": A Framework for the Study of State Socialization, *European Journal of International Relations* 12(1): 89–118.

Gabel, M.J. and C.J. Anderson (2001) *Exploring the European Demos (or Lack Thereof): The Structure of Citizen Attitudes and the European Political Space*, http://www.monnet-centre.uni-bremen.de/pdf/wp/2001-4-Gabel-Anderson.pdf (accessed 28 April 2015).

Habermas, J. (1992) Citizenship and National Identity: Some Reflections on the Nature of Europe, *Praxis International* 12(1): 1–19.

Havel, V. (2000) Address by Vaclav Havel, President of the Czech Republic, before the Members of the European Parliament, Strasbourg, 16 February, http://old.hrad.cz/president/Havel/speeches/2000/1602_uk.html (accessed 28 April 2015).

Havelka, M. (2002) Historické a tématické předpoklady tematizace problému mentalit [Historical and systematic thematization of mentalities], in J. Havelka, M. Tuček, J. Černý, J. Česal and M. Hudema (eds.), *Skupinové mentality*

[Group mentalities], Sociological Papers, pp. 10–34, Prague: Academy of Sciences of the Czech Republic, Institute of Sociology.

Klicperová-Baker, M. (ed.) (1999) *Ready for Democracy? Civic Culture and Civility with a Focus on Czech Society*, Prague: Academy of Sciences of the Czech Republic, Institute of Psychology.

Klicperová-Baker, M. and J. Košťál (2012) Ethno-national, Religious, Ideological and Sexual Diversity: Elite and Citizen Views Compared, *Javnost – The Public* 19(1): 85–102.

Klicperová-Baker, M. and J. Košťál (2015) European Sociopolitical Mentalities: Identifying Pro- and Antidemocratic Tendencies, Part I – Individual Citizens' Perspective, *European Societies* 17(3): 301–332.

Klicperová-Baker, M., S. Kovacheva, L. Titarenko, I.K. Feierabend and C.R. Hofstetter (2003) *Democratic Citizenship: Psychological Theory and Empirical Studies in Four Central and Eastern European Nations*, San Diego, CA: Montezuma Publishing, San Diego State University.

Klicperová-Baker, M., I.K. Feierabend, S. Kovacheva, L. Titarenko, J. Košťál and C.R. Hofstetter (2007) *Demokratická kultura v České republice: Občanská kultura, éthos a vlastenectví ze srovnávacího pohledu* [Democratic culture in the Czech Republic: civic culture, ethos and patriotism in a comparative perspective], Prague: Academia.

Košťál, J. and M. Klicperová-Baker (2015) European Sociopolitical Mentalities: Identifying Pro- and Antidemocratic Tendencies, Part II – Group (Ideological, Partisan, Regional) Perspective, *European Societies* 17(3): 333–350.

Lacey, J. (2014) Must Europe Be Swiss? On the Idea of a Voting Space and the Possibility of a Multilingual Demos, *British Journal of Political Science* 44(1): 61–82.

Lane, R.L. (1972) *Political Man*, New York: Free Press.

Lasch, C. (1996) *The Revolt of the Elites and Betrayal of Democracy*, New York: W.W. Norton & Company.

Lengyel, G. (2011) Supranational Attachment of European Elites and Citizens, *Europe–Asia Studies* 63(6): 1033–1054.

Makarovič, M. (2008) Patterns of Political Participation in Europe, *Innovative Issues and Approaches in Social Sciences of Slovenian Association for Innovative Political Science* 1(3): 43–61.

Makarovič, M., A. Ivančič and D. Podmenik (2007) Social and Political Participation: Is There a European Convergence? in F. Adam (ed.), *Social Capital and Governance: Old and New Members of the EU in Comparison*, pp. 51–90, Berlin: LIT Verlag.

Miller, A., V.L. Hesli and W.M. Reisinger (1995) Comparing Citizen and Elite Belief Systems in Post-Soviet Russia and Ukraine, *Public Opinion Quarterly* 59(1): 1–40.

Mouffe, C. (2009) *The Democratic Paradox*, London: Verso.

Müller, J.-W. (2006) On the Origins of Constitutional Patriotism, *Contemporary Political Theory* 5(3): 278–296.

Nicholson, M. (1987) *The New Environmental Age*, Cambridge: Cambridge University Press.

Nissen, S. (2003) Who Wants Enlargement of the EU? Support for Enlargement among Elites and Citizens in the European Union, *Sociologický Časopis/Czech Sociological Review* 39(6): 757–772.

Nitoiu, C. (2013) The European Public Sphere: Myth, Reality or Aspiration? *Political Studies Review* 11(1): 26–38.

Risse, T. (2010) *A Community of Europeans? Transnational Identities and Public Spheres*, Ithaca, NY: Cornell University Press.

Risse, T. (2014) No Demos? Identities and Public Sphere in the Euro Crisis, *JCMS – Journal of Common Market Studies* 52(6): 1207–1215.

Scharpf, F.W. (1999) *Governing in Europe: Effective and Democratic?* New York: Oxford University Press.

Sternberger, D. (1979) Verfassungspatriotismus, *Frankfurter Allgemeine Zeitung*, 23 May.

Teney, C. and M. Helbing (2014) How Denationalization Divides Elites and Citizens, *Zeitschrift für Soziologie* 43(4): 258–271.

Tudoroiu, T. (2010) Post-communist Democratization Revisited: An International Relations Approach, *Perspectives on European Politics and Society* 11(1): 80–108.

10. The role of EU policies in the making of the European public sphere

Hakan G. Sicakkan

The political history of European nation states teaches us that states, political elites, groups and individuals created, in interplay with each other, three different channels through which citizens manifest themselves in politics: the numerical channel (electoral democracy), the corporate-plural channel (negotiation democracy) and the media channel (mediated democracy). The former two channels were conceptualized and theorized by Stein Rokkan (1966). The media channel, that is, 'the press', was introduced by Jürgen Habermas as 'the public sphere's preeminent institution' (Habermas 2011 [1962]: 181), comprising 'newspapers and magazines, radio and television' which function as 'the media of the public sphere' (Habermas et al. 1974 [1964]: 49).

The numerical channel is about the election of legislators by voters. It entails relations of exchange between political elites and citizens. In this channel one talks about voters, elections, electorates, political parties, party systems and parliaments. The interactions are between citizens and legislators, or legislator candidates, the majority of whom are organized in political parties. The corporate-plural channel concerns public and corporate interest groups' negotiation with policymakers. This entails bargaining in policymaking processes whereby social movements, civil society organizations and other non-state political actors focusing on specific policy issues exert pressure on governments to generate policy outcomes or policy implementation in favour of their members. Interactions in this channel occur between policymakers and citizens who are organized in non-state organizations. Whereas the numerical channel is used by political actors for determining who will have how much power in decision-making (party composition in parliament and government) based on the degree of popular support (election results), the corporate-plural channel is about negotiations on specific policy issues between policymakers (governments and parliamentary commissions) and non-state organizations. The numerical and corporate-plural channels are, then, respectively about distribution of decision power and bargaining on policy proposals and outcomes. Following Fraser's typology of 'strong and weak publics' (Fraser 1990: 75–76), the numerical and corporate-plural channels can be termed strong public spheres because their outputs are both public opinion and collective decisions made through voting and bargaining.

The media channel, on the other hand, is not about collective decision-making or policymaking but rather opinion and will formation. Thus, using Fraser's (1990) terminology, it is a weak public sphere. The media channel is also designated as a 'general public sphere', because mass media, including digital media, is usually considered to be the best empirical equivalent and the tangible institutional setting of the notion of a general public sphere. The general public sphere is about states', citizens' and civil society's efforts to spread and diffuse their views into contesting publics. It appears first and foremost as a space that empowers citizens by enabling them to criticize and hold the power-holders accountable for their decisions and policies between elections. The outcomes of a general public sphere are, depending on one's ontological point of departure, aggregation of interests, formation of public opinion, formation of general will, or formation of common citizen identity.

Agonistic politics, understood as adversary contestation among various political actors, publics and power-holders happening in the numerical, corporate-plural and media channels, and the political cleavages that these channels accommodate, constitutes the political public sphere. Conceived as a corollary of such an institutional framework the modern public sphere arose as a democratic nation-state phenomenon. This is so although formations of national democracies were historically elite-led processes. As outlined in Chapter 4, in order to diffuse peripheries, state building elites built resilient links and alliances with influential local elites. Which local elites they sought alliances with depended on overlaps and gaps between the political objectives of central and local elites. This meant also new polarizations and contestations generated by the polity building process.

The European Union appears to be following a historical path that is similar to the trajectory its member states once followed when establishing direct links between political institutions and citizens. The Union has been attempting to create a European public sphere by setting up and sponsoring numerical, corporate-plural and media channels on a European scale. For this purpose, the European Union has introduced six key components of a public sphere: (1) a political power centre through supranationalization in increasingly more policy areas (Chapter 1); (2) a more unified territorial space with increasingly more diverse local societies (Chapter 2); (3) a trans-European network of civil society, that is, the Eurosphere, to link the European citizenry with the European Commission, European Parliament, and other bodies of the European Union (Chapters 1, 4, 6 and 7); (4) direct election of the members of the European Parliament and formation of trans-European party groups in the European Parliament (Chapter 8); (5) a European demos through Eurobarometer, European citizenship and identity politics with European symbols (Chapter 9); and (6) a pan-European media through a single media market and centralized information distribution, the latter of which has not been realized (Chapters 3, 4 and 5).

Have these efforts of supranational elites to create a European public sphere had any impact at all? If their policies did foster even an embryonic European public sphere, what are its distinguishing features? My task here is to provide at least partial answers to these questions by using the results of the chapters in this volume. This chapter is organized as follows. In section 1, I evaluate the extent to which the European Union policies have created links between the supranational political institutions and citizens. Here, I focus on the links created with the leaders of national civil society organizations, think tanks, political parties, mass media and citizens. In section 2, I portray the ways in which European Union policies have created political cleavages with integrative effects on a European scale that can be considered as the basis of an agonistic European public sphere. Finally, in section 3, I discuss the theoretical implications of these.

1 LINKING THE EUROPEAN UNION INSTITUTIONS WITH CITIZENS

The European Union's policies of 'creating an ever closer union', 'closing the gap', 'connecting with citizens', 'unity in diversity', 'Europe of the regions' and 'subsidiarity' all aim to establish links with citizens, bypassing the member states. In Chapter 1, I showed that this has been a pronounced objective of the supranational institutions since the 1950s. The European Union first tried to reach citizens directly in the period between 1951 and 1962. When it realized that achieving this objective was not realistic with the resources at hand it adopted in 1963 a new strategy of linking with citizens less directly by forming alliances with national and local elites whom it perceived as influential opinion makers. Recent historical research designates these two periods as, respectively, 'the popularist approach' and 'the opinion leader approach' (Harrison and Pukallus 2015).

This method adjustment in efforts to link the European Union with citizens was followed with a series of new policies that are still in use. Concerning linking through political parties in the numerical channel, European party federations outside the European Parliament and ideology-based pan-European party groups in the European Parliament were founded. Concerning citizen connection through civil society organizations and think tanks in the corporate-plural channel, the European Union supported the foundation and activities of pan-European networks of these organizations. Supranational leaders of pan-European networks and formal and opinion leaders of their member organizations operating within national numerical and corporate-plural channels constitute today an extended, complex and more advanced version of what the founding fathers once called the 'Eurosphere' (cf. Sicakkan, this volume, Chapter 1). As to creating links through the media channel, several attempts at instituting pan-European media were made, such as Eurikon, Europa TV, Eurosport and Euronews, as well as creation of digital media channels and a single media market (cf. Mokre, this volume, Chapter 3). Since these policies did not generate citizen interest in following the daily news from the pan-European media, the European Union opted for getting national media actors interested in European Union-related news and convincing them to adopt European perspectives when reporting news.

1.1 Linking with Citizens through the Media Channel

The European Union has not yet been able to create what we may call the basic media institutions of a general European public sphere. The pan-European media channels that were created as a result of European Union initiatives dissolved (e.g. Europa TV), did not topically contribute to a political public sphere (e.g. Eurosport) or ended up reporting national news in neutral ways rather than adding European perspectives to the political landscape (e.g. Euronews). Policies aiming to prepare the conditions for the development of pan-European media resulted in the creation of a single media market but not common infrastructures for information sharing and news distribution (Mokre, this volume, Chapter 3). In these senses, the European Union's top-down policies did not help achieve the originally targeted objectives. However, this does not mean that the European Union failed to generate constitutive agons, adversaries, alliances and polarizations on a European scale.

Through interviews with almost 750 national elites conducted in the Eurosphere project, we observe that lack of a pan-European media is noticed not only by media elites themselves but also by elites within political parties, civil society organizations and think tanks. In particular, elites with more pro-diversity and pro-EU attitudes recognize the necessity of having common European media channels available to all European citizens. However, although the European Union policies aiming to create a shared media channel did not serve the desired ends, there are some bottom-up structures that contribute to the formation of a European public sphere. Namely, journalists and media institutions do collaborate with each other on a regular basis in information sharing and news distribution.

> [The Eurosphere project's] empirical results have shown a possible way out of this dilemma in transnational exchange of news and the attempts of journalists to include a European dimension in media coverage. Maybe one could speak here of a hidden form of EPS [European public sphere] – the audience is addressed as a national audience but shares similar themes and outlooks with other national audiences. In the long run, this could lead to ... [the] Europeanization of public spheres. (Mokre, this volume, Chapter 3)

Such bottom-up, transnational collaboration between national media institutions in information sharing and news distribution should result in at least some degree of Europeanizing perspectives and framings in national media's reporting of news which correspond to the pro-EU and pro-diversity preferences of the media elites who engage in news and information exchanges across national borders. Is this the case? In line with findings in earlier research, media studies in the Eurosphere project show that there is a visible share of Europeanizing perspectives in national media on all the themes we studied. Chapter 4 by this author, for example, found that 27.6 per cent of news reported by national print and broadcast media in 15 European countries is framed with a Europeanist perspective. The share of news reported with Europeanizing perspectives has been gradually increasing over 30 per cent in the current decade (e.g. cf. Trenz 2004). On the other hand, the percentages of nation-statist and nativist framings are 57.4 and 15.0 respectively.

Earlier research conducted within and outside the Eurosphere project suggests that variation in media discourses is still partly explained by national borders and national media regimes (Peters et al. 2005). Variation in themes of media's interest along national lines is largely explained by the East–West and old member–new member divides (Bakalova and Zografova 2011). From an agonistic pluralism perspective, the sheer existence of national impact on themes of media's interest does not tell us much about the European public sphere. What is important is whether such impact contributes to the formation and perpetuation of political cleavages on a European scale, a question which I will address in section 2 of this chapter.

The European Union has also been actively digitizing its direct links with citizens. The internet is the European Union's main tool of transparency. The internet medium hosts, among other things, the European Union's law database, EuroparlTV, stakeholder registers and consultation procedures. Parallel to the European Union's top-down digital media policies (cf. Mokre, this volume, Chapter 3), we see digital public spaces developing through bottom-up initiatives that are linking Europe's citizens and publics transnationally. We observe the impacts of elite networking and exchanges of information in the digital public spaces outside the infrastructures set up by the European Union. As of February 2016, there were nearly 450 Facebook pages directly addressing the European Union.[1] Initiators of these social media networking pages include both pro-EU and anti-EU actors. The majority of page owners are trans-European and national civil society, social movement and non-governmental organizations, political parties, think tanks, media organizations and individual public figures. That is, in addition to virtual national and transnational actors who participate only through digital media, we observe the same actors are participating in both traditional media channels and digital social networking media in order to link with citizens. The Facebook pages and tweets with thematic hashtags on Twitter, for example, provide platforms for everybody to declare their stances on specific policy issues rather than discuss or deliberate, thus generating both aggregative and agonistic functions.

According to Duru and Trenz, who present a case study of elite expats' social networking pages on the internet in Chapter 5, social networking media facilitate virtual meeting platforms between highly mobile expats and other groups in local society. This contributes to development of transnational public spheres on the local scale. The crucial factor leading to this outcome is that free mobility in the European Union has not transformed the digital spheres that accommodate elite expats' interactions into an insular public space of mobile elites. On the contrary, expats' social networking brings individuals from different backgrounds, elites and non-elites, and mobiles and locals, to engage in communication and exchanges on topics of common interest.

> Mobility and citizenship rights as facilitated by the Europe of free movement do not in this sense lead to the seclusion of a distinct group of privileged EU citizens but contribute to the consolidation of a transnational public sphere in which communicative exchanges and encounters are kept in flow between the well-established group of high-skilled EU (and also non-EU) mobiles and

> other newly arriving groups of less privileged migrants (e.g. those escaping the economic crisis in Southern Europe, or working migrants in low-skilled jobs from South-eastern Europe). (Duru and Trenz, this volume, Chapter 5)

The main purpose of the European Union's mobility policy is to strengthen the common market by making skills throughout Europe available to all European employers. The aim of digital media policy is to connect the supranational institutions directly with citizens through citizen and civil society participation in consultation processes and through public access to information coming from the supranational institutions. However, by using mobility and digital technology, non-state organizations and elites have managed to create their own horizontal links across and beyond the boundaries of the publics and public spaces that they belong to. The European Union's media policies aiming to create a European public sphere have not only generated a single media market but also prompted bottom-up initiatives by national media actors to exchange information and distribute news across borders. We observe the same trend in the digital social networking media on the internet. Rather than the European Union's attempts to create pan-European media, it is the unintended consequences of the European Union media policies, combined with the creation of a single media market, that contribute to the emergence of an agonistic European public sphere.

1.2 The European Civil Society and Its Corporate-plural Channel

The corporate-plural channel is where the impact of the Eurosphere is the most significant (cf. Sicakkan, this volume, Chapter 1). By creating the Eurosphere – a top-down, pro-EU and pro-diversity public of elites and citizens – the European Union generated a corporate-plural channel on a European scale. Initiatives facilitating the emergence of the Eurosphere are entrenched in various policy documents, primarily in its communication, governance and civil dialogue policies (cf. Sicakkan, this volume, Chapter 1). One of the main policy tools was the creation and funding of European networks of civil society through which national- and local-level civil societies could aggregate their common interests, form a common will and reach the supranational organizations. These networks' participation in civil dialogue, communication and governance activities, as European-level civil society actors, is seen as part of involving society and citizens in supranational policymaking. The question posed in this book is whether these networks really involved the sub-European publics.

In spite of using different conceptual, theoretical and methodological approaches, Chapters 4, 6 and 7 have similar findings on the participation of civil society organizations, including both majority and minority organizations and think tanks that are operating in the corporate-plural channel. Together, these chapters constitute an evaluation of the European Union policies aiming to create a European civil society as the foundation of a common European public sphere.

One important finding throughout these chapters is that trans-European networks of civil society have a socializing impact, especially when European Union institutions actively participate in their activities. This puts their representation capacity, legitimizing function and democratizing role into question in the eyes of the national- and subnational-level organizations, whose interests they are supposed to transmit upwards in the European Union's policymaking processes. One significant finding here is that trans-European networks adopt the values of the European Union and often transmit them downwards to their constituencies instead of (or in addition to) carrying the voices from below to the European Union-level policymaking instances. In the case of the trans-European networks of ethnic and religious minority organizations, the goals of the European Union and minority organizations – i.e. protection and development of the rights of minorities – largely overlap (van de Beek and Vermeulen, this volume, Chapter 7). However, concerning other types of national organizations, there are significant gaps between the goal sets (Sicakkan 2012b, this volume, Chapters 1, 4).

Choosing to conceive the European Union-initiated trans-European networks of civil society and think tanks as capable representatives of the European civil society, the European Union policy lacks a clear focus on the social and political actors that do not participate in the vertical structures of communication created by the trans-European networks. Thus, another important consequence of European Union policies attempting to create a European civil society is that those civil society organizations that refuse to partake in the Eurosphere (because they view it as not promoting democracy) continue to develop alternative, critical horizontal trans-European spaces which are distant from both the European Union and the Eurosphere.

At the same time, this strategy of the European Union has resulted in expansion and diffusion of the Eurosphere into Europe with peculiar discourses and vertical alliance patterns that contest the historically existing essentializing, nationalizing and transnationalizing public spaces. Moreover, as earlier research on the Eurosphere project (Sicakkan 2012a, 2012b) and the chapters in this volume show, the same strategy has partly transformed the historically existing public spaces into critical horizontal trans-European public spaces by putting them in relationships of conflict and contestation with the Eurosphere. This picture tells us that the

European Union's goals of legitimacy and democracy cannot be achieved without effectively including these new horizontal transnational publics in the corporate-plural channel.

1.3 The European Demos, Political Parties and the Numerical Channel

The chapters by Sata (Chapter 8) and Klicperová-Baker and Košťál (Chapter 9) assess how the European Union policies aiming to create a common numerical channel and a European electorate have performed. Sata finds in Chapter 8 that

> The legislative outcomes of the EP can be well aligned with the preferences of the EP party groups, but, given the great variety of parties EP party groups must accommodate as members, it is very plausible these outcomes will be far away from the preferences of at least some of the national parties. This will leave ample room for agonistic politics both within the party groups and among the different national parties, underlining that the emerged European public sphere of political actors is not one of consensus but rather one of contestation.

Underlining the differences between national political parties, the EP party groups and the legislative outcomes of the European Parliament, this finding documents the existence of a general centre–periphery cleavage between European party groups and national parties. This cleavage is based on the extent to which national constituencies endorse European integration. More importantly, Sata finds that

> differences among the member parties of a given EP party group with regard to positions on European integration and ideology do not affect the loyalty of these parties to the group; even the most distant member parties vote most often in line with the rest of the EP party group. This suggests EU policies – or the EP itself – have indeed managed to create a vertical trans-European public space that integrated national constituencies well into trans-European party groups … [T]he trans-European public sphere of political parties is very much linked to existing national public spheres, and the two often compete with each other, underlining the agonistic character of the emerging European public sphere of political parties.

On the other hand, Klicperová-Baker and Košťál (2012) suggest that, while elites generally manifest more embracing and tolerant attitudes to diversity than the general public, at the same time, they express a heightened awareness of relevant social problems. In Chapter 9, they further investigate traces of a European demos and argue that their analysis in this volume reveals a possible classification of European citizenry based on their various shared values. They find here that 'Almost two-thirds … of the European general public seemed to lean to skeptically non-democratic or anti-democratic mentalities'. Moreover, in another work, Klicperová-Baker and Košťál (2013) document that this general pattern is also mirrored amongst the party sympathizers at national levels. That is, the views of citizens in general are observed proportionally in the views of party sympathizers, who constitute the link between national parties and citizens. However, citizen views are truncated within both national party elite circles and national elite circles. Finding that the democratic values and views required to constitute a national or European demos are prevalent amongst elites, the authors of Chapter 9 conclude that 'Still, the vertical … perspective [social status paradigm] reassures us that the democratic spirit seems to significantly and reliably prevail (or at least hold plurality) among the European elites and hence may have a stronger influence than sheer numbers suggest'.

In the Eurosphere project, we also examined the influence that civic engagement and participation in different European Union actions and initiatives have on citizen attitudes. Zografova and Bakalova find that

> The willingness to be involved in and utilize the EU civic initiative in certain fields and to optimize the integration processes in the Union is a clear indicator that the communicative channels between citizenship and the Commission function regardless of the difficulties and the delays. It is also indicative for the EPS [European public sphere] in a process of constitution and the relations between citizens and public sphere. (Zografova and Bakalova 2013: 249)

These chapters trace the links between citizens and the European Union within the numeric channel, and each finds clear effects of interacting with the European Union within the structures of communication that are provided by the European Union. They uncover the issues of conflict and contestation in the numerical channel between different levels of the EU political system, from individual citizens and national parties to the European Parliament party groups. They give a rather detailed picture of the extent to which the European numerical channel actually gives voice to citizens by conveying their concerns to the European level, that is, to the European Parliament and supranational policymaking. The overall finding concerning the numerical channel is that citizens' preferences are filtered upwards in the system in favour of democratic and pro-diversity views. This starts with underrepresentation of non-democratic and anti-democratic views in national party elite circles. Then, although left- and right-wing extremes are overrepresented in the European Parliament, the higher degree of voting cohesion in party groups that are pro-European integration gives more voice to elite views on the European level.

1.4 The Links between Citizens and Supranational Institutions

There is a pattern that we observe in connection with the formation of bottom-up trans-European networks in the numerical, corporate-plural and media channels: (a) the European Union introduces top-down institutions and policies to achieve transnational integration in an area; (b) the desired policy objectives may be achieved, only partly achieved or not achieved at all; (c) bottom-up initiatives arise either as a protest reaction to the Union's top-down 'undemocratic' approaches or in order to meet a need that the European Union could not satisfy with its policies; and (d) civil actors create alternative, regular and structured transnational interactions outside the Union's institutional domain. This is a dynamics that explains the emergence of new transnational collective actors, structures, alliances and polarizations in different sectors in Europe. The new transnational formations affect the existing associations between citizens and political institutions at different levels and create new ones. Some links are weakened; some are strengthened.

We find weak links in the relationship between citizens' views and the premises in which the European Union's policies are ingrained. On their bottom-up ways from individual citizens, through national and trans-European elites, in the numerical, corporate-plural and media channels citizens' perspectives, views and preferences are either (1) transformed from particularistic, exclusionary, non-democratic and anti-EU feelings into universalistic, inclusive and democratic ones or (2) filtered by national- and European-level elite circles and the national mass media. Anti-integration, particularistic and non-democratic views are rendered less visible in the European public sphere. Moreover traditional national media also truncate the Europeanist values and views that are associated with the Eurosphere public, whereas they follow suit with the preferences of national civil society leaders (Sicakkan forthcoming).

A strong link is found between citizens' views and the European Union policies aiming to transform different kinds of national and subnational publics into trans-European publics. Citizens and organizations that interact with the European Union institutions within the European Union-initiated frames of representation in the numerical and corporate-plural channels, that is, the Eurosphere, become partly socialized into the European Union values and perspectives, and they increasingly find themselves in situations whereby they have to act as messengers of the

European Union downwards to their constituencies. This happens especially in Eurosphere platforms that facilitate encounters between the European Union's supranational elites, the Eurosphere civil society elites, national civil societies and citizens (Perez 2013; Sicakkan 2012b).

These two links – the weak link and the strong link – function in combination with each other as a gatekeeper against the surfacing of particularistic, exclusionary and non-democratic perspectives in the European Union political system. In this sense, it may be considered undemocratic to exclude any political views from a procedural democracy perspective (cf. Dahl 1989). However, these two links may also be conceived as promoting democracy in Europe from a substantive democracy perspective, which places equal emphasis on democratic institutions, procedures and the fairness of outcomes for all citizen groups involved (cf. Fraser 2007; Mouffe 1992, 1999, 2002a, 2002b; Sicakkan forthcoming; Young 1990; cf. Shapiro 1994 for a middle-way account). Further, in addition to contestations between various publics arising from diverging political visions and public opinions, the ongoing exclusion of views and values at different levels is generating new political cleavages on the European scale and strengthening the existing ones. The emergence of Europe-wide political cleavages is the theme of the next section.

2 POLITICAL CLEAVAGE SYSTEMS AND THE AGONISTIC EUROPEAN PUBLIC SPHERE

The European Union has been transforming the publics and public spaces of Europe into an agonistic European public sphere by creating direct links between the European Union and citizens, building a more unified territorial space and reducing national barriers for broadcasting and establishing a single European media market. Tallying the Eurosphere into the relatively less interdependent co-existence of historical public spaces has started transforming them by linking them to each other through collaboration, conflict and contestation with the Eurosphere. The particular links established between the European Union's supranational institutions, the Eurosphere, national social and political actors and individual citizens have generated new political cleavages on the European scale. The emergence of the Eurosphere in the form of elite and citizen alliances in the numerical, corporate-plural and media channels is a central factor in the creation of the European-level political cleavages. Thus, conceptualized in an agonistic pluralism framework, the Eurosphere has a causal status in relation to the formation of a European public sphere.

2.1 Emerging Constitutive Political Cleavages on the European Scale

Establishment of the Eurosphere not only added a top-down trans-European public space and a new elite public into the European Union's political system but also prompted formation of alternative transnational public spaces and publics in Europe that emerged as reactions to the top-down, elitist and exclusionary nature of the Eurosphere. The majority of the civil society organizations that chose to remain outside the political opportunity structures provided by the Eurosphere allied as a protest against the exclusion of bottom-up initiatives and the relative lack of citizen voice in supranational policymaking.

This has led to three vertical political cleavages on the European scale between the Eurosphere and the three alternative trans-European publics advocating 'another Europe' (Europeanists), 'a Europe of nation states' (nation-statists) and 'a Europe of natives' (populist nativists). The Europeanist public is concerned with the democratic qualities of the European Union's supranational institutions, and how European integration should proceed in the future. The nation-statist public voices a preference on re-empowerment of nation states against the European Union. The nativist public is concerned about the fate of their nations, if not the democratic nation states, and the impact of immigration and minorities. On the other hand, these three trans-European publics are also contesting each other, resulting in three additional horizontal transnational political cleavages. Both the vertical and the horizontal cleavages I identify here are constitutive in relation to the European public sphere. In the following, I focus mainly on the vertical trans-European political cleavages.

The forerunners of current nativist publics in Europe (e.g. national defence leagues and Pegida) were relatively more confined to their countries before they organized transnationally in order to collaborate on policy issues of their common interest. Our interviews contain statements from the leaders of nativist organizations in Europe demonstrating that, in addition to migration and integration policies and increasing diversity that are undesirable to them, the challenges posed by the Eurosphere elite public and the European Union are the primary motivation for their horizontal transnational collaboration. Also leaders of horizontal Europeanist organizations mention, in addition to the necessity generated by the European Union's supranational competency areas, the existence of the inaccessible elite public sphere and selective approaches of both the Eurosphere elites and the European Union institutions as the most important motivations for their efforts for forming horizontal trans-European networks aiming to democratize the European Union. In one sense, collective actors that are against the European Union are becoming transnationalized and Europeanized through shared political goals, including challenging the same political centre. While doing so, they are becoming constitutive elements of an emerging agonistic European public sphere, increasing the functionality of the other publics and public spaces that contest them and catalysing European integration.

'Another Europe', 'Europe of nation states' and 'Europe of natives' are critical publics towards the European Union and the Eurosphere, something which forms three vertical centre–periphery political cleavages. The political cleavage between the Eurosphere and 'Europe of nation states' is the classical struggle between intergovernmentalists and supranationalists. This cleavage links nationalizing publics and public spaces of Europe with the Eurosphere through contestation on the status of the member states in the emerging European public sphere. The vertical political cleavage between the Eurosphere and alternative horizontal Europeanist publics ('another Europe') is about democratization of the European Union, disempowerment of the Eurosphere public and choice of bottom-up or top-down strategies of European integration. This cleavage puts the transnationalizing publics and public spaces of Europe into a relationship of contestation about the power of the Eurosphere elites. The third vertical political cleavage is between the Eurosphere and the alternative nativist public advocating 'a Europe of natives'. The point of contestation linking this public with the Eurosphere is about diversity, immigration, and the status of migrant minorities. In addition to the publics mentioned above, there are regional ('Europe of the regions') and minority ('Europe of diversity') publics. These two publics are relatively well incorporated into the Eurosphere through the political opportunity structures provided for them by the Eurosphere (cf. van de Beek and Vermeulen, this volume, Chapter 7; Dressler, this volume, Chapter 2; Sicakkan, this volume, Chapters 1, 4), adding new dimensions to contestation between the Eurosphere and publics and public spaces.[2]

2.2 Structure of the Agonistic European Public Sphere

Considering the preceding chapters altogether, we observe one overall finding: the different types of publics in Europe have all come into enduring agonistic relationships with the trans-Europeanizing public (elites) operating in and from the Eurosphere. The alliances, conflicts and contestations have resulted in the political and social actors involved in them being structurally linked to each other across public spaces because of a desire to defend or promote their positions and stances. While these cross-public spaces and cross-public agonistic relations offer a set of new opportunity structures, getting out of them can be penalized with losses in terms of decision power, access to supranational power-holders, recognition and negotiation of belongings and access to resources. The networks operating from the Eurosphere provide opportunities to influence European Union policymaking. Being an outsider means having less opportunity to have a voice in the making of policies that may affect these publics.

On the other hand, the aforementioned transnational European publics with anti-EU attitudes have chosen to remain outside the trans-European networks because of a concern for the European Union's and these networks' democratic qualities. They are operating outside the institutional domain set up by the European Union, but this does not mean that they are outside the agonistic relations. They have their own horizontal European networks that do not take the European political institutions or the European Union-created trans-European networks as their addressees. They are for an alternative European integration which it is desired will advance bottom up. Whereas the strength of the actors working through the Eurosphere comes from their easier access to supranational decision-makers, the strength of the alternative networks outside the Eurosphere comes from their large numbers and sizes. Such horizontal networks include both conservative and nation-statist organizations and groups that advocate a Europe of nations and postnationalist democrats and humanists who want to have a Europe of citizens.

Thus, Europe is structurally divided between a handful of actors that interact with the Eurosphere and those that do not accept it as a democratic channel of influence. The latter have their Europe-wide networks that are not initiated or sponsored by the European Union. Further, there are actors that are members of the Eurosphere networks and those that regularly interact with them without having membership. In all four categories, one finds actors from all types of public spaces. Most of these relations have found their (quasi-)institutional expressions in the European Union through trans-European networks and the meeting platforms that these have created between the representatives of European publics and the political institutions of the European Union.

2.3 Crises, New Political Cleavages and the Future of the European Public Sphere

The financial and refugee crises have had severe consequences for European integration in general, and for the formation of the European public sphere in particular. Concerning consolidation of the European public sphere, the two crises facilitated a development towards an agonistic European public sphere that cannot be captured by aggregative and deliberative approaches to the public sphere. The crises brought the aforementioned political cleavages more to the surface, intensified them and rooted them deeper. Although it remains to be seen whether they will have an integrative effect or lead to institutional dissolution, I foresee more integration through strengthened political cleavages between the Eurosphere, horizontal Europeanists, nation-statists and nativists.

Firstly, the global financial crisis has revealed the severity of the ideological clash between the supranationalists in the Eurosphere and the nation-statists. Here is a clear mismatch between the integrated structure and demands of the internal market and the divergent economic policies of the member states. The Eurosphere elites blame member states for the inability of national policymakers to manage their national economies. The necessary response, for the Eurosphere elites, is more power to the political centre of the European Union, and a limiting of national options. This response is tempered by promises to further democratize European institutions. Nation-statists, by contrast, blame the inadequate design of European institutions. From their perspective, the European Union's problems are the result of constitutional asymmetries, a suboptimal currency union, a European Court of Justice with a mission to integrate, or centralized institutions that are unresponsive to local demands. The necessary response, for the nation-statists, is to regain sovereignty over national markets. Linking this efficiency-oriented delineation with the notion of democracy, Dani Rodrik's 'trilemma' summarizes the current status of the European Union as follows:

> We cannot have globalization, democracy, and national sovereignty simultaneously. We must choose two among the three … If European leaders want to maintain democracy, they must make a choice between political union and economic disintegration. They must either explicitly renounce economic sovereignty or actively put it to use for the benefit of their citizens. The first would entail coming clean with their own electorates and building democratic space above the level of the nation-state. The second would mean giving up on monetary union in order to be able to deploy national monetary and fiscal policies in the service of longer-term recovery. The longer this choice is postponed, the greater the economic and political cost that ultimately will have to be paid. (Rodrik 2012, cf. Rodrik 2011: 200)

On this issue, the Eurosphere elites made clear progress by convincing the Eurozone states to give additional power to the European Union on economic policy. Regarding the problem of crisis response as both a problem of national policymakers' incompetence and the Union's 'too intergovernmental' institutional design that separates monetary policy (e.g. the European Central Bank steers the currency and interest rates) from other economic policy (e.g. employment policy, national spending), the Eurosphere elites pushed for Rodrik's first option. The result is that every year member states have to submit their draft national budgetary plans to the European Union, before they propose them to national parliaments, for an assessment of whether they follow the European Union's economic governance rules. Still, the euro currency is under serious danger because of restrictive austerity measures that national governments have to implement but are unable to explain to their suffering citizens. Increased unemployment and poverty, especially youth poverty, are obviously benefiting the nativist approaches in European countries.

On the other hand, as a consequence of the asylum crisis, the Eurosphere elites, horizontal Europeanists and nation-statists have all lost ground against the transnationally organized nativists concerning issues of diversity, immigration and asylum. Countries like Denmark, the Netherlands and Norway (a member of the Schengen Agreement), which have traditionally been willing to actively contribute to protection of human rights, have turned against international conventions because of nativist pressure and demands for more favourable treatment of the natives compared to aliens. Huge migration and asylum pressure from the Middle East and Africa, accompanied by the fact that a majority of the migrants arriving are Muslim and that political-Islamic terror is on the rise, intensify further the political cleavages between the nativists and other publics of Europe. The European Union's response to the Syria-related asylum crisis was, with Germany in the lead, more generous than the response to the Mediterranean boat refugees. Further, the basic policy measure was to create more effective measures for burden-sharing among the member states, which is categorically rejected by many new member states. Some member states even responded by suspending their obligations in the Schengen Agreement to provide open internal borders in order to prevent the flow of asylum seekers into their countries.

Further supranationalization in economic policymaking is repelling countries like the United Kingdom and Greece from the European Union. If the member states push more for increasing their sovereignty over economic policymaking, there may be a risk of the dissolution of the Eurozone. Also, in the context of the asylum crisis, free mobility of persons, and the Schengen Agreement itself, is in danger of suspension. This will mean a significant weakening of the very fundament of the European Union, that is, the common market. However, from an extended agonistic pluralism perspective, these are more unlikely than likely to happen. This is because the European Union is, in its current form, the physical manifestation of existing symbiotic interdependencies in Europe in economic, political and societal terms. Capital ownership in Europe is much less national and much more European than in 1950. Capital owners and states need these institutions – the common market, the euro currency, the four freedoms, the Schengen and Dublin Agreements – to sustain their dominance and share in both the European Union's common market and the global market. Therefore, I hypothesize, any problems arising from power and competence asymmetries between the European Union, the member states and the regions will result in increased supranationalization in the Union's institutional design rather than more national sovereignty, subsidiarity or exit. For example, the Greek sovereign debt crisis brought in the Grexit scenario as a threat rather than a realistic option for Greece. The European Union ended up, as mentioned above, further supranationalizing its economic policy-making as a result of the Eurozone crisis, and the Greek crisis in particular. On the other hand, owing to the fact that the UK is outside the Eurozone and at the same time embedded in multiple transnational economic systems, the ongoing Brexit process seems likely to end up as a soft exit, which involves relatively minor modifications to the status quo and continued access to the single market. This ambiguous status of the UK within the Union may in turn decrease its political influence within the European Union, releasing the British brakes on the supranationalization process.

From an agonistic pluralism perspective of the public sphere, conflicts are an ordinary part of politics as long as they involve encounters between adversaries and not enemies. The danger for institutional dissolution lies in the extent to which parties perceive each other as enemies that need to be eliminated. Currently, this is not the case in Europe. As long as symbiotic interdependencies continue to exist, conflicts and contestations arising from crises will contribute to the further building of the agonistic European public sphere just as they did in the past.

3 THEORETICAL IMPLICATIONS: CONCEPTUALIZATION AND CAUSALITY

In Chapter 1, I stated that we can start talking about a European public sphere only when the already existing public spaces come into a relationship of conflict and contestation with the vertical trans-European public sphere and the EU's political institutions. The Eurosphere project results document that this necessary condition is more than fulfilled. The

European Union policies have managed to create a vertical trans-European public space, the Eurosphere, linking and de-linking national constituencies with the European Union – a new public space which is in conflict and contestation with the already existing essentializing, nationalizing and transnationalizing public spaces. This is so in spite of the adverse effects of the ongoing financial and political crises, whose outcomes might lead to some degree of dissolution. The dominant discourse in the Eurosphere is still that of democratization, pro-diversity, inclusion, Europeanization and partly also supranationalization.

As this book shows, the Eurosphere is constituted by trans-European networks of various kinds of non-state actors, for example political parties, civil society organizations and think tanks. These networks are elite-led and elitist, and they are quite closed towards political visions and ideas other than Europeanism. Reactions against the elitist, hierarchical and exclusionary nature of the Eurosphere have been an integrative factor in transforming the other types of historical publics and public spaces within Europe into horizontal trans-European publics and public spaces. These horizontal trans-European spaces are not linked with the EU political institutions, and their discourses vary from being more democratic and more pro-diversity than the European Union's perspectives to anti-democratic, authoritarian, racist and exclusionary discourse. This very simplified empirical result has two theoretical implications. The first implication concerns conceptualization of a transnational public sphere. The second implication concerns the causal factors associated with the emergence of a transnational public sphere.

Concerning conceptualization, the European public sphere is distinguished from other public spheres by its incorporation of a co-constitutive Eurosphere, that is, a trans-European public space and a trans-European public that is in conflict and contestation with other co-constitutive publics (e.g. transnational, national, subnational). This includes society-initiated and EU-initiated publics and the new spaces of communication, interaction and collective action that they create. This conceptualization stands in stark contrast to the mainstream notions of the public sphere. I will address this in only very brief terms here, as this is the topic of a forthcoming work (see also Sicakkan 2013).

The mainstream notions of public sphere are inspired by discussions between, and important contributions by, individualists, communalists, multiculturalists and pluralists. To accommodate individual differences, individualists suggest a single, discursive public sphere (e.g. Habermas 2011 [1962]; Mouffe 2002a, 2002b). For Europe, this implies 'Europeanization of national public spheres' (Eriksen 2005; Gerhards 2000). Communalists and multiculturalists propose multiple, segmented public spheres at two levels to accommodate separate historical communities which meet at the higher 'non-local' level (Taylor 2002: 113–114). For Europe, this implies a segmented public sphere divided along the lines of national cultures (e.g. Kielmannsegg 2003). Pluralists advocate the midway perspective of accommodating both individual and group differences in multiple and multi-level public spheres (cf. Nancy Fraser's 2007 'subaltern counter-publics'). The implication of this for Europe is 'a European sphere of publics' (cf. Schlesinger 1999, 2003). The Habermas-inspired 'Europeanization of national public spheres' is currently the dominant notion being used as a point of departure in empirical research. Apart from the multiculturalist notion of the public sphere, the common denominator of the above-mentioned conceptualization is the idea of a single, unified public sphere.

The current trend is to understand this single, unified public sphere by observing it 'directly' through its appearance mirrored by the national mass media (e.g. Koopmans 2004, 2007; Peters et al. 2005; Trenz 2000, 2003) and at the same time overlooking its two preordained components: publics (except Olesen 2005) and their public spaces (except Risse 2010; Risse and Van de Steeg 2003). In this book, an analytical distinction between public spaces and public spheres is introduced. The former is a space of interaction and deliberation separate from the state, but in which the state representatives may also participate on equal terms with other actors. It is a discursive social and political space in which individuals, groups, and social and political actors with a certain level of in-group feeling and the ability to form a public opinion, that is, publics, form and articulate the interests and views to be conveyed outwards. It is also an arena where persons' belongings and identities are mediated, confirmed, shaped and re-shaped. The public sphere, on the other hand, is an arena at another level where views articulated in communicative public spaces confront and are confronted by state actors and actors representing other publics and speaking from other public spaces. Public spaces and publics are thus constitutive components of a public sphere. This conceptualization allows for segmentation and fragmentation along integrative political cleavages and asserts that a public sphere does not cease to exist because of segmentation or fragmentation as long as segments and fragments are tied to each other by political cleavages.

Concerning causality, that is, the factors to explain the emergence of transnational public spheres, recent work attempting to explain the emergence of transnational public spheres is rare despite substantive elucidations in the works of Habermas (e.g. 2011 [1962]) and suggestions by Taylor (2002). The general trend is a focus on the barriers against them – e.g. diversity of languages, religions, cultures, identities, nationalisms, national media systems, and ownership structures – but studying the obstacles to a phenomenon alone is not the same as exploring its causes. The few theorists who do address the causes of the emergence of transnational public spheres highlight shifts of political power from nation states to new global, regional and local power centres; that is, wherever you get a new power centre, you get mobilizations at corresponding geographical scales in the form of new, bottom-up collective groups and networks that attempt to hold accountable the new power-holders (e.g. Bohman 1998; Castells 2008; Sicakkan 2012a). Some underline democracy types as an explanatory factor (e.g. Feree et al. 2002).

Causal approaches that focus exclusively on the European public sphere, on the other hand, conceive the emergence of a European public sphere either as a consequence of the Europeanization of national public spheres or as expanding overlaps between national public spheres. Approaches that overlook the impact of power and the central political elites such as these have been especially widespread since the European Union policies failed to create a pan-European media space. Both approaches presume that national public spheres will gradually fade away and be replaced by a Europe-wide public sphere through overlaps, Europeanization or both. They also assume that a European demos with a common identity is a necessary condition for the emergence of a full-grown European public sphere. Observing the historical patterns of new public sphere formations, we have to acknowledge that existing public spaces need not fade away or overlap with each other for new ones to emerge, and that a public sphere is constituted by trespassers between multiple historical and new public spaces that co-exist. In conjunction with the political cleavages approach, my explanatory frame puts emphasis on the trespassers between public spaces, the European Union's own attempts to create a European public sphere, and its unintended consequences deriving from the political cleavage structures.

Theoretical and conceptual frames based on these considerations were introduced in Chapter 1, along with a brief history of the establishment of the Eurosphere by the European Union's founding fathers. The empirical facts that we have discovered and presented in this book cannot be properly understood with conceptual frameworks deriving from aggregative, deliberative or minimalist notions of democracy and the public sphere. A turn toward substantive and agonistic pluralist notions of democracy and the public sphere is required, which allows acknowledgement of the possibility of a transnational public sphere. This has to be an extended notion of agonistic pluralism that recognizes the multiplicity of public spaces in a public sphere and the possibility of a segmented and fragmented public sphere.

NOTES

1. This information is based on this author's ongoing research on the European public sphere on the internet, which is not published yet.
2. Turning to the typology of public spaces in Europe's political history that I introduced in Chapter 1, the above-mentioned publics correspond to the trans-Europeanizing, transnationalizing, nationalizing and essentializing publics. Sicakkan (this volume, Chapter 4), Sata (this volume, Chapter 8) and Klicperová-Baker and Košťál (this volume, Chapter 9) map out the vertical and horizontal political cleavages between trans-Europeanizing, transnationalizing, nationalizing and essentializing publics. Dressler (this volume, Chapter 2), Mokre (this volume, Chapter 3) and Perez (this volume, Chapter 6) elaborate on the European-scale political cleavages spreading across the boundaries of trans-Europeanizing and nationalizing public spaces. Van de Beek and Vermeulen (this volume, Chapter 7) demonstrate the political cleavages between trans-Europeanizing, nationalizing and essentializing public spaces. Duru and Trenz (this volume, Chapter 5) study ethnographically the horizontal political cleavage arising from the confrontations between nationalizing and transnationalizing publics and public spaces. Mokre (this volume, Chapter 3) covers the political cleavages between trans-Europeanizing and nationalizing publics.

REFERENCES

Bakalova, D. and Y. Zografova (2011) *The Role of Print and Broadcast Media in the Articulation of the European Public Sphere: Qualitative Case Studies: Reform Treaty and Constructing Europe and the EU*, Eurosphere Comparative Studies No. 5.4.2, Brussels: Eurosphere Consortium.

Bohman, J. (1998) The Globalization of the Public Sphere: Cosmopolitanism, Publicity, and Cultural Pluralism, *Globalization* 75(2): 101–117.

Castells, M. (2008) The New Public Sphere: Global Civil Society, Communication Networks, and Global Governance, *Annals of the American Academy of Political and Social Science* 616(1): 78–93.

Dahl, R. (1989) *Democracy and Its Critics*, New Haven, CT: Yale University Press.

Eriksen, E.O. (2005) An Emerging European Public Sphere, *European Journal of Social Theory* 8(3): 341–363.

Feree, M.M., W.A. Gamson, J. Gerhards and D. Rucht (2002) Four Models of the Public Sphere in Modern Democracies, *Theory and Society* 31: 289–324.

Fraser, N. (1990) Rethinking the Public Sphere: A Contribution to the Critique of Actually Existing Democracy, *Social Text* 25(26): 56–80.

Fraser, N. (2007) Transnationalizing the Public Sphere: On the Legitimacy and Efficacy of Public Opinion in a Post-Westphalian World, *Theory, Culture and Society* 24(4): 7–30.

Gerhards, J. (2000) Europäisierung von Ökonomie und Politik und die Trägheit der Entstehung einer europäischen Öffentlichkeit, in M. Bach (ed.), *Die Europäisierung nationaler Gesellschaften*, Sonderheft 40 der *Kölner*

Zeitschrift für Soziologie und Sozialpsychologie, pp. 277–305, Wiesbaden: Westdeutscher Verlag.
Habermas, J. (2011 [1962]) *The Structural Transformation of the Public Sphere: An Inquiry into a Category of Bourgeois Society*, Cambridge: Polity Press.
Habermas, J., S. Lennox and F. Lennox (1974 [1964]) The Public Sphere: An Encyclopedia Article (1964), *New German Critique* 3: 49–55.
Harrison, J. and S. Pukallus (2015) The European Community's Public Communication Policy 1951–1967, *Contemporary European History* 24(2): 233–251.
Kielmannsegg, P.G. (2003) Integration und Demokratie, in M. Jachtenfuchs and B. Kohler-Koch (eds), *Europäische Integration*, 2nd edn, pp. 49–83, Opladen: Leske + Budrich.
Klicperová-Baker, M. and J. Košťál (2012) Ethno-national, Religious, Ideological and Sexual Diversity: Elite and Citizen Views Compared, *Javnost – The Public* 19(1): 85–102.
Klicperová-Baker, M. and J. Košťál (2013) European Demos in the Horizontal and Vertical Perspective: Value Orientations of Citizens, Party Sympathizers and Elites, in H.G. Sicakkan (ed.), *Linking the European Union with the Citizens: Evaluation of the EU's Policies Aiming to Create a Democratic European Public Sphere*, pp. 216–234, Eurosphere Final Report, Vol. 1, Brussels: Eurosphere Consortium.
Koopmans, R. (2004) Movements and Media: Selection Processes and Evolutionary Dynamics in the Public Sphere, *Theory and Society* 33(3–4): 367–391.
Koopmans, R. (2007) Who Inhabits the European Public Sphere? Winners and Losers, Supporters and Opponents in Europeanised Political Debate, *European Journal of Political Research* 46(2): 183–210.
Mouffe, C. (1992) *Dimensions of Radical Democracy: Pluralism, Citizenship, Democracy*, London: Verso.
Mouffe, C. (1999) Deliberative Democracy or Agonistic Pluralism? *Social Research* 66(3): 745–758.
Mouffe, C. (2002a) For an Agonistic Public Sphere, in Okwui Enwezor (ed.), *Democracy Unrealized: Documenta 11, Platform 1*, pp. 87–97, Berlin: Hatje Cantz.
Mouffe, C. (2002b) Which Public Sphere for a Democratic Society? *Theoria: A Journal of Social and Political Theory* 99: 55–65.
Olesen, T. (2005) Transnational Publics: New Spaces of Social Movement Activism and the Problem of Global Long-sightedness, *Current Sociology* 53(3): 419–440.
Perez, M. (2013) Can European Networks Contribute to the Reproduction of Common Views of the European Public Sphere among National Think Tanks? in H.G. Sicakkan (ed.), *Linking the European Union with the Citizens: Evaluation of EU Policies Aiming to Create a Democratic European Public Sphere*, Eurosphere Final Comparative Study, Vol. 1, pp. 111–128, Brussels: Eurosphere Consortium.
Peters, B., S. Sifft, A. Wimmel, M. Brüggemann and K. Kleinen-von Königslöw (2005) National and Transnational Public Spheres: The Case of the EU, *European Review* 3(1): 139–160.

Risse, T. (2010) *A Community of Europeans? Transnational Identities and Public Spheres*, Ithaca, NY: Cornell University Press.

Risse, T. and M. Van de Steeg (2003) An Emerging European Public Sphere? Empirical Evidence and Theoretical Clarifications, Paper presented to the conference Europeanization of Public Spheres, Political Mobilization, Public Communication and the European Union, Science Center Berlin, 20–22 June.

Rodrik, D. (2011) *The Globalization Paradox: Democracy and the Future of the World Economy*, New York: Norton.

Rodrik, D. (2012) The Truth about Sovereignty in *Project Syndicate*, October 8.

Rokkan, S. (1966) Norway: Numerical Democracy and Corporate Pluralism, in R.A. Dahl (ed.), *Political Oppositions in Western Democracies*, pp. 70–115, New Haven, CT: Yale University Press.

Schlesinger, P. (1999) Changing Spaces of Political Communication: The Case of the European Union, *Political Communication* 16(3): 263–279.

Schlesinger, P. (2003) *The Babel of Europe? An Essay on Networks and Communicative Spaces*, ARENA Working Papers WP 22/2003, Oslo: University of Oslo, Centre for European Studies.

Shapiro, I. (1994) Three Ways to Be a Democrat, *Political Theory* 22(1): 124–151.

Sicakkan, H.G. (2012a) Diversity, Polity and the European Public Sphere, *Javnost – The Public* 19(1): 5–18.

Sicakkan, H.G. (2012b) Trans-Europeanizing Public Spaces in Europe, *Javnost – The Public* 19(1): 103–124.

Sicakkan, H.G. (2013) *Diversity and the European Public Sphere: Towards a Citizens' Europe*, Eurosphere Final Comparative Study, Vol. 3, Brussels: Eurosphere Consortium.

Sicakkan, H.G. (forthcoming) Is the European Public Sphere Good for Democracy? in Y. Peters and M. Tatham (eds), *Democratic Transformations in Europe 31: Challenges and Opportunities*, Abingdon: Routledge.

Taylor, C. (2002) Modern Social Imaginaries, *Public Culture* 14(1): 91–124.

Trenz, H.-J. (2000) Korruption und politischer Skandal in der EU: Auf dem Weg zu einer europäischen politischen Öffentlichkeit, in M. Bach (ed.), *Die Europäisierung nationaler Gesellschaften*, Sonderheft 40 der *Kölner Zeitschrift für Soziologie und Sozialpsychologie*, pp. 332–359, Wiesbaden: Westdeutscher Verlag.

Trenz, H.-J. (2003) Media Coverage on European Governance: Testing the Performance of National Newspapers, EUSA Biennial International Conference, Nashville, TN, 27–29 March.

Trenz, H.-J. (2004) Media Coverage on European Governance: Exploring the European Public Sphere in National Quality Newspapers, *European Journal of Communication* 19(3): 291–319.

Young, I.M. (1990) *Justice and the Politics of Difference*, Princeton, NJ: Princeton University Press.

Zografova, Y. and D. Bakalova (2013) EU Citizens – A Key Resource for Articulation of European Public Sphere? in H.G. Sicakkan (ed.), *Linking the European Union with the Citizens: Evaluation of the EU's Policies Aiming to Create a Democratic European Public Sphere*, Eurosphere Final Report, Vol. 1, pp. 235–263, Brussels: Eurosphere Consortium.

Index